SEVEN STEPS TO INFOSEC NIRVANA

DEFEND WHAT MATTERS MOST

By

AJAI KUMAR SRIVASTAVA

and

SUSHEELA GUPTA

notionpress.com

INDIA • SINGAPORE • MALAYSIA

ISBN
Paperback 979-8-90584-804-9
Hardcase 979-8-90584-805-6

Part of The Wisdom Code Series of Practitioner Books by Seven Step Consulting Private Limited

CIN: U72200DL2009PTC193149

Website: www.sevenstepconsulting.com

Email: info@sevenstepconsulting.com

Cover Design: Padmapada Nayak

Printed and published by : Notion Press Media Pvt. Ltd.

7, Red Cross Road, Egmore, Chennai – 600008, Tamil Nadu, India

Email: publish@notionpress.com

Intellectual Property Notice

The author(s)of the book has/have taken all reasonable care to ensure that the contents of the book do not violate any existing copyright or intellectual property rights of any person in any manner whatsoever. In the event that the author(s) has/have been unable to track any source and if any copyright has been inadvertently infringe, please notify the publisher in writing for corrective action

TrustOS™, S.T.E.P.S.™, Seven Pillars of AI Governance™, ComplAi™, The Compliance First™, 9 P Paradigm™, and ENABLING TRUST! ™ are trademarks or proprietary frameworks of Seven Step Consulting Pvt. Ltd. All other trademarks, service marks, and product names mentioned in this book are the property of their respective owners.

ComplAi™ is Seven Step Consulting's proprietary AI-powered compliance readiness platform. The Compliance First™ is its structured methodology for governance and compliance implementation. These and related frameworks are explored in greater depth in forthcoming titles within The Wisdom Code Series™.

Part of The Wisdom Code Series of Practitioner Books by Seven Step Consulting Private Limited

CIN: U72200DL2009PTC193149

Website: www.sevenstepconsulting.com

Email: info@sevenstepconsulting.com

Cover Design: Padmapada Nayak

Printed and published by : Notion Press Media Pvt. Ltd.

7, Red Cross Road, Egmore, Chennai – 600008, Tamil Nadu, India

Email: publish@notionpress.com

The writing and development of this book was supported by advanced AI tools (Claude, ChatGPT, Perplexity) which assisted with the research, content organization, idea generation, language refinement, and editorial enhancement. All AI-assisted outputs were reviewed by the authors for accuracy and alignment with the intended objectives of this publication.

Intellectual Property Notice

ComplAi™ is Seven Step Consulting's proprietary AI-powered compliance readiness platform. The Compliance First™ is its structured methodology for governance and compliance implementation. These and related frameworks are explored in greater depth in forthcoming titles within The Wisdom Code Series™.

Annexure 419

Epilogue 457

Abbreviations 459

Bibliography 463

About the Authors 467

CONTENTS

Dedication		7
Foreword		9
Nirvana: Etymology, History, and Its Relevance to Information Security		11
Acknowledgements		23
Introduction		25
Chapter 1:	The Bit and the Bridle	31
Chapter 2:	An Introduction to Management Systems	52
Chapter 3:	An Overview of ISO/IEC 27001:2022 Requirements	83
Chapter 4:	Risk-Based Security Decision-Making	112
Chapter 5:	The 7-Step Framework Defined	155
Chapter 5:	Organizational Controls	277
Chapter 6:	People Controls	322
Chapter 7:	Physical Controls	338
Chapter 8:	Technological Controls	358
Chapter 9:	Ensuring Success for Your Organisation with ISO/IEC 27002:2022	395
Chapter 10:	The Future of Information Security, Cybersecurity and Privacy Protection	407

DEDICATION

This book is dedicated to every security practitioner, risk manager, compliance professional, and organizational leader who rises each day to guard the invisible frontiers of the digital world — often unheralded, always essential.

To our families, for their unwavering patience and encouragement. To the organizations that trust us with their most sensitive assets. And to the next generation of information security professionals: may you find in these pages the clarity, confidence, and conviction to pursue Infosec Nirvana.

FOREWORD

Information security has never been more consequential — or more misunderstood. Boardrooms that once treated it as an IT housekeeping matter are now grappling with ransomware that shuts down hospitals, supply-chain breaches that cascade across continents, and data privacy regulations that reshape how entire industries operate. The stakes have never been higher, and the complexity has never been greater.

Yet the fundamentals remain stubbornly constant. Well-designed governance, clear risk ownership, systematic control implementation, and a culture of security awareness continue to distinguish resilient organizations from those that become the next cautionary tale. What has changed is the urgency of getting these fundamentals right, the breadth of threats that test them, and the sophistication demanded of those who lead them.

Seven Steps to Infosec Nirvana addresses this reality head-on. Ajai Kumar Srivastava and Susheela Gupta bring decades of combined experience advising organizations across BFSI, healthcare, government, and technology sectors. Their 7-Step Framework — Define, Discover, Design, Document, Do and Deploy, Deploy & Check, Drive — is not a theoretical construct. It is a practitioner's roadmap, forged in the crucible of real implementations, audit findings, and boardroom conversations about risk that cannot wait.

What sets this book apart is its integration of the internationally recognised ISO/IEC 27001:2022 standard with practical insight drawn from three decades of implementation experience, the Brotby model of security metrics and governance, and the latest guidance from the Australian Signals Directorate's Information Security Manual (March 2026). Together, these sources provide a triangulated view of information security that is simultaneously strategic and operational, principled and pragmatic.

The clause-by-clause treatment of ISO/IEC 27001:2022 in Chapter Three, followed by the control-by-control analysis of all 93 controls from ISO/IEC 27002:2022 across Chapters Five through Eight, makes this book an indispensable reference for anyone implementing, auditing, or improving an Information Security Management System. The authors wisely root each control in its business context, linking technical requirements to board-level governance outcomes and measurable security metrics.

The future chapter is a sober reminder that the horizon is never still. Artificial intelligence, quantum computing, increasingly sophisticated nation-state threat actors, and the relentless expansion of the Internet of Things mean that the ISMS of today must be built with tomorrow's challenges already in view.

Read this book as a practitioner's companion: consultable, quotable, and rich with the kind of structured common sense that only comes from people who have lived these challenges.

Your journey to Infosec Nirvana begins here.

NIRVANA: ETYMOLOGY, HISTORY, AND ITS RELEVANCE TO INFORMATION SECURITY

The concept of **Nirvana** is one of humanity's oldest and most profound ideas about freedom, wisdom, and liberation. While it originated in spiritual traditions more than 2,500 years ago, its underlying principles have surprising relevance to modern information security, governance, risk management, and cyber resilience.

1. Etymology of Nirvana

Nirvana comes from the Sanskrit word **निर्वाण (Nirvāṇa)** and the Pali word **Nibbāna**.

The word is generally derived from:

- **nir** = out, away, without
- **vā** = to blow

Literally, it means:

"To blow out" or **"to extinguish."**

What is extinguished?

Not life.

Rather:

- ignorance
- attachment
- craving

- hatred
- suffering
- illusion

The image is often compared to a flame going out—not because something has been destroyed, but because the fuel sustaining the flame has been exhausted.

In ancient India, fire was believed to exist because of fuel. Remove the fuel, and the fire naturally ceases.

Similarly,

Remove greed.

Remove fear.

Remove ignorance.

Suffering naturally ends.

2. Historical Origins

Before Buddhism

The idea existed in early Indian philosophy before Siddhartha Gautama.

Ancient Vedic thinkers discussed liberation from:

- repeated suffering
- attachment
- worldly cycles

However, the meaning was not clearly defined.

Buddha's Interpretation (5th Century BCE)

The Buddha transformed the concept. He taught that Nirvana was not:

- heaven
- paradise
- a place
- reward after death

Instead, it was:

A state of complete freedom from mental suffering.

He identified the root cause of suffering as:

- craving (Tanha)
- ignorance (Avijja)

When these disappear,

Nirvana appears naturally.

Four Noble Truths

Nirvana forms the destination of the Buddha's central teaching.

1. Life contains suffering.

Not only pain.

Also:

- anxiety
- uncertainty
- dissatisfaction
- insecurity

2. Suffering has causes.

Mainly:

- attachment

- ego
- desire
- illusion

3. Suffering can end.

Liberation is possible.

4. There is a path.

The Eightfold Path.

Not belief.

Practice.

Discipline.

Wisdom.

The Eightfold Path

The path consists of:

- Right View
- Right Intention
- Right Speech
- Right Action
- Right Livelihood
- Right Effort
- Right Mindfulness
- Right Concentration

Notice something remarkable.

It is a governance framework.

Not unlike:

- ISO standards
- quality systems
- continuous improvement

3. Evolution Across Traditions

Theravāda

Nirvana means complete liberation from the cycle of rebirth.

Focus:

Individual enlightenment.

Mahāyāna

Greater emphasis on compassion.

A Bodhisattva delays personal Nirvana to help others.

Interesting cybersecurity analogy:

An experienced CISO does not secure only themselves.

They raise the security maturity of the entire ecosystem.

Zen

Nirvana is not distant.

It is experienced through complete awareness of the present.

Security analogy:

The best defenders remain fully aware of the present environment rather than reacting only after incidents occur.

4. What Nirvana Is Not

Many misunderstand Nirvana.

It is NOT:

- extinction
- death
- unconsciousness
- heaven
- paradise
- escape

Instead, it is:

Perfect clarity.

Freedom.

Peace.

Wisdom.

5. Philosophical Meaning

Nirvana represents freedom from:

- fear
- attachment
- illusion
- uncontrolled desire
- reactive thinking

This creates:

- stability
- resilience
- clarity
- ethical action

These qualities are equally valuable in leadership and security.

6. Why Nirvana Matters in Information Security

At first glance, spirituality and cybersecurity appear unrelated.

Yet both deal fundamentally with **reducing suffering by eliminating root causes rather than merely reacting to symptoms**.

The parallels are striking.

Nirvana Principle	Information Security Equivalent
Remove ignorance	Security awareness
Remove craving	Reduce unnecessary data collection and privilege
Remove attachment	Avoid dependence on single systems or vendors
Mindfulness	Continuous monitoring
Right action	Secure operational practices
Wisdom	Risk-based decision making
Discipline	Governance and compliance
Inner resilience	Cyber resilience

7. Ignorance Is the Greatest Vulnerability

In Buddhism:

Ignorance creates suffering.

In cybersecurity:

Ignorance creates breaches.

Most incidents begin because someone:

- clicked a phishing email
- reused passwords

- ignored warnings
- misunderstood risk
- bypassed policy

Technology rarely fails first.

Human understanding does.

Security awareness is therefore analogous to removing ignorance (Avijja).

8. Attachment Creates Risk

Buddhism teaches that attachment causes suffering.

Information security teaches that excessive dependence creates systemic risk.

Examples include attachment to:

- legacy systems
- outdated passwords
- obsolete software
- manual processes
- insecure convenience
- unrestricted administrator privileges

Organizations often delay change because of attachment to familiar systems.

Attackers exploit this reluctance.

9. Craving Equals Excess

Modern organizations often collect data simply because they can.

This creates unnecessary exposure.

Examples include:

- excessive customer information
- indefinite retention
- duplicate databases
- over-collection of logs
- unnecessary employee monitoring

Privacy laws increasingly promote data minimization because unnecessary data becomes unnecessary risk.

The fewer valuable assets exposed, the smaller the attack surface.

10. The Flame Analogy

Nirvana literally means extinguishing the fire.

Cybersecurity also seeks to extinguish:

- malware propagation
- ransomware spread
- insider threats
- privilege abuse
- attack persistence

Good incident response removes the “fuel”:

- vulnerable systems
- compromised credentials
- excessive privileges
- exposed services

Without fuel, the attack dies.

11. The Eightfold Path Compared with ISO 27001

Eightfold Path	Security Governance
Right View	Risk Assessment
Right Intention	Security Strategy
Right Speech	Security Communication
Right Action	Security Controls
Right Livelihood	Ethical Technology Use
Right Effort	Continuous Improvement
Right Mindfulness	Monitoring & Detection
Right Concentration	Incident Response

The similarities reflect a shared emphasis on disciplined practice and continual refinement.

12. Nirvana as the Ultimate Security State

If we define security as:

The absence of unacceptable risk,

then Nirvana can be viewed metaphorically as:

The absence of the internal conditions that generate insecurity.

This does **not** imply perfect or absolute security—an unattainable goal in information security—but rather a mature state where root causes are understood, risks are managed, and responses are grounded in wisdom rather than fear.

A mature security organization:

- anticipates threats
- reduces unnecessary exposure
- learns continuously

- acts ethically
- builds resilience
- responds calmly under pressure

These qualities echo the disciplined mindset associated with Nirvana.

13. Lessons for Cybersecurity Leaders

A modern CISO can draw practical inspiration from the philosophy of Nirvana by focusing on enduring principles:

1. Eliminate ignorance through continuous education.
2. Remove unnecessary complexity to reduce attack surfaces.
3. Minimize data collection and retention.
4. Build resilience instead of relying solely on prevention.
5. Practice continuous awareness through monitoring and threat intelligence.
6. Base decisions on ethics, governance, and long-term trust.
7. Seek continual improvement rather than perfection.

Conclusion

Although conceived over two millennia ago, the philosophy of Nirvana offers a powerful metaphor for contemporary information security. Both disciplines recognize that lasting safety comes not from endless reaction to external threats, but from addressing the underlying conditions that create vulnerability. By replacing ignorance with knowledge, excess with restraint, and reactive behavior with disciplined governance, organizations can cultivate stronger security, greater resilience, and deeper trust.

For cybersecurity professionals, the lesson is enduring: the highest level of security is achieved not merely by deploying more controls, but by removing the causes that allow risk to flourish. In that sense, the journey toward cyber resilience resembles the journey toward Nirvana—not a destination of perfection, but a disciplined path of continual awareness, wise action, and freedom from avoidable vulnerabilities.

ACKNOWLEDGEMENTS

The authors wish to express their deep gratitude to the many colleagues, clients, and contributors who have shaped the thinking embedded in this book.

To the entire team at Seven Step Consulting: your dedication to excellence in governance, risk, and compliance advisory work is reflected on every page. Your field experience has been the real laboratory from which the 7-Step Framework emerged.

To the organizations and leaders who trusted us with their most complex information security challenges: your environments, your constraints, and your questions taught us things no standard alone could teach.

To W. Krag Brotby, whose foundational work on Information Security Management Metrics continues to be an invaluable guide for practitioners seeking to move security from intuition to measurement. To the Australian Signals Directorate, whose Information Security Manual (March 2026) remains one of the most practically useful national-level frameworks in existence.

To the International Organization for Standardization and the International Electrotechnical Commission: the ISO/IEC 27000 family of standards is the backbone of this book and the global language of information security.

To our families: your patience, encouragement, and willingness to share us with a manuscript that seemed to grow faster than it could be finished made this book possible.

Finally, to you, the reader: thank you for investing your most scarce resource — time — in this work. We hope it returns that investment many times over.

INTRODUCTION

Why This Book?

This book was written to serve as a compass for organizations charting their Information Security and Privacy strategies, and a cogent roadmap to implementing them effectively. It is designed for the leaders and senior managers of corporations — the CISOs, CIOs, Risk Officers, and Boards — who must make high-stakes decisions about information security, but who are often overwhelmed by the volume, complexity, and technical depth of the subject.

The authors have deliberately focused on developing an overarching strategic vision rather than tactics and technologies. Where technical controls are addressed — as they must be, given the subject matter — they are presented in their business context: why they matter, what they protect, how their effectiveness should be measured, and what governance outcomes they support.

What This Book Will Help You Achieve

- A clear understanding of trends, experiences, and perspectives in the Information Security, Cybersecurity, and Privacy arena
- Insight into the key drivers and challenges of managing Information Security, Cybersecurity, and Privacy in the enterprise context
- A grounding in the history and evolution of the standards-based approach to these disciplines

- A systematic approach to evolving holistic strategies for managing risk through Information Security, Cybersecurity, and Privacy controls
- A practical roadmap for implementing the various policies, procedures, and controls required by ISO/IEC 27001:2022 and ISO/IEC 27002:2022
- A framework for maintaining and ensuring ongoing compliance through audits and measurement programmes
- An awareness of statutory and regulatory obligations that must be integrated into any ISMS

Why Seven?

The 7-Step Framework forms the keystone for successful Information Security, Cybersecurity, and Privacy protection design in an organizational context. The number seven has deep significance:

- George A. Miller's celebrated 1956 paper in Psychological Review, "The Magical Number Seven, Plus or Minus Two," established that seven chunks of information represent the maximum that can be processed by humans in short-term memory — making a seven-step framework an optimally memorable structure.
- Seven layers of security: as security practitioners observe, no single layer of defence is sufficient. The 7-Step Framework addresses all seven layers simultaneously.
- The 7 D framework and STEPS methodology of Seven-Step Consulting reflects the PDCA (Plan-Do-Deploy & Check-Act) cycle and ISO's Annex SL high-level structure

— creating natural alignment with other management systems an organization may already operate.

How This Book Is Organized

This book is designed to serve both as a structured learning guide and as a practical implementation reference for professionals at every stage of their information security journey.

Part I (Chapters 1–4) establishes the strategic and conceptual foundation. It explains the evolving relationship between information security, cybersecurity, privacy, and digital trust, introduces the principles of management systems and the Plan-Do-Deploy & Check-Act (PDCA) methodology, provides a comprehensive clause-by-clause interpretation of ISO/IEC 27001:2022, and demonstrates how the Seven Step Consulting's 7 D Framework translates the standard's requirements into a practical implementation roadmap.

Part II (Chapters 5–10) moves from theory to practice. It provides detailed guidance on implementing all 93 controls of ISO/IEC 27002:2022, organized according to the four control themes—Organizational, People, Physical, and Technological. The later chapters focus on integrating these controls into a resilient and continually improving Information Security Management System (ISMS), measuring effectiveness, sustaining certification, and preparing organizations for emerging challenges such as artificial intelligence, cloud-native environments, digital privacy, supply-chain security, quantum computing, and evolving regulatory expectations.

Whether you read the book cover to cover or consult it as a practical reference, it is designed to support your needs at every stage of implementation. Read it sequentially for a comprehensive understanding of ISO/IEC 27001 and modern information security governance or use individual chapters to address specific challenges. For example, refer to Chapter Three when preparing for clause-specific implementation or certification audits, and Chapters Five through Eight when designing, implementing, or assessing specific security controls and operational safeguards.

The Annexures complement the main text with practical implementation resources, including templates, checklists, sample policies, audit questions, evidence requirements, maturity assessment tools, cross-reference matrices, recommended reading, and a carefully curated bibliography. These resources are intended to help readers move beyond understanding the standard to successfully implementing, maintaining, and continually improving an effective Information Security Management System.

Ultimately, this book aims to bridge the gap between compliance and capability, enabling organizations not only to achieve certification but also to build enduring cyber resilience, strengthen stakeholder trust, and establish security as a strategic business enabler.

PART I

THE CONTEXT AND CHALLENGES

Understanding the landscape before building the fortress

The first part of this book focuses on information security, cybersecurity, and privacy — the three main priorities of organizations and companies in the hyper-digitalized societies of the 21st century.

Caught in the day-to-day pressures of competitive markets and operational demands, the vital issue of managing risks to business survival on account of information security breaches is too often treated as a secondary concern — until a major incident forces it to the top of the agenda.

The book highlights the necessity of adopting a structured, standards-based approach, integrating Information Security Risk Management as an increasingly important part of the Total Business Management System.

The Seven Golden Rules encapsulated in the 7-Step Framework, postulated by the authors, provide the path that Senior Management must follow to protect themselves and their organizations.

CHAPTER

1

THE BIT AND THE BRIDLE

Building an ISMS for Digital Trust in the Knowledge Economy

The forces shaping our digital reality

Chapter Overview

The knowledge economy has made information the decisive asset of the modern organisation and, with it, the protection of information a decisive responsibility of leadership. That responsibility cannot be discharged by treating security as a technical state to be purchased; it must be understood as a probabilistic discipline governed through risk. Information security, cybersecurity and privacy are distinct fields, but they fail together, as the Marriott breach and the Indian and Australian cases each demonstrate: a lapse in due diligence or configuration becomes a privacy catastrophe and a governance crisis. Seeing this reality clearly — honestly naming what the organisation depends on, what it is worth, and how much risk it carries — is the foundation on which the S.T.E.P.S.™ journey to Infosec Nirvana is built.

Chapter Objectives

By the end of this chapter, the reader will be able to:

- Define information as an asset and explain why, in the knowledge economy, its protection is a board-level responsibility rather than an IT chore.
- Articulate the CIA Triad — confidentiality, integrity, availability — as the foundational model of information security.
- Distinguish information security, cybersecurity and privacy protection, and explain why all three must be governed together.
- Explain why security is a probabilistic discipline and how the question "how much security is enough?" is answered through risk, not absolutes.
- Draw the lessons of the Marriott breach and leading regional incidents for governance, due diligence and privacy.

S.T.E.P.S.™ Engine — Operational Anchor: The Foundation Beneath DEFINE

Before an organisation can DEFINE the scope of its security journey, its leaders must first see reality clearly: what information is, why it has become the most valuable asset class on earth, and how security, cybersecurity and privacy differ yet depend on one another. This chapter is the ground on which the entire

S.T.E.P.S.™ cycle is built.

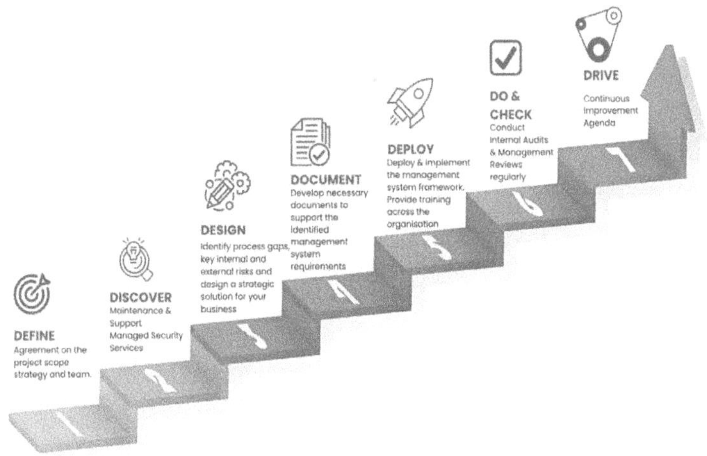

The S.T.E.P.S.™ Governance Trust Cycle — the engine beneath every chapter.

A quarrel had arisen between the Horse and the Stag, so the Horse came to a Hunter to ask his help to take revenge on the Stag. The Hunter agreed but said: "If you desire to conquer the Stag, you must permit me to place this piece of iron between your jaws..." The Horse agreed to the conditions, and the Hunter soon saddled and bridled him. Then with the aid of the Hunter, the Horse soon overcame the Stag. "Now get off," said the Horse. "Not so fast, friend," said the Hunter. "I have now got you under bit and spur and prefer to keep you as you are at present."

— The Horse, the Stag, and the Hunter — Aesop's Fables

The Bit and the Bridle

Aesop's horse won its quarrel with the stag — and lost its freedom forever. It accepted the bit and bridle to gain a short-term advantage and discovered, too late, that the instrument of its victory had become the instrument of its captivity. It is a fable about dependence, and it describes the modern enterprise with uncomfortable precision. Organisations have saddled themselves to information technology to outpace their rivals, and in doing so have accepted a bridle of dependence whose risks most boards have only begun to understand.

This chapter establishes the reality that the rest of the book builds upon. Information has become the most valuable asset class in the world, the discipline of protecting it is probabilistic rather than absolute, and the three fields most leaders blur together — information security, cybersecurity and privacy — are distinct disciplines that nonetheless rise or fall together. Seeing this clearly is the precondition for every decision that follows.

Executive Insight

Dependence is not the danger; *ungoverned* dependence is. The organisations that thrive are not those that use less technology, but those that understand precisely how much risk their technology carries and have decided, deliberately, to accept it.

1.1 What Is Information — and Why It Must Be Protected

Information is data that has been given meaning. It is the meaning, not the raw bits and bytes, that must be protected in accordance with its worth to the organisation. Phenomena become information only when they are perceived and interpreted: a tree falling in an empty forest produces pressure waves, but "noise" — the information denoting a falling tree — exists only when an ear detects those waves and a brain interprets them. Information is technology-independent; what we can do with it, and how fast, is utterly technology-dependent.

Information as Something That Gives Form to the Mind

The English word **"information"** derives from the Latin verb ***informare***, meaning **"to give form to," "to shape," or "to instruct."** At its core, information is not merely data—it is the process of shaping human understanding. It transforms uncertainty into knowledge, confusion into clarity, and observation into action.

Information: The Invisible Architect of Human Decisions

Every significant human decision is built upon information.

Thus, information has always been more than a collection of facts—it is the invisible architecture upon which power, prosperity, and survival are built.

Information as a Source of Power Throughout History

History repeatedly demonstrates that those who controlled information often controlled outcomes.

Sun Tzu and the Intelligence Advantage

More than 2,500 years ago, the Chinese military strategist Sun Tzu emphasized that victory depended not merely on superior weapons but on superior knowledge.

In *The Art of War*, he wrote:

"Know the enemy and know yourself; in a hundred battles you will never be defeated."

Renaissance Trade Networks: Information as Economic Capital

During the Renaissance, merchants competing across Europe discovered that commercial success depended as much on information as on goods.

Information could generate enormous competitive advantage.

Information became economic power.

The Enigma Code: Protecting Information to Protect Nations

The importance of protecting information reached extraordinary significance during the World War II.

Germany relied heavily on the Enigma machine to encrypt military communications, believing its messages were secure.

However, cryptanalysts led by Alan Turing and teams at Bletchley Park successfully deciphered Enigma traffic.

The ability to read encrypted communications provided Allied forces with unprecedented strategic intelligence about troop movements, naval operations, and military plans.

Information only creates advantage when it remains protected. Once confidentiality is lost, strategic superiority can disappear overnight.

From Data to Knowledge to Wisdom

Information occupies a critical place in the hierarchy of human understanding.

- **Data** consists of raw facts and observations.
- **Information** organizes data into meaningful context.
- **Knowledge** emerges when information is interpreted and understood.
- **Wisdom** develops when knowledge is applied with judgment and experience.

Protecting information therefore safeguards the pathway that leads from observation to intelligent action.

Why Information Must Be Protected

Because information shapes decisions, it also shapes power.

Unauthorized disclosure can expose national secrets.

Manipulation can influence elections or financial markets.

Corruption can lead to catastrophic engineering failures.

Loss can cripple businesses and critical infrastructure.

In the digital age, organizations increasingly recognize that their most valuable assets are often intangible:

- Customer databases
- Intellectual property
- Research findings
- Source code
- Financial records
- Strategic plans
- Personal data
- Artificial intelligence models

Unlike physical assets, information can be copied instantly, transmitted globally, and exploited without visibly disappearing from its owner.

Its value lies not in its physical form but in the trust placed in its **confidentiality, integrity, and availability**.

A Modern Interpretation

The original meaning of *informare*—"to give form to"—remains remarkably relevant.

It shapes minds before it shapes actions.

This is why information security is not merely an IT discipline. It is the discipline of preserving the integrity of human decision-making itself. Every encryption algorithm, access control mechanism, privacy regulation, and cybersecurity framework ultimately exists to protect the resource that has driven civilizations for millennia: **the information that gives form to thought, guides action and determines success or failure.**

An information asset is a definable piece of information, stored in any form, recognised as valuable to the organisation — valuable, hard to replace, part of the organisation's identity, or classified as confidential. Information assets take many forms, and a security programme that protects only the electronic ones is protecting a fraction of the estate.

Type of asset	Examples
Paper	Contracts, company documentation, invoices, system documentation, continuity plans, manuals
Electronic	Databases, data files, intellectual property, training material, operational procedures, fallback arrangements
People	Employees, customers, subscribers, contractors, consultants
Physical	Computers, network equipment, communication equipment, magnetic media, buildings and facilities
Services	Internet providers, courier services, utilities, environmental controls
Software	Applications, development tools, utilities, operating systems, databases
Image & reputation	Corporate image, brand equity, stakeholder trust, customer confidence

1.2 Information in the Knowledge Economy

Information has played a vital role in every civilisation, but in the knowledge economy it has become the lifeblood of the modern organisation. As the archaeologist Tim Kohler observed, there is a fundamental relationship between how a society processes information and how large it can grow; early innovations such as writing and coinage were as decisive for our ancestors as the internet is for us.

Information is far more than digital data stored on computers. Rooted in the Latin *informare*—"to give form to"—it is the force that shapes understanding, enables sound decisions, and creates strategic advantage.

From Sun Tzu's battlefield intelligence to Renaissance merchant networks and the breaking of the Enigma code, history consistently shows that societies and organizations that generate, preserve, and protect information gain enduring advantages. In the modern world, safeguarding information is therefore not only a technical necessity but a strategic imperative for resilience, trust, and long-term success.

Gartner's judgement is blunter: information is the most important asset class in the world. Yet it rarely commands the senior-management attention its value warrants, and corporations and governments alike sacrifice enormous resources to breaches that threaten not just data but organisational survival.

1.3 Information Security and the CIA Triad

Information security is concerned with the confidentiality, integrity and availability of data — in any form, in motion or at rest — keeping it secure from unauthorised access, disclosure, modification or destruction. ISO/IEC 27000 frames it as the application and management of appropriate controls across a wide range of threats, with the aim of sustaining business success and minimising the consequences of incidents.

The CIA Triad — the foundational model

Confidentiality: information is accessible only to those authorised to have access.

Integrity: the accuracy and completeness of information and its processing methods are safeguarded.

Availability: authorised users can access information and associated assets when required.

NIST SP 800-12 establishes eight foundational "enduring principles" designed to guide organizations in integrating security into their management culture. Originally introduced in the classic computer security handbook and preserved in subsequent revisions, these principles form the philosophical backbone of federal and enterprise information security

The eight principles outline the holistic approach organizations must take:

1. **Support the Organizational Mission:** Security must align directly with the organization's goals, culture, and operational vision.
2. **Integral Element of Sound Management:** Cybersecurity shouldn't be an afterthought; it is a core management function that enhances planning and governance.
3. **Cost-Effective:** The cost of security measures must be justified by the risk being mitigated. Security is a cost of doing business.

4. **Explicit Responsibilities:** Security roles, duties, and accountability must be clearly documented for users, administrators, and executives.
5. **System Owner Responsibilities:** System owners hold obligations beyond their local network—they must ensure their systems don't negatively impact the broader organization or interconnected external networks.
6. **Comprehensive and Integrated Approach:** Security must be viewed as a unified system, integrating physical, personnel, administrative, and technical controls.
7. **Periodically Reassessed:** Because the threat landscape constantly evolves, security programs must be continually monitored and periodically re-evaluated.
8. **Constrained by Societal Factors:** All security policies and implementations are limited by human behavior, laws, and ethical/privacy constraints

Disclosure is irreversible. Once information is released it can never be "recalled" — the email is sent, the post goes viral, the leak is permanent. This is a sharper way to motivate confidentiality than the usual "data is valuable" line, and it sets up breach case studies beautifully.

The worst assumption a leader can make is to believe the organisation is secure when it is not. Security is a game that is never fully won.

1.4 Understanding Cybersecurity

Cybersecurity is the practice of protecting networks, devices and data from unauthorised access or criminal use, ensuring confidentiality, integrity and availability across cyberspace. It is a subset of information security: information security protects data across all media, while cybersecurity focuses on data stored in or transmitted through cyberspace.

The discipline has crossed decisively from the server room to the boardroom — Gartner reports that a large majority of boards now treat cybersecurity as a business risk rather than a purely technical IT problem and increasingly write cyber-risk accountability into executive performance terms.

Security Is About Probability

Security is a probabilistic, statistical discipline. There is always some probability that something bad will happen to your information; merely hoping it will not is unlikely to change that probability. The objective of risk assessment is therefore to identify what could happen, to prioritise the important risks over the trivial ones, and to act on the priorities — an application of the Pareto principle in which treating the critical few removes most of the potential loss.

The 95/5 Rule

Roughly 95% of organisations are not attractive targets for serious, determined attackers; their principal threats are commodity malware and low-level intrusion, against which patched systems, antivirus and firewalls are largely sufficient. The remaining 5% — those whose information is genuinely valuable or whose systems are genuinely vital — are real targets, and they need a strategically designed, risk-based programme, not a compliance checklist. The first task of leadership is to know honestly which group the organisation is in.

1.5 What Is Privacy — and How It Differs from Security

Privacy concerns the rights and obligations of individuals and organisations with respect to the collection, use, retention, disclosure and disposal of personal information. The concept is ancient, but its modern legal form began with Warren and Brandeis, whose 1890 Harvard Law Review article framed privacy as "the right to be let alone." In the twenty-first century, processing personal data has become integral to social and economic life, and legal systems worldwide — the GDPR, India's Digital Personal Data Protection Act 2023, California's CCPA — have transformed privacy from a philosophical right into a legal obligation with financial consequences.

Privacy and security are closely related but not the same. Privacy governs the use and governance of personal data — ensuring it is collected, shared and used appropriately. Security protects data from attack and misuse. Security is necessary for privacy but not sufficient for it: a perfectly secure system still violates privacy if it processes personal data without a lawful basis. This is why the two disciplines must be governed together, a theme that the regional cases below make vivid.

1.6 The Case for a Structured Approach

Risk: Beyond Threats to Opportunity

The concept of risk is often misunderstood. In many organizations, risk is viewed solely as the possibility of loss—a cyberattack, a financial setback, a compliance violation, or an operational failure. This narrow perspective leads to defensive strategies that focus only on preventing bad outcomes. However, the true nature of risk is far broader and far more strategic.

The internationally accepted definition in ISO 31000: Risk Management – Guidelines defines risk as **"the effect of uncertainty on objectives."** This deceptively simple statement fundamentally changes how organizations should think about risk. It shifts the conversation away from isolated threats and toward the achievement of business goals. Risk is not merely about what can go wrong; it is about how uncertainty—whether positive or negative—affects an organization's ability to achieve its intended outcomes.

The Evolution of Risk

The history of the word risk itself reflects humanity's changing relationship with uncertainty.

In today's interconnected digital economy, risk encompasses both dimensions simultaneously. Organizations operate across global supply chains, cloud infrastructures, remote workforces, and digital ecosystems where uncertainty exists across both space and time. Cyber incidents in one geography can disrupt operations worldwide within minutes. Strategic decisions made today may create compliance, reputational, or operational consequences years later.

Modern enterprises therefore face uncertainty across a vast portfolio of assets, including:

- Financial capital
- Intellectual property
- Information and data
- Technology infrastructure
- Human resources
- Business processes
- Reputation and brand value

- Regulatory compliance obligations
- Customer trust and stakeholder confidence

Risk management is no longer confined to protecting physical assets or financial investments; it has become the discipline of preserving and enhancing organizational value in an environment of constant uncertainty.

Risk Has Two Faces: Threat and Opportunity

One of the most misunderstood aspects of risk is that it encompasses both danger and opportunity. Every strategic decision exposes an organization to potential losses while simultaneously creating possibilities for growth, innovation, and competitive advantage.

This dual nature is reflected in the ISO 31000 definition of risk as the "effect of uncertainty on objectives." That effect may be negative, positive, or both. The goal of management is not to eliminate risk—which is impossible—but to understand and manage uncertainty in a way that supports organizational objectives.

Consider a FinTech organization launching an AI-powered lending platform. Potential risks include cybersecurity breaches, algorithmic bias, regulatory non-compliance, and service disruptions. However, when these risks are effectively managed, the same platform can deliver faster loan approvals, lower operating costs, improved customer experience, and expanded market reach. The ability to manage uncertainty becomes a source of competitive advantage.

Healthcare presents a similar example. Electronic Health Records (EHRs), telemedicine platforms, and AI-assisted diagnostics introduce privacy, security, and compliance risks. Yet, when supported by strong governance and safeguards, these technologies improve patient care, enable remote access to services, reduce clinical errors, and accelerate medical research.

The lesson is clear: organizations that focus only on avoiding threats often miss valuable opportunities, while those that pursue innovation without managing risk expose themselves to unnecessary losses. Effective governance seeks the right balance—reducing unacceptable risks while enabling growth and value creation.

A mature security program takes a different view. This perspective transforms the role of information security. Rather than acting as a barrier to change, security becomes a strategic enabler. Strong governance, cybersecurity controls, privacy safeguards, and compliance frameworks create the trust required for digital transformation, cloud adoption, innovation, and business expansion.

By establishing strong governance, protecting information assets, ensuring regulatory compliance, and building stakeholder confidence, security creates the conditions under which organizations can innovate with confidence. It enables secure digital transformation, accelerates cloud adoption, facilitates trusted partnerships, protects intellectual property, and strengthens customer relationship. In this sense, security is far more than a defensive function. It does not merely prevent failure—it creates the confidence that enables organizations to succeed.

In other words, effective security management does not merely prevent failure—it enables success.

From Risk Management to Trust Management

This broader understanding of risk lays the foundation for a more strategic perspective on information security.

A mature understanding of risk naturally leads to a broader objective: trust. Organizations that manage risk effectively do more than avoid losses—they create an environment where employees collaborate confidently, customers share information willingly, investors commit capital with assurance, regulators recognize responsible governance, and business partners engage without hesitation.

Trust is not a vague or intangible concept; it is a strategic and economic asset. High-trust organizations benefit from stronger customer loyalty, faster decision-making, lower transaction costs, enhanced reputation, and greater resilience. In today's digital economy, trust has become one of the most powerful sources of sustainable competitive advantage.

Viewed through this lens, information security is far more than a technical or compliance function. It is a business enabler that transforms uncertainty into confidence and risk into opportunity. Organizations that embrace this perspective move beyond a narrow focus on controls and compliance toward resilience, innovation, and long-term value creation.

The path from risk management to trust management begins by recognizing that risk is not the enemy of progress. Every worthwhile objective involves uncertainty. Success depends not on eliminating risk, but on managing it intelligently and consistently.

The challenge facing organizations today is clear. Cyber threats continue to grow in scale and sophistication, the cybersecurity skills shortage remains severe, and regulatory requirements are becoming increasingly complex. Yet many organizations still rely on fragmented controls, reactive responses, and individual expertise rather than systematic, repeatable processes.

The need for a structured, standards-based approach has never been greater. Frameworks such as ISO/IEC 27001:2022, supported by the S.T.E.P.S.™ Governance Trust Cycle and meaningful security metrics, provide organizations with a practical roadmap for building trust, strengthening resilience, and enabling secure growth. The chapters that follow present that roadmap.

When Cybersecurity Fails: Lessons from Marriott, AIIMS, Medibank, and Optus

The true impact of information security failures becomes clear when examining some of the most significant cyber incidents of recent years. Although these events occurred in different industries and countries, they reveal a common truth: cybersecurity is not merely a technical issue—it is a business, governance, and trust issue.

In 2018, Marriott International disclosed that attackers had maintained unauthorized access to the Starwood guest reservation system for several years. The breach, which originated before Marriott acquired Starwood in 2016, exposed the personal information of approximately 339 million guests worldwide, including passport details, payment card information, travel records, and dates of birth. The incident demonstrated a critical governance failure: cybersecurity risks had not been adequately assessed during the acquisition process. Marriott inherited not only Starwood's assets but also its vulnerabilities. The financial penalties, legal settlements, and reputational damage that followed underscored the importance of cybersecurity due diligence in mergers and acquisitions.

A similar lesson emerged in India during the 2022 ransomware attack on the All India Institute of Medical Sciences (AIIMS), Delhi. The attack disrupted appointment systems, laboratory services, billing, and clinical operations, affecting millions of patients. The incident highlighted how cyberattacks on healthcare institutions are no longer simply IT problems—they directly affect patient care and safety. Weak network segmentation, inadequate backup strategies, and insufficient resilience planning amplified the impact of the attack.

Australia experienced its own wake-up call in 2022 through the Medibank and Optus breaches. Medibank suffered the theft and public release of sensitive health information, transforming a cybersecurity incident into a major privacy and trust crisis. Optus, meanwhile, exposed customer identity information through weaknesses in API security and excessive data retention practices. Both incidents demonstrated that privacy protection depends on strong cybersecurity controls and responsible data governance.

Together, these cases reveal a consistent lesson: organizations must view cybersecurity, privacy, resilience, and governance as interconnected disciplines. Whether in hospitality, healthcare, telecommunications, or financial services, trust can take years to build and only moments to lose. Effective information security is therefore not simply about preventing breaches—it is about protecting the confidence of customers, patients, employees, regulators, and investors. In a digital economy, that trust has become one of an organization's most valuable assets.

Key Takeaways

- Information is the most valuable asset class in the world, and its protection is a board-level responsibility.
- Information security, cybersecurity and privacy are related but distinct; a complete programme governs all three together.
- The CIA Triad — confidentiality, integrity, availability — remains the foundational model.
- Security is probabilistic: the objective is risk management, not the impossible goal of risk elimination.

- The cybersecurity talent gap is structural; systematic processes, not heroic individuals, are what endure.
- A structured, standards-based approach is both necessary and achievable for an organisation of any size.

Reflection Questions

1. Could your board state, in one sentence, why information is your organisation's most valuable asset — and name the assets that matter most?
2. Are you in the 95% or the 5%? What evidence supports your answer, and who has tested it?
3. Where in your organisation does a perfectly 'secure' system still process personal data without a clearly documented lawful basis?
4. When you last acquired or onboarded a business or vendor, what cyber due diligence did you perform — and what might you have inherited?
5. If your most critical digital service failed today, is the consequence an inconvenience, a financial loss, or a safety event?

Action Deploy & Checklist

- Commission a plain-language inventory of your most valuable information assets across all seven asset types — not just the electronic ones.
- Hold an honest 95/5 conversation at the leadership level and document which category you are in and why.
- Map every system that processes personal data to a documented lawful basis, purpose and retention limit.

- Add a cyber due-diligence requirement to your M&A and vendor-onboarding playbooks.
- Confirm that confidentiality, integrity and availability each have an owner and a measure for your top services.
- Brief the board on the distinction — and the dependence — between security, cybersecurity and privacy.

CHAPTER

2

AN INTRODUCTION TO MANAGEMENT SYSTEMS

Building the governance foundation for information security

S.T.E.P.S.™ Engine — Operational Anchor: The PDCA Cycle Beneath the Whole Staircase

A management system is the machinery that turns intent into consistent, improvable performance. The Plan–Do–Deploy & Check–Act cycle is the heartbeat of that machinery — and the S.T.E.P.S.™ staircase (Define → Discover → Design → Document → Deploy → Do & Deploy & Check → Drive) is how this book operationalises PDCA across every clause of ISO/IEC 27001:2022.

The S.T.E.P.S.™ Governance Trust Cycle — the engine beneath every chapter.

Chapter Overview

Security becomes reliable only when it is governed as a system. A management system supplies the policies, processes, accountabilities and feedback loops that turn isolated controls into a coherent, improving whole, and the ISO/IEC 27000 family

— anchored by the certifiable 27001:2022 and the 93 controls of 27002:2022 — is the global standard for doing so.

The Plan–Do–Deploy & Check–Act cycle is its engine, and the S.T.E.P.S.™ staircase is how this book makes that engine walkable, mapping each of its seven steps to specific ISO clauses.

Complementary frameworks and a disciplined metrics model keep the system aligned to business value rather than drifting into compliance ritual.

The Cosmos Bank heist is the warning that frames the rest of the journey: an organisation can possess every tool and still fail catastrophically if the management system that connects them does not function. Building that system is the work of the steps that follow.

Chapter Objectives

By the end of this chapter, the reader will be able to:

- Define a management system and explain why it, not technology, is what makes security consistent and improvable.
- Describe the seven common elements of any ISO management system (the Annex SL High-Level Structure).
- Explain the process approach and the Plan–Do–Deploy & Check–Act cycle and map them to the S.T.E.P.S.™ staircase and the clauses of ISO/IEC 27001:2022.
- Navigate the ISO/IEC 27000 family of standards and the evolution that produced the 2022 editions.
- Use complementary frameworks — the Balanced Scorecard and SABSA — and a three-tier metrics model to make the ISMS measurable and business-aligned.

Why a Management System, Not Just Security Tools

Most organisations that suffer a serious breach were not short of security tools. They had firewalls, monitoring, antivirus and skilled people. What they lacked was the connective tissue that turns those parts into a functioning whole — the documented processes, clear accountabilities and feedback loops that ensure a control selected on paper is actually operated, measured and improved in practice. That connective tissue is a management system, and it is the difference between an organisation that is occasionally secure by luck and one that is reliably secure by design.

> **Executive Insight**
>
> Tools answer the question "what protects us?" A management system answers the harder question "how do we know our protection actually works, and how does it get better?" Boards should fund the second question at least as generously as the first.

2.1 What Is a Management System?

A management system is the framework of policies, processes and procedures an organisation uses to ensure it can fulfil the tasks required to achieve its objectives.

ISO/IEC 27000 defines it as a set of interrelated elements that establish policies, objectives and the processes to achieve those objectives.

For information security, the Information Security Management System (ISMS) supplies the structure, policies, responsibilities, practices, processes and resources through which security is systematically governed, implemented, monitored and improved.

Management systems are not bureaucratic overlays; they are the machinery by which strategy becomes consistent, measurable operational performance.

2.2 The Common Elements: ISO's Annex SL Structure

Every modern ISO management system is built on the same High-Level Structure (Annex SL), which is why an organisation running ISO 9001 for quality can integrate ISO/IEC 27001 for security with far less friction than it expects.

The seven elements below recur in every discipline.

Element	What it covers
1. Context	Internal and external issues, and interested parties, that affect intended outcomes
2. Leadership	Top-management commitment, policy, and assignment of roles and authority
3. Planning	Risk-based thinking: actions to address risks and opportunities; objectives and plans
4. Support	Resources, competence, awareness, communication and documented information
5. Operation	Planning and controlling the processes that meet requirements
6. Performance evaluation	Monitoring, measurement, analysis, internal audit and management review
7. Improvement	Nonconformity, corrective action and continual improvement

2.3 The Process Approach

A central tenet of every ISO management system is the process approach: any activity that uses resources to transform inputs into outputs is a process, and security is managed by systematically identifying these processes and — crucially — the interactions between them.

Risk assessment, access management, incident response and management review are all processes, each with inputs, activities, controls, outputs and an accountable owner. Combined with risk-based thinking, the process approach lets an organisation understand its context, determine its risks, select proportionate controls, monitor performance and continually improve.

2.4 What Is an Information Security Management System?

An ISMS is a systematic approach to managing sensitive information so that it remains secure — encompassing people, processes and technology under a single risk based-management discipline.

A well-run ISMS lets an organisation satisfy stakeholder security requirements, meet its own security objectives, comply with legal and regulatory mandates, and manage information assets in a way that supports continual improvement.

The recurring lesson is that security limited to technical means is insufficient: technical controls must be supported by management policies and procedures, and control selection must involve the whole organisation and its supply chain, not the IT department alone.

2.5 The ISO/IEC 27000 Family

The ISO/IEC 27000 family is the most widely deployed body of information-security management standards in the world. A working knowledge of its structure is a prerequisite to implementation.

Standard	Purpose and Scope
ISO/IEC 27000	Overview and vocabulary — defines the terms and concepts used across the family
ISO/IEC 27001:2022	Requirements for establishing, implementing, maintaining, and continually improving an ISMS — the certifiable standard
ISO/IEC 27002:2022	Information security controls — guidance on 93 controls across four control categories (organizational, people, physical, technological)
ISO/IEC 27003	Guidance on implementing the requirements of ISO 27001
ISO/IEC 27004	Monitoring, measurement, analysis, and evaluation — guidance on metrics and performance evaluation
ISO/IEC 27005	Information security risk management — guidance on risk assessment and treatment
ISO/IEC 27006	Requirements for bodies providing audit and certification of ISMS
ISO/IEC 27017	Code of practice for information security controls for cloud services
ISO/IEC 27018	Code of practice for protection of personally identifiable information (PII) in public clouds
ISO/IEC 27701	Extension for privacy information management — adds requirements for a PIMS that complements the ISMS

The complete family, organised by job

Group	Members (illustrative)	What it gives you
Overview & vocabulary	27000	Shared terms; free of charge; the on ramp
Requirements (certifiable)	27001	The management-system specification you certify to
Reference controls	27002	The catalogue of controls you select from
Supporting guidance	27003 (implementation), 27004 (measurement), 27005 (risk)	How to implement, measure and manage risk
Audit & certification	27006, 27007, 27008, 27009	Rules for certification bodies and auditors
Sector & topic specific	27017/27018 (cloud, PII), 27701 (privacy), 27019, etc.	Tailoring for cloud, privacy and industry sectors
Interrelated	27031 (ICT continuity), 27032 (cyber), 27035 (incident), 27037 (forensics)	Adjacent disciplines the ISMS draws on

2.6 How the Standard Evolved

The family's history charts the rise of information security from a technical code of practice to a strategic discipline. It began with the UK's BS 7799 (Part 1 in 1995, Part 2 in 1998, which introduced the PDCA model), became ISO/IEC 17799:2000 and then ISO/IEC 27001:2005, and was restructured in 2013 onto the Annex SL High-Level Structure.

The current 2022 editions completed a fundamental redesign of the control set: ISO/IEC 27002:2022 replaced the old fourteen-domain, 114-control structure with 93 controls across four categories — organizational, people, physical and technological — adding controls for cloud services, threat intelligence, data masking, information deletion and ICT supply-chain security to reflect the threat landscape of the 2020s.

The Evolution of ISO 27001: A Legacy Built on Experience

Its origins can be traced back to the **British Standard BS 7799**, developed by the British Standards Institution (BSI) in the mid-1990s. Recognizing that organizations needed structured guidance to protect increasingly valuable information assets, BSI introduced **BS 7799 Part 1** in 1995 as a **Code of Practice for Information Security Management**. Rather than prescribing certification requirements, it provided a comprehensive collection of recommended security controls and best practices that organizations could adopt according to their needs.

The success and international recognition of BS 7799 led to its adoption by the International Organization for Standardization (ISO) and the International Electrotechnical Commission (IEC). In 2000, **BS 7799 Part 1** evolved into **ISO/IEC 17799**, extending its influence beyond the United Kingdom and becoming a globally recognized code of practice. In 2005, it was renumbered as **ISO/IEC 27002**, where it continues to serve as detailed guidance on information security controls.

At the same time, **BS 7799 Part 2** formed the foundation of **ISO/IEC 27001**, first published in 2005 as the international standard specifying the requirements for an Information Security Management System. Subsequent revisions in 2013 and 2022 modernized the standard to address emerging technologies, cloud computing, digital transformation, privacy considerations, and evolving cyber threats while preserving its fundamental risk-based management philosophy.

This lineage demonstrates that ISO/IEC 27001 is not a passing management trend or a fashionable compliance exercise. It is a battle-tested framework that has evolved through decades of real-world implementation across governments, financial institutions, healthcare providers, technology companies, manufacturers, and critical infrastructure organizations around the world.

2.7 The Benefits of an ISO/IEC 27001:2022 ISMS

Organisations that implement a well-designed ISMS derive benefits well beyond the certificate: systematic risk reduction; a structured route to legal and regulatory compliance; customer and partner confidence (certification is increasingly a precondition for enterprise contracts and public tenders); business resilience through integration with continuity planning; competitive differentiation in markets where data handling is a selection criterion; a genuine culture of security that reaches beyond IT; and measurable, continual improvement driven by monitoring and management review. As the original code of practice observed, the critical success factors are consistent: objectives that reflect business goals, visible management commitment, sound risk management, effective internal marketing of security, and balanced measurement.

— ISO/IEC 17799:2000

ISO/IEC 27001 vs. ISO/IEC 27002: Understanding the Difference Between Certification and Conformance

One of the most common misconceptions in information security is the belief that an organization can be **certified to**

ISO/IEC 27002. In reality, organizations are **certified to ISO/IEC 27001**, while they may **conform to or use ISO/IEC 27002 as guidance**. Understanding this distinction is essential for anyone involved in information security governance, compliance, or audit.

At its core, **ISO/IEC 27001** and **ISO/IEC 27002** serve different but complementary purposes.

ISO/IEC 27001: The Management System Standard

ISO/IEC 27001 specifies the **requirements for establishing, implementing, maintaining, and continually improving an Information Security Management System (ISMS).** It follows the management system approach adopted by many other ISO standards, such as ISO 9001 for quality management and ISO 14001 for environmental management.

The standard requires organizations to:

- Understand their business context and stakeholders.
- Identify and assess information security risks.
- Select and implement appropriate controls.
- Define policies, roles, and responsibilities.
- Monitor performance and conduct internal audits.
- Review the ISMS through management oversight.
- Drive continual improvement through corrective actions and ongoing risk management.

Because ISO/IEC 27001 contains auditable requirements expressed using terms such as **"shall,"** accredited certification bodies can independently assess an organization against these requirements. If the organization demonstrates compliance, it may be awarded **ISO/IEC 27001 certification**.

In simple terms:

An organization can be certified to ISO/IEC 27001 because it defines the requirements for a management system.

ISO/IEC 27002: The Guidance Standard

ISO/IEC 27002 serves a different purpose. It is **not a management system standard**, nor does it prescribe mandatory requirements for certification.

Instead, it provides **guidance on information security controls** that organizations may consider when treating identified risks. The standard explains the objectives, implementation guidance, and practical considerations for controls covering areas such as:

- Access management
- Cryptography
- Physical security
- Human resource security
- Supplier relationships
- Incident management
- Business continuity
- Cloud services
- Threat intelligence
- Secure development
- Information deletion and masking
- Monitoring activities

The language of ISO/IEC 27002 is intentionally advisory rather than mandatory. It describes **what organizations should consider** rather than **what they must implement**.

As a result:

Organizations do not become "ISO/IEC 27002 certified." Instead, they use or conform to ISO/IEC 27002 as a reference framework when selecting and implementing controls appropriate to their risk environment.

A Simple Analogy

An easy way to understand the relationship is to compare the two standards to constructing and operating a building.

- **ISO/IEC 27001** is the blueprint for managing the entire building project. It defines how planning, governance, responsibilities, inspections, reviews, and continual improvements should be carried out.
- **ISO/IEC 27002** is the catalogue of recommended building materials and engineering practices. It offers guidance on the types of locks, fire protection systems, surveillance equipment, and structural safeguards that may be appropriate depending on the building's design and risk profile.

The blueprint can be independently certified. The catalogue provides expert recommendations but is not itself certifiable.

Risk-Based Rather Than Deploy & Checklist-Based

Another important distinction is that ISO/IEC 27001 does **not require every control described in ISO/IEC 27002 to be implemented.**

Instead, organizations perform a risk assessment and select controls that are appropriate to their business objectives, legal obligations, regulatory requirements, customer expectations, and risk appetite. Controls that are not applicable may be excluded, provided the organization can justify its decision.

For example:

The flexibility to tailor controls based on risk is one of the defining strengths of the ISO/IEC 27000 family.

The Practical Distinction

ISO/IEC 27001	ISO/IEC 27002
Specifies requirements for an Information Security Management System (ISMS).	Provides guidance on selecting and implementing information security controls.
Uses mandatory language ("shall").	Uses advisory guidance and recommendations.
Can be independently audited and certified.	Cannot be certified independently.
Focuses on governance, risk management, and continual improvement.	Focuses on practical security controls and implementation guidance.
Organizations achieve certification against ISO/IEC 27001.	Organizations **conform to or use** ISO/IEC 27002 as a best-practice reference.

Understanding this distinction prevents one of the most frequent misunderstandings in information security. **ISO/IEC 27001 tells an organization how to build and operate an effective information security management system; ISO/IEC 27002 helps it decide which security controls are appropriate to support that system.** Together, they provide a comprehensive and internationally recognized foundation for managing information security in a structured, risk-based, and business-aligned manner.

ISO/IEC 27000:2018

Information technology — Security techniques — Information security management systems — Overview and vocabulary

The foundational ISO/IEC 27000 standard is available at no cost through the official ISO Store. https://www.iso.org/standard/73906.html

2.8 PDCA, the S.T.E.P.S.™ Staircase, and the ISO Clauses

The Plan–Do–Deploy & Check–Act cycle, named for the quality pioneer W. Edwards Deming, is the engine of continual improvement. ISO/IEC 27001:2022 does not mandate PDCA explicitly, but the structure of its clauses mirrors it precisely — and the S.T.E.P.S.™ staircase is how this book turns that abstract cycle into seven concrete, sequenced steps an organisation can actually walk. The mapping below is the operational backbone of the entire book.

S.T.E.P.S.™ step	PDCA phase	ISO/IEC 27001:2022 clauses	What happens
1 — DEFINE	Plan	Clause 4 (Context); Clause 5 (Leadership)	Establish context, interested parties, scope, leadership commitment
2 — DISCOVER	Plan	Clause 6.1.2	Identify, analyse and evaluate information-security risk
3 — DESIGN	Plan	Clause 6.1.3, 6.2	Decide risk treatment, select controls, produce the Statement of Applicability and objectives

S.T.E.P.S.™ step	PDCA phase	ISO/IEC 27001:2022 clauses	What happens
4 — DOCUMENT	Plan / Support	Clause 5.2, 7.5	Codify policy and the documented information the system needs
5 — DEPLOY	Do	Clause 7, 8	Resource, train, communicate and operate the controls
6 — DO & CHECK	Check	Clause 9	Monitor, measure, audit internally and review at management level
7 — DRIVE	Act	Clause 10	Correct nonconformities and continually improve

2.9 Complementary Frameworks: Balanced Scorecard and SABSA

An Information Security Management System (ISMS) cannot succeed in isolation. While ISO/IEC 27001 provides a structured framework for managing information security risks, organizations often struggle to communicate its value to senior executives and boards of directors. Security teams frequently report technical metrics—such as vulnerabilities patched, firewall events, or malware detections—that fail to resonate with business leaders whose primary concerns are revenue, profitability, customer trust, resilience, and regulatory compliance.

Two complementary frameworks help bridge this communication gap by translating security activities into business language: the **Balanced Scorecard (BSC)** and the **Sherwood Applied Business Security Architecture (SABSA)**. Together, they enable organizations to demonstrate that information security is not merely a technical function but a strategic business capability that supports organizational objectives.

2.9.1 The Balanced Scorecard: Measuring Security Through a Business Lens

Developed by Robert Kaplan and David Norton, the Balanced Scorecard was originally designed as a strategic performance management framework that goes beyond traditional financial metrics. Instead of measuring success solely through profit and loss statements, it evaluates organizational performance across four interrelated perspectives:

- Financial
- Customer
- Internal Processes
- Learning and Growth

The Four Perspectives Applied to Information Security

When adapted for information security, the Balanced Scorecard provides a powerful mechanism for aligning cybersecurity initiatives with business strategy.

Financial Perspective: Security as an Investment

- By demonstrating tangible financial outcomes, security leaders can justify investments based on business value rather than fear.

Customer Perspective: Security Creates Trust

- Customers increasingly choose organizations based on their ability to protect personal and confidential information.

Internal Process Perspective: Security Enables Reliable Operations

- Information security is deeply integrated into business operations. Effective governance improves internal processes through:

Learning and Growth Perspective: People as the First Line of Defence

- Technology alone cannot protect an organization. Human behaviour remains one of the most significant sources of both vulnerability and resilience.

Perspective	Strategic Objective	Example Metrics	Business Outcome
Financial	Reduce cyber-related losses and optimize security investment	Cost per incident, Return on Security Investment (ROSI), cyber insurance premiums	Lower operational losses and improved financial performance
Customer	Build trust and protect customer experience	Service availability, breach notification timeliness, customer privacy complaints	Stronger customer confidence and brand loyalty

Perspective	Strategic Objective	Example Metrics	Business Outcome
Internal Processes	Improve governance and operational effectiveness	Audit compliance rate, patch management performance, incident response time	Better governance, resilience, and process maturity
Learning & Growth	Develop security culture and workforce capability	Security awareness scores, phishing simulation success rates, training completion	Reduced human risk and stronger organizational culture

A workforce that understands and practices secure behaviour significantly reduces organizational risk while strengthening overall security culture.

2.9.2 SABSA: Aligning Security Architecture with Business Objectives

Developed by John Sherwood, Andrew Clark, and David Lynas, SABSA is a business-driven enterprise security architecture framework that begins not with technology but with the organization's mission, strategy, and stakeholder requirements.

Its fundamental principle is simple:

- Every security control should exist because it protects a specific business requirement.

This represents a profound shift from traditional security approaches that implement controls simply because they are considered industry best practices or regulatory expectations.

Only after defining the business priorities does the framework determine the security services and technical controls required to protect them.

For example:

Business Attribute	Security Requirement	Technical Control
Customer Trust	Protect personal information	Encryption and access control
Operational Resilience	Ensure uninterrupted service	High availability architecture and disaster recovery
Regulatory Compliance	Meet legal obligations	Audit logging and retention controls
Reputation	Prevent unauthorized disclosures	Data Loss Prevention (DLP) and monitoring
Business Continuity	Minimize downtime	Backup and recovery systems

This traceability ensures that every security investment can be justified in terms of measurable business value.

Traceability from Boardroom to Firewall

One of SABSA's greatest strengths is its ability to create a clear line of sight between strategic objectives and technical implementation.

Consider a board-level objective:

"Maintain customer trust while expanding digital services."

This objective translates into business requirements.

These requirements then drive architectural decisions:

Finally, they result in specific technical implementations such as identity management systems, security information and event management (SIEM) platforms, endpoint protection, and network segmentation.

When a board member asks why the organization invested millions in identity security or encryption technologies, the CISO can answer not with technical jargon but with business language:

"These controls protect customer trust, support regulatory compliance, reduce fraud risk, and enable secure digital transformation."

The conversation shifts from technology expenditure to business value creation.

Combining the Balanced Scorecard and SABSA

The Balanced Scorecard and SABSA complement each other exceptionally well.

The Balanced Scorecard measures whether security initiatives are delivering strategic outcomes.

SABSA ensures that every security initiative is designed to achieve those outcomes in the first place.

Together they create a closed-loop governance model:

- Business objectives define required business attributes.
- SABSA translates those attributes into security architecture and controls.
- The ISMS manages risks and implements the controls.
- The Balanced Scorecard measures whether those controls are producing the intended business outcomes.

- Management reviews the results and continually improves performance.

This integrated approach aligns perfectly with ISO/IEC 27001's philosophy of continual improvement and risk-based decision-making.

From Cost Centre to Business Enabler

Frameworks such as the Balanced Scorecard and SABSA bridge this divide by translating cybersecurity into the language of strategy and value creation. They demonstrate that security is not merely about preventing attacks—it is about enabling innovation, supporting digital transformation, protecting organizational reputation, and sustaining stakeholder trust.

Ultimately, the most successful Information Security Management Systems are not those with the largest number of controls but those in which every control can be traced to a clear business objective and every security investment can be measured by the value it creates. In this way, the ISMS evolves from a compliance-driven obligation into a strategic capability that helps the organization achieve its mission with confidence, resilience, and trust.

2.10 Security Metrics: From Intuition to Evidence

One of the most under-appreciated parts of an ISMS is its measurement infrastructure. As W. Krag Brotby observed, security is one of the few management areas without a well-understood canon of measurement — and without metrics, decisions about investment, prioritisation and risk acceptance are made on intuition. Brotby distinguishes three tiers of measurement, each for a different audience:

1. **Technical metrics** — narrow IT measures (patch rates, IDS alerts, hardening scores): useful for managing technologies, insufficient for managing security.

2. **Programme metrics** — trends in incident rates, control-maturity scores, remediation rates: used by security management to steer the programme.

3. **Strategic / governance metrics** — board-level indicators of overall risk posture: residual-risk levels, alignment of security with business objectives.

Case Study: The Cosmos Bank Cyber Heist (Pune, 2018)

Between 11 and 13 August 2018, attackers stole approximately ₹94 crore (US$13.5 million) from Cosmos Cooperative Bank, one of India's oldest cooperative banks. The attack, later attributed by a United Nations panel to a North Korean advanced persistent threat (APT) group, unfolded in two stages.

First, malware implanted in the bank's ATM switch created a malicious proxy that intercepted and manipulated ISO 8583 transaction messages. This enabled nearly 14,000 fraudulent ATM withdrawals across 28 countries, resulting in losses of about ₹80 crore within hours. Two days later, the attackers exploited the compromised SWIFT environment to transfer an additional ₹13.92 crore to a Hong Kong account.

The root cause was not a lack of security technology but a failure of governance and system integration. Because transaction requests never reached the core banking system, fraud-detection mechanisms remained blind to the attack. There was no effective monitoring of switch-level activity, inadequate segregation between environments, and delayed incident escalation.

Mapping the Failure to ISO/IEC 27001:2022

Clause 6.1.2 – Risk Assessment: The ATM switch and SWIFT systems were not assessed as a single critical ecosystem, leaving switch-level manipulation unaddressed.

A.8.15–A.8.16 – Logging and Monitoring: Insufficient monitoring and correlation of transaction flows allowed malicious activity to remain undetected.

A.5.19–A.5.22 – Supplier Security: Weak change management and inadequate oversight of vendor-managed systems increased exposure.

A.5.24–A.5.27 – Incident Management: Abnormal transaction patterns were not identified and escalated quickly enough to contain the attack.

Key Lessons

1. Critical systems must be assessed as interconnected ecosystems rather than isolated components.
2. Effective detection requires monitoring the right control points and correlating events across systems.
3. Cyber resilience depends on integrating risk management, supplier governance, monitoring, and incident response into a unified management system.
4. Security controls alone are insufficient; without disciplined execution, governance remains little more than documentation.
5. A management system is what connects supplier control, configuration, monitoring and response into a working whole. PDCA without execution is just paperwork

Governance in Practice: Australia's APRA CPS 234

Australia's Prudential Standard CPS 234 provides a practical example of how cybersecurity governance can be embedded into organizational management systems. Rather than prescribing a detailed checklist of technical controls, CPS 234 requires regulated entities to maintain information security capabilities that are proportionate to the threats and risks facing their information assets. This risk-based approach closely aligns with the principles of ISO/IEC 27001:2022.

The standard places clear accountability on boards and senior management, making cybersecurity a governance responsibility rather than merely an IT function. Organizations are expected to establish security policies, define cyber-risk appetite, oversee third-party risks, test controls regularly, and report significant incidents. In practice, boards receive cybersecurity metrics, critical systems undergo periodic security testing, and vendors are required to demonstrate appropriate security controls through certifications or independent assessments.

CPS 234 mirrors many of the core requirements of ISO/IEC 27001:

Management System Thinking in Practice

For example:

ISMS Principle (ISO/IEC 27001)	Comparable CPS 234 Expectation
Leadership commitment and governance	Board accountability for information security capability
Risk assessment and treatment	Security measures proportional to vulnerabilities and threats
Asset identification	Identification and classification of information assets
Control implementation	Maintenance of appropriate security controls
Monitoring and review	Systematic testing and assurance activities
Supplier security management	Oversight of third-party information security arrangements
Incident management	Timely detection, response, and notification of material incidents
Continual improvement	Ongoing review and enhancement of security capability

The result is a regulatory framework that focuses not merely on implementing controls but on ensuring that security is embedded within organizational governance and business decision-making

One of the standard's most significant features is its focus on third-party and supply chain risk. Financial institutions increasingly depend on cloud providers, software vendors, payment processors, and managed service providers. CPS 234 makes it clear that while services may be outsourced, accountability cannot. Organizations remain responsible for protecting information assets regardless of where they are processed.

The standard also emphasizes continuous assurance rather than point-in-time compliance. Controls must be regularly tested, vulnerabilities assessed, incidents reviewed, and improvements implemented. This reflects the Plan–Do–Deploy & Check–Act (PDCA) cycle that underpins ISO/IEC 27001 and effective management systems.

Although CPS 234 applies specifically to Australian banks, insurers, and superannuation funds, its principles are increasingly relevant across industries worldwide. It demonstrates a fundamental shift in regulation—from prescribing technical controls to requiring organizations to establish governance, manage risk systematically, verify effectiveness, and continually improve.

In essence, CPS 234 illustrates how cybersecurity becomes a business discipline, enabling trust, resilience, and sustainable growth.

Managing Third-Party and Supply Chain Risk

Modern financial institutions rely extensively on cloud providers, payment processors, software vendors, managed service providers, and other external partners. Recognizing this dependency, CPS 234 requires organizations to ensure that third parties maintain security capabilities appropriate to the information assets they manage.

The organization remains accountable for protecting its information even when processing is outsourced.

This requirement reflects a fundamental ISMS principle:

Risk can be delegated, but accountability cannot.

Continuous Assurance Rather Than Point-in-Time Compliance

Another hallmark of CPS 234 is its emphasis on ongoing assurance. Controls are expected not only to exist but also to be tested regularly to confirm that they remain effective against evolving threats.

Examples include:

This reflects the Plan–Do–Deploy & Check–Act (PDCA) philosophy that underpins ISO/IEC 27001, where continual evaluation and improvement are essential elements of the management system.

Lessons for Organizations Beyond Australia

Although CPS 234 applies specifically to APRA-regulated entities such as banks, insurers, and superannuation funds in Australia, its principles have broader relevance.

Organizations in healthcare, fintech, critical infrastructure, government, and technology sectors increasingly face similar expectations from regulators, customers, and investors:

For many organizations, implementing an ISO/IEC 27001-compliant ISMS provides a structured foundation for meeting these expectations.

Regulation Meets Management

APRA CPS 234 illustrates an important evolution in cybersecurity regulation. Instead of prescribing an exhaustive list of technical controls, it adopts a **management system mindset**, requiring organizations to establish governance structures, assess risks, implement appropriate safeguards, monitor effectiveness, and continually improve their security capability.

Latitude Financial (2023): When Data Governance Fails

The 2023 cyberattack on Latitude Financial, one of Australia's largest consumer finance providers, demonstrates how information security failures often stem from governance weaknesses rather than technology alone. Following the compromise of a third-party service provider with privileged access, attackers gained unauthorized access to sensitive customer information, ultimately exposing more than 14 million records, including identity documents and financial data.

The breach highlighted two critical management system failures.

Failure 1: Excessive Data Retention

A significant volume of identity documents had been retained long after their original business purpose had ended. These historical records became valuable targets for attackers despite no longer serving operational needs. The incident reinforces a fundamental security principle:

The safest sensitive data is the data that no longer exists.

This aligns with ISO/IEC 27001:2022 Annex A.8.10 (Information Deletion), which requires organizations to securely dispose of information that is no longer required.

Failure 2: Weak Third-Party Governance

The attack originated through a trusted external provider, demonstrating that supplier vulnerabilities can quickly become organizational vulnerabilities. Outsourcing services does not outsource accountability. ISO/IEC 27001 addresses this through controls covering supplier relationships, contractual security requirements, ICT supply chain security, and ongoing supplier monitoring.

The Missing PDCA Cycle

The breach also exposed weaknesses in the "Deploy & Check" and "Act" stages of the Plan–Do–Deploy & Check–Act (PDCA) cycle. Regular management reviews should have identified excessive data retention, assessed supplier risks, and verified the effectiveness of security controls before the incident occurred.

Key Lessons

1. Data minimization reduces risk.
2. Retention policies must be actively enforced and reviewed.
3. Third-party risk is organizational risk.
4. Strong governance is as important as technical controls.
5. Continuous improvement helps identify weaknesses before attackers do.

Beyond Cybersecurity

The Latitude incident was ultimately a governance failure rather than a purely technical one. It demonstrates that effective information security depends on disciplined data lifecycle management, supplier oversight, and continual review. The lesson is simple yet powerful: organizations cannot lose data they no longer retain, and they cannot effectively manage cyber risk if suppliers operate outside their security management system.

The enduring lesson is clear: **you cannot lose data you no longer retain, and you cannot effectively manage cyber risk if your suppliers fall outside your security management system.**

Key Takeaways

- A management system — not a collection of tools — is what makes security consistent, measurable and improvable.
- Every ISO management system shares the seven Annex SL elements, which is what makes integration across disciplines achievable.
- PDCA is the engine of continual improvement; the S.T.E.P.S.™ staircase (Define Drive) is how this book maps PDCA onto every clause of ISO/IEC 27001:2022.
- ISO/IEC 27002:2022 restructured controls into 93 controls across four categories — organizational, people, physical and technological.
- The Balanced Scorecard and SABSA translate security into business outcomes; three tiers of metrics serve technical, programme and governance audiences.
- The Cosmos Bank heist shows that tools without an integrated management system are no defence: PDCA without execution is paperwork.

Reflection Questions

1. If you scored your organisation 1–5 on each of the seven Annex SL elements today, where would the lowest scores fall — and who owns them?

2. Can your security leader explain each major control in terms of the business attribute it protects, or only in technical terms?
3. Which of your critical systems have never been risk-assessed as an ecosystem, including their vendor and integration points?
4. What security metrics reach your board, and do they describe residual risk and business alignment — or only technical activity?
5. If a regulator-imposed CPS 234-style obligations on you tomorrow, how much of it could you already evidence?

Action Deploy & Checklist

- Score your management system against the seven Annex SL elements on a 1–5 scale to create an ISMS gap register.
- If no formal ISMS exists, stand up the three highest-value elements first: a documented scope, an asset inventory and a formal incident-response process.
- Map the S.T.E.P.S.™ staircase to your current state and identify which ISO clauses are unaddressed.
- Establish a monthly security-metrics dashboard with at least five KPIs reaching senior management.
- Review every third-party contract with system access for security clauses and minimum baselines within 90 days.
- Appoint a C-suite (not IT-only) sponsor for information security and schedule quarterly management reviews for the first year.

CHAPTER

3

AN OVERVIEW OF ISO/IEC 27001:2022 REQUIREMENTS

A clause-by-clause guide to the world's leading ISMS standard

A Clause-by-Clause Guide to the World's Leading ISMS Standard

S.T.E.P.S.™ Engine — Operational Anchor: Clauses 4–10 ARE the Staircase

ISO/IEC 27001:2022 is not an abstract specification. Read correctly, its seven clause-groups are the seven treads of the staircase: Clause 4 is DEFINE, Clause 6.1.2 is DISCOVER, Clause 6.1.3 is DESIGN, Clause 7.5 is DOCUMENT, Clauses 7–8 are DEPLOY, Clause 9 is DO & DEPLOY & CHECK, and Clause 10 is DRIVE.

Chapter Overview

ISO/IEC 27001:2022 is best read not as a compliance burden but as the codified experience of every organisation breached for want of structure. Its seven clause-groups map precisely onto the seven steps of the S.T.E.P.S.™ staircase: Clauses 4 and 5 define context and leadership, Clause 6 discovers and designs the response to risk, Clauses 7 and 8 document and deploy it, Clause 9 checks that it works, and Clause 10 drives its improvement.

The 2022 revision modernised the control set for a cloud-and-supply-chain world, and regulators from India's CERT-In and SEBI to Australia's ASD now turn these clauses into hard, sector-specific obligations. The NHS WannaCry disaster is the chapter's standing lesson: the clauses exist because their absence carries a measurable, sometimes life-threatening cost, and the disciplined application of basic, documented, managed processes is what separates resilience from catastrophe.

Chapter Objectives

By the end of this chapter, the reader will be able to:

- Summarise what changed in the 2022 revision and why the control set was restructured.
- Walk Clauses 4 through 10 and explain the intent and key requirements of each.
- Explain the central role of risk assessment, risk treatment and the Statement of Applicability.
- Identify the documented information the standard requires and why each artefact matters at audit.
- Map every clause to the S.T.E.P.S.™ staircase and to real regulatory expectations in India and Australia.

Why the Clauses Exist

It is tempting to read a standard as bureaucracy — a checklist imposed from outside. ISO/IEC 27001 is better understood as institutional memory: each clause exists because organisations that lacked that discipline suffered the consequences its absence enables. The NHS lost two weeks of care to WannaCry because it lacked the patch-management process Clause 8 would have required. This chapter walks the clauses in that spirit — not as requirements to satisfy an auditor, but as the seven disciplines that make security reliable.

3.1 The Standard and the 2022 Update

ISO/IEC 27001:2022 specifies the requirements to establish, implement, maintain and continually improve an ISMS within the context of the organisation, including the assessment and treatment of information-security risk. It uses the Annex SL High-Level Structure — enabling integration with ISO 9001, 14001, 22301 and 27701 — and is organised into Clauses 4 to 10, with Annex A providing the reference control set. The 2022 edition, the first revision in nine years, made modest changes to the management-system clauses and a major reorganisation of the controls.

- **Clauses 4–10:** a new Clause 6.3 (Planning of changes) requires ISMS changes to be managed; Clause 7.4 (Communication) was expanded; Clauses 9.2 and 9.3 were broken into sub-sections for clearer auditing.

- **Annex A:** the old 114 controls across 14 domains were consolidated into 93 controls across four categories — organisational (37), people (8), physical (14) and technological (34) — and each control now carries attribute tags (control type, security properties, cybersecurity concepts, operational capabilities, security domains).

- **Eleven new controls:** threat intelligence (A.5.7), ICT supply-chain security (A.5.21), cloud-service security (A.5.23), ICT readiness for continuity (A.5.30), physical security monitoring (A.7.4), configuration management

(A.8.9), information deletion (A.8.10), data masking (A.8.11), data-leakage prevention (A.8.12), monitoring activities (A.8.16), web filtering (A.8.23) and secure coding (A.8.28).

3.2 Clause 4 — Context of the Organisation (DEFINE)

Understanding context is not a compliance exercise — it is the process by which the ISMS becomes relevant to the actual business rather than a generic template. An ISMS that does not reflect the organisation's unique risk profile is unlikely to be effective.

Clause 4.1 requires the organisation to determine the external and internal issues relevant to its purpose that affect the intended outcomes of its ISMS. External issues span the regulatory, competitive, technological and macro-environment (PESTLE gives useful structure); internal issues span culture, governance, capabilities, contracts, infrastructure and strategic direction. The point is to make the ISMS "at one" with the business it serves rather than a parallel bureaucracy of templated policies — an ISMS disconnected from business reality inevitably becomes shelf-ware that satisfies auditors but adds little value.

Clause 4.2 requires identifying interested parties and their relevant requirements — anyone who can affect, be affected by, or perceive themselves affected by the ISMS. Clause 4.3 then sets the documented scope (locations, assets and processes), accounting for those issues, interested-party requirements, and all interfaces and dependencies. Clause 4.4 is brief but binding: establish, implement, maintain and continually improve the ISMS — it is not optional, partial or temporary.

From Interested Parties to ISMS Requirements

Every policy, risk-treatment plan and control should trace back to an expectation held by an interested party, following a simple chain: Interested Party → Need or Expectation → ISMS Requirement. Shareholders expect cyber risk to be managed because incidents destroy enterprise value; customers expect their data protected and services available; regulators expect compliance and prompt incident reporting; suppliers and partners expect clear, fair contractual security expectations.

Interested Party	Need / Expectation	ISMS Requirement / Obligation
Shareholders & Investors	Protect enterprise value, manage cyber risk, ensure resilience, avoid financial or reputational loss	Risk-based ISMS with board oversight, regular risk assessments, effective controls, performance monitoring, assurance that risks are actively managed
Customers	Data protection, confidentiality, breach notification, SLA compliance	Access controls, encryption, incident response, retention and deletion, continuity and privacy safeguards
Regulators	Compliance with legal and contractual obligations; timely incident reporting	Compliance registers, aligned policies, internal audits, retained evidence, regulatory-reporting processes
Suppliers / Partners	Security clauses, supply-chain risk management, audit rights, fair oversight	Contractual security requirements, supplier due diligence, third-party monitoring, lifecycle supply-chain risk management

Viewed this way, Clause 4 is the bridge between business strategy and information-security governance — the ISMS exists not only to satisfy auditors but to protect shareholder value, preserve customer trust and demonstrate compliance.

3.3 Defining the Scope (Clause 4.3): Object, Boundary, Connections

Many organisations treat scope as merely a boundary drawn around a department or location. In reality scope has both a boundary and an object. The real question is not only "Where does the ISMS apply?" but "What exactly are we protecting, and what dependencies could affect it?" A well-defined scope has three interrelated elements:

- **The Object** — the information assets, products, services, business activities and supporting processes covered.
- **The Boundary** — the organisational units, locations, technologies and legal entities included.
- **The Connections** — the internal and external interfaces through which information flows or on which scoped activities depend.

The object is often overlooked. A hospital's true object of protection is not its building but its electronic health records, diagnostic and telemedicine services and patient-care processes; a fintech's object includes transaction data, identity verification, fraud detection, APIs and mobile apps. Equally, connections rarely stay inside one boundary — information flows through cloud providers, identity providers, outsourced SOCs, payroll processors and remote staff. Such functions may sit outside the formal boundary yet remain critical connections that must be identified and managed, because failure in any one can compromise the scoped service.

Scope Element	Key Question	Example
Object	What are we protecting?	Customer data, payment services, intellectual property, healthcare records
Boundary	Where does the ISMS formally apply?	Business unit, legal entity, geographic location, cloud environment
Connections	What dependencies cross that boundary?	Suppliers, cloud providers, shared services, regulators, APIs, remote users

Beware of Artificial Exclusions

A common cause of certification difficulty is artificial exclusions designed to avoid hard controls — excluding cloud infrastructure that hosts critical applications, omitting development teams, or carving out third-party managed environments that process sensitive data. The rule is simple: if an asset, process or supplier is essential to delivering an in-scope product or service, it should either be included in the ISMS or explicitly managed as a connected dependency through documented governance and risk controls. The purpose of Clause 4.3 is not a narrow scope that simplifies certification, but a management system that accurately reflects operations and protects what truly matters — making certification a consequence of good governance rather than its objective.

3.4 Clause 5 — Leadership (DEFINE)

An ISMS succeeds or fails not because of technology but because of leadership. Firewalls, encryption and policies cannot compensate for a lack of executive direction. Clause

5 places top management at the centre: the ISMS must be driven from the top, aligned with strategy, adequately resourced, and supported by a culture in which security is everyone's responsibility. Clause 5.1 imposes explicit, non-delegable obligations on top management — align policy and objectives with strategic direction, integrate ISMS requirements into business processes, provide resources, communicate the importance of security, ensure intended outcomes, and promote continual improvement. It is the most frequently cited success factor, and its absence the most common cause of failure.

Leadership Is a Documented Act

Commitment that exists only in conversation is invisible to employees and auditors alike. Its most visible expression is a formally approved and signed Information Security Policy, endorsed by the highest level of management. During audits, assessors look for objective evidence rather than declarations: a signed policy, board minutes discussing security risk, management-review records, approved objectives and budgets, resource allocations for people, technology and training, executive-level performance reporting, and leadership communications promoting awareness. Together these demonstrate that leadership is embedded in governance rather than delegated by default.

Leadership Creates Culture

Employees observe what leaders prioritise. Where executives bypass controls or treat security as "an IT issue," staff follow suit; where leaders visibly comply, participate in awareness and discuss cyber risk alongside financial and operational risk, they reinforce that security is integral to business success. Signing the policy is a milestone, not the destination — effective leadership means setting objectives, ensuring risks are treated, providing resources, removing barriers, reviewing performance and promoting accountability at every level.

A Practical Test of Leadership

"If an auditor asked for evidence of top-management commitment today, what documents, decisions and actions could we present?" If the answer is only verbal assurance, leadership has not been demonstrated. If the organisation can produce a signed policy, board-approved objectives, management-review records, resource allocations and governance reports, leadership is visible, measurable and embedded.

3.5 Clause 5.2 & 5.3 — Policy, Roles and Accountability

An ISMS is expressed through two governance instruments: a clear Information Security Policy and clearly defined roles, responsibilities and authorities. Together Clauses 5.2 and 5.3 ensure everyone understands what the organisation intends to achieve and who is accountable for achieving it.

Clause 5.2 — The Information Security Policy

Clause 5.2 requires top management to establish, approve, maintain and communicate a policy that gives strategic direction. It should not be a lengthy technical manual but concise enough to be read, simple enough to be understood, and meaningful enough to influence behaviour — answering why security matters, what principles guide protection, how security supports objectives and manages risk, and who must comply. Crucially it should reflect the organisation's risk appetite (a global bank and a small consultancy will differ), align with business strategy, provide a framework for objectives, commit to legal and contractual compliance and continual improvement, and be available as documented information. The best policies are clear, business-focused and principle-based, supported by detailed standards where needed. (See example IS policy in the Appendix.)

Clause 5.3 — Roles, Responsibilities and Authorities

A policy cannot protect information unless responsibility for it is assigned. Clause 5.3 requires roles, responsibilities and authorities to be determined and communicated so that every person knows what they are responsible for, what authority they hold, and to whom they are accountable:

- **Board & top management** — set strategic direction, approve policy, allocate resources, oversee risk, and integrate security into business processes.
- **Security leadership (CISO)** — coordinates the ISMS, advises on risk, develops policy, monitors compliance, reports performance and drives improvement; this role facilitates governance but does not own all risk — risk ownership stays with the business leaders responsible for affected processes.
- **Department managers** — implement security within their functions, ensure staff follow policy, and maintain controls.
- **Employees & contractors** — comply with policy, protect information, use systems responsibly, report incidents promptly and complete required training.

Governance Depth: ISO 27001 vs Australia's ASD ISM

ISO 27001 Clause 5 asks "Has leadership demonstrated commitment?" and stays intentionally flexible so it applies to organisations of all sizes — evidence is an approved policy, defined objectives, assigned responsibilities, management-review minutes and resource records. Australia's ASD Information Security Manual asks the sharper question "How exactly is leadership governing cyber security?" and sets a higher maturity benchmark: a board-approved cyber strategy, formal board accountability, a designated CISO, cyber risk in the enterprise risk register, regular board reporting, executive-reviewed KPIs and resilience assurance. The two align closely — ASD GOV controls map to ISO Clauses 4, 5, 7.1, 9.1, 9.3 and 10 — but ASD elevates routine management activity to explicit board governance.

Maturity Level	ISO 27001 Perspective	ASD ISM Perspective
Level 1	Security policy exists	Security policy exists
Level 2	Responsibilities assigned	CISO appointed
Level 3	Risks assessed	Risks integrated into ERM
Level 4	Management reviews conducted	Board reviews cyber risk regularly
Level 5	ISMS continually improved	Board actively governs cyber resilience and risk appetite

The lesson for a book is that ISO 27001 compliance is not merely about policies and audits — it is fundamentally about governance, accountability and leadership.

3.6 Clause 6 — Planning (DISCOVER & DESIGN)

Clause 6 is the heart of the ISMS, where governance becomes concrete risk management. Clause 6.1.1 requires planning actions to address the risks and opportunities arising from Clause 4. Clause 6.1.2 (Risk assessment) requires a defined, repeatable process that sets risk criteria, produces consistent and comparable results, identifies risks to confidentiality, integrity and availability, and analyses and evaluates them for prioritisation — supported by ISO/IEC 27005, using asset-based, scenario-based or quantitative (FAIR) methods as appropriate. Clause 6.1.3 (Risk treatment) requires selecting treatment options, determining controls, comparing them against Annex A to confirm none are omitted, producing the Statement of Applicability, formulating a risk-treatment plan and obtaining risk owners' approval and explicit acceptance of residual risk. Clause 6.2 requires measurable, monitored, communicated objectives; Clause 6.3 (new in 2022) requires changes to the ISMS to be planned, since unplanned change is a frequent source of incidents.

Once Is Not Enough: Risk Assessment Is Continuous

Risk assessment is not a one-time implementation task. The risks found in DISCOVER and the treatments chosen in DESIGN are a snapshot in time, but objectives evolve, technologies change, threat actors adapt, suppliers and regulations shift, and new vulnerabilities emerge. Risks and treatments must therefore be periodically reassessed, with Step 07 — monitoring, internal audit, management review and continual improvement — providing the feedback loop: Discover → Design → Implement → Monitor → Review → Improve → Rediscover. This continual reassessment is what turns risk management from a compliance exercise into an enduring capability.

The Statement of Applicability (SoA)

The SoA lists all 93 Annex A controls, states whether each is applicable, justifies every inclusion and exclusion, and records implementation status. It is the master control register and a key audit artefact — the single page from which an auditor, a customer or a board can see exactly what the organisation has chosen to do and why.

The SoA is among the most misunderstood documents in ISO 27001 — often treated as a spreadsheet for the certifier when it is in fact the architectural blueprint of the entire ISMS. If the policy defines what leadership intends to achieve, the SoA defines how those intentions become actual controls. It is the only document that connects business objectives, context, risk assessment, treatment decisions, controls, policies, compliance obligations, audits, management reviews and continual improvement into one coherent system, and it provides the documented logic that controls are selected to address real risks rather than because they appear in Annex A.

Because of this, the SoA is the auditor's roadmap — it tells them which controls to verify, which are excluded and why, which risks drove selection, and where evidence should exist; sampling plans are often built directly from it, and a weak SoA invites deeper questioning. It also serves customers during due diligence (a concise control summary in place of hundreds of pages of policy), defines the internal-audit universe, gives management a consolidated view of control coverage and residual-risk decisions, and — because it evolves with new technologies, regulations and threats — becomes a living record of the organisation's security maturity. Auditors scrutinise exclusions closely: a poorly justified exclusion signals a weak risk assessment, while a well-justified one demonstrates mature governance.

If the ISMS were a city, the policy would be its constitution, the risk assessment would identify threats, the treatment plan would decide the defences, and the SoA would be the master map showing every road, checkpoint and defence and explaining why each exists. Without the map the city still functions, but no one fully understands how. The SoA is therefore the control architecture, governance register, audit roadmap, customer-assurance document and risk-to-control bridge of the ISMS — arguably its most important operational document.

3.7 Clause 7 — Support (DOCUMENT & DEPLOY)

If Clauses 4–6 answer why, who and what, Clause 7 answers the practical question: do we have the people, resources, skills, communications and information to make the ISMS work? Many implementations fail not because the risk assessment was poor but because the organisation never provided these enablers.

7.1 Resources

The organisation must provide the resources needed to establish, run and improve the ISMS — people, technology, budget, infrastructure, external expertise, training, audit support and monitoring tools. The standard recognises a simple truth: you cannot secure what you are unwilling to invest in. A SaaS firm facing ransomware, account compromise and source-code theft might fund MFA, EDR, awareness training, vulnerability scanning, penetration testing and certification; a hospital facing device compromise and data breach might fund SOC monitoring, device assessments, compliance training and disaster-recovery testing.

To justify that spend, the Brotby Return-on-Security-Investment (ROSI) model quantifies control value. Worked example for a customer database valued at $5M, with 40% exposure and a once-in-five-years likelihood (ARO = 0.20):

Step	Calculation
Annualised Loss Expectancy (ALE)	$5M × 40% × 0.20 = $400,000
Residual ALE after a 75% control	$400,000 × 25% = $100,000
Annual risk-reduction value	$300,000
Control cost	$80,000 per year
ROSI	($300,000 – $80,000) ÷ $80,000 × 100 = 275%

A 275% return gives management a defensible business case for the investment.

7.2 Competence

People whose work affects security must be competent by education, training, skills and experience; the organisation must determine required competence, assess it, train where needed and retain evidence. Developers need OWASP Top 10, secure SDLC and input-validation knowledge (evidenced by certificates, assessments and a competency matrix); administrators need cloud-security and hardening skills. Competence is not the same as training: training is an activity, competence is a demonstrated ability — and auditors increasingly seek evidence of the latter, not attendance records.

7.3 Awareness

Personnel must be aware of the policy, relevant objectives, their role in security, the benefits of compliance and the consequences of non-compliance. Awareness training is what lets an employee recognise and report a phishing email instead of surrendering credentials, or verify identity before releasing another customer's data. Awareness is not one annual email but an ongoing programme — campaigns, phishing simulations, newsletters, town halls, leadership messaging and security-champion networks — aimed at behavioural change, not policy acknowledgement.

7.4 Communication

Communication must be planned, not ad hoc: the organisation determines what to communicate, when, with whom, how and by whom. A communication matrix typically covers monthly awareness updates (CISO → employees), a quarterly risk dashboard (→ executives), a quarterly ISMS report (→ board), incident notifications as required, audit findings to process owners, and supplier requirements at contract renewal. For a ransomware incident the plan specifies immediate employee notification, customer notice within contractual terms, regulatory reporting as required by law, an executive board briefing and media handled by an approved spokesperson only. Without a plan, incidents often become worse than the technical event itself.

7.5 Documented Information

The organisation must create, update, protect, control, retain and dispose of the documented information the ISMS needs. An ISMS is evidence-based — an auditor cannot audit intentions, only evidence. Documentation spans governance documents (policy, scope, risk methodology, SoA), operational records (risk and asset registers, access reviews, incident logs, vulnerability and audit reports) and management records (review minutes, objectives, metrics). A policy stating "access shall be reviewed quarterly" is meaningless to an auditor without the review records, approvals and corrective actions that prove it happens.

In one sentence: Clause 7 ensures the ISMS is not merely a collection of policies and registers but a functioning system supported by adequate resources, competent people, effective awareness, structured communication and reliable documentation. If the ISMS were an aircraft, Clause 4 sets the destination, Clause 5 assigns the pilot, Clause 6 creates the flight plan — and Clause 7 provides the fuel, crew, radio, navigation and flight records without which it never leaves the ground.

The standard mandates specific documented information — the audit trail that proves the system is real:

Required documented information	Clause
ISMS scope	4.3
Information security policy	5.2
Risk-assessment criteria, process and results	6.1.2 / 8.2

Required documented information	Clause
Risk-treatment plan and decisions	6.1.3 / 8.3
Statement of Applicability	6.1.3 d)
Information security objectives	6.2
Evidence of competence	7.2
Monitoring and measurement results	9.1
Internal-audit programme and results	9.2
Management-review results	9.3
Nonconformities and corrective actions	10.2

3.8 Clause 8 — Operation (DEPLOY)

Clauses 4–7 establish the foundation, but none of them actually protect information — protection begins with Clause 8, where plans become actions, policies become practices and controls become operational reality. If Clause 6 is the blueprint, Clause 8 is the construction site: the DEPLOY tread of the staircase.

Clause 8.1 — Operational Planning and Control

The organisation must plan, implement, control and review the processes that meet security requirements, manage planned changes, review unintended ones, and control externally provided processes. The intent is simple: do not just design controls — operate them. Many organisations have policies, registers and procedures but never confirm the controls are consistently executed. For user-access management, that means an actual workflow — request, manager approval, provisioning, logging, quarterly review — with evidence the process runs, not just a policy on file. For vulnerability management, a "15-day remediation" policy is meaningless without scans performed, findings reviewed, remediation tracked, closure verified and exceptions approved. Operational control is ultimately about consistency: backups monitored daily, awareness completion tracked, incident-response exercises conducted.

Because unmanaged change is a leading cause of incidents, planned changes (a new CRM, say) require a prior security review — where is data stored, is it encrypted, is MFA available, what data is processed, who has admin access? Unintended changes (emergency patches, outages, incidents, vendor failures) must also be reviewed afterwards, with risks reassessed, documentation updated and lessons recorded. And because outsourcing responsibility never outsources accountability, externally provided processes — cloud hosting, payroll, support, monitoring — must be controlled through supplier assessments, contract reviews, SOC reports and security questionnaires; the cloud provider may run the infrastructure, but the organisation remains responsible for access control, data classification and compliance.

Clause 8.2 — Risk Assessment in Operation

Risk assessments must be performed at planned intervals and whenever significant change occurs — not only at the annual audit. Typical triggers include business changes (a European expansion raising GDPR risk), technology changes (deploying generative AI introduces data-leakage, prompt-injection and IP-exposure risks), security incidents (a ransomware attack prompting a review of control adequacy), audit findings (unreviewed privileged accounts revealing a control failure), and regulatory changes (India's DPDPA creating new obligations). Even with no major change, threats and vulnerabilities evolve, so annual reassessment remains essential. Risk assessment is the organisation's security radar: without it, emerging threats stay unseen, controls drift out of date and resources are misallocated.

Clause 8.3 — Risk Treatment in Operation

The organisation must implement the treatment plan, apply controls, monitor effectiveness, formally accept residual risk and update decisions as circumstances change — answering "what did we actually do about the risks we identified?" For a ransomware risk treated with MFA, EDR, offline backups and awareness training, Clause 8.3 requires evidence the controls were implemented: configuration screenshots, monitoring dashboards, restore-test reports and training records. Without evidence, treatment remains a plan, not a control.

No control eliminates risk entirely. Where a control reduces a risk from 25 (High) to 8 (Medium), management must consciously decide to accept the residual risk, add controls, transfer it (insurance) or avoid the activity. "Residual risks have not been formally approved" is one of the most common audit findings — without documented approval, there is no evidence leadership accepted the risk and accountability is unclear. Treatment also evolves: antivirus sufficient one year, EDR needed the next, managed detection and response after that. Clause 8 is the execution engine of ISO 27001 — the point where strategy becomes action and governance becomes operational control.

3.9 Clause 9 — Performance Evaluation (DO & DEPLOY & CHECK)

If Clause 8 deploys and operates the controls, Clause 9 asks: how do we know the ISMS is actually working? A common weakness is assuming that implementing controls automatically produces security. Clause 9 closes that gap, giving management assurance that controls operate as intended, risks stay within limits, objectives are met, resources are used well and the ISMS continues to support the business — the DEPLOY & CHECK stage of PDCA.

Clause 9.1 — Monitoring, Measurement, Analysis and Evaluation

The organisation must determine what to monitor and measure, how, when, by whom, and how results are analysed, evaluated and reported — because if you cannot measure it, you cannot manage it.

When a CEO asks, "we spent $250,000 on security this year; are we more secure than last year?", only measurement can answer.

By Brotby's principle, every metric must answer three questions:

1. what is being measured,
2. why (its link to business objectives or risk reduction), and
3. what action the result requires.

A metric that supports no decision is merely a statistic.

Effective examples trend over time — phishing click-rates falling 18% → 12% → 7%, critical vulnerabilities open beyond SLA dropping 15 → 10 → 4, mean-time-to-detect improving 18h → 9h → 4h. "Number of firewall rules" is a poor metric (no link to outcomes); "percentage of unauthorised connections blocked" is a good one. A balanced programme spans governance, operational, compliance and risk metrics.

Clause 9.2 — Internal Audit

The organisation must conduct planned internal audits to determine whether the ISMS conforms to its own and the standard's requirements and is effectively implemented and maintained. *Treating internal audit as mere certification rehearsal is a mistake — its real purpose is independent assurance, the organisation's own health check.*

An access-control audit might sample twenty new accounts for approval evidence and check that quarterly reviews were completed; finding 18 compliant and 2 lacking approval triggers a finding and corrective action.

Effective audits are risk-based (high-risk processes get greater scrutiny), planned (an annually approved programme, e.g. risk management, access control, supplier security and incident management across four quarters), objective and independent (auditors do not audit their own work). A good internal audit finds weaknesses before customers, regulators, certifiers or attackers do.

Clause 9.3 — Management Review

Top management must review the ISMS at planned intervals for suitability, adequacy, effectiveness and alignment with strategy — because leadership owns risk, allocates resources, approves objectives and accepts residual risk.

ISO specifies the inputs: status of previous actions; changes in internal and external issues; changes in interested parties; security performance (objectives, KPIs, incidents); feedback from interested parties; audit results; risk-assessment results; and improvement opportunities.

A concise review dashboard — objectives 92% achieved, 5 high risks open, 3 critical vulnerabilities, 2 audit findings, 4 incidents, 98% awareness completion, 0 customer complaints — turns these into governance decisions on improvements, resources, ISMS changes and risk acceptance. This is where the board obtains assurance that investments are effective, risks remain within appetite and compliance is met, mirroring the executive-reporting expectations of frameworks like the ASD ISM.

If Clause 8 is driving the car, Clause 9 is reading the dashboard: monitoring is the instrument panel, internal audit inspects the vehicle, and management review decides whether the journey stays on course. Clause 9 transforms security from an act of faith into evidence-based management and links operational performance to executive decision-making.

3.10 Clause 10 — Improvement (DRIVE)

Clause 10 closes the loop. Clause 10.1 (Continual improvement) requires the organisation to keep improving the suitability, adequacy and effectiveness of the ISMS — ideally informed by threat intelligence and real-world exercises, as the ASD ISM expresses in its GOV-07 principle. Clause 10.2 (Nonconformity and corrective action) requires the organisation to react to each nonconformity, address its consequences, eliminate its root cause, verify the effectiveness of the correction and update the ISMS — retaining evidence throughout. This is the DRIVE tread: the discipline that turns every failure into a permanent improvement.

The Clauses as the Staircase — a Recap

S.T.E.P.S.™	ISO/IEC 27001:2022 clause(s)
DEFINE	Clause 4 (Context) + Clause 5 (Leadership)
DISCOVER	Clause 6.1.2 (Risk assessment)
DESIGN	Clause 6.1.3 + 6.2 (Risk treatment, SoA, objectives)
DOCUMENT	Clause 5.2 + 7.5 (Policy, documented information)
DEPLOY	Clause 7 + 8 (Support, operation)
DO & DEPLOY & CHECK	Clause 9 (Monitoring, audit, management review)
DRIVE	Clause 10 (Improvement, corrective action)

Case Study: NHS WannaCry (2017) — The Cost of an Unstructured ISMS

On Friday 12 May 2017 the WannaCry ransomware disrupted one of the world's largest healthcare systems. Within hours, NHS hospitals and practices across England lost access to critical systems: patient records became inaccessible, appointments were cancelled, ambulances were diverted and staff reverted to paper. At least 80 of England's 236 NHS Trusts and nearly 600 GP practices were affected; roughly 19,000 appointments and operations were cancelled, including an estimated 139 urgent cancer referrals. The National Audit Office later estimated the cost at about £92 million.

What made it significant is that WannaCry was not a sophisticated zero-day. It exploited EternalBlue, an SMB vulnerability for which Microsoft had released patch MS17-010 two months earlier, in March 2017. Multiple warnings had been issued, yet many organisations had not applied the patch. The NAO's conclusion was blunt: the attack was largely preventable. The NHS was defeated not by a nation-state adversary but by the absence of disciplined, documented, consistently executed information-security management.

The Root Cause Was Governance, Not Malware

Ransomware was only the final symptom. The real causes were unsupported operating systems such as Windows XP, failure to deploy available patches, no centralised vulnerability management, inconsistent asset inventories, weak change and configuration management, insufficient monitoring, the absence of a formal ISMS and a lack of executive visibility into cyber risk. Every one of these maps directly to an ISO/IEC 27001 requirement — WannaCry succeeded because the management system protecting the environment was inadequate.

How an Effective ISMS Would Have Interrupted the Chain

Under Clause 4, electronic patient records, clinical and diagnostic systems and emergency services would have been identified as business-critical assets, and the question "what happens if these are unavailable for 24 hours?" would have exposed unacceptable clinical risk.

Clause 5 would have made patching a governance issue rather than "an IT issue," putting unsupported systems on management dashboards and forcing the question of why critical clinical systems still ran unsupported software.

Clause 6 would have rated unsupported Windows XP as a High/Critical risk and prescribed upgrades, segmentation, isolation and accelerated patching;

Clause 7 would have surfaced the resource and competence gaps that left ageing infrastructure unmaintained.

Clause 8 is the crux: a compliant patch-management process — identification, classification, testing, scheduling, verification, exception management and escalation — had two clear months between MS17-010 and the attack to act. Annex A.8.8 (management of technical vulnerabilities) is almost a textbook description of what was missing: the vulnerability was known, the patch existed, the exposure was understood; the missing step was action.

Clause 9 metrics (critical vulnerabilities patched within 14 days, zero unsupported operating systems, patch compliance >95%) and management review would have revealed the growing technical debt through routine governance rather than a ransomware outbreak, and

Clause 10 would have kept any un-patchable systems visible through risk-acceptance reviews and corrective-action plans until formally addressed.

The NHS possessed firewalls, antivirus, IT departments, guidance, government warnings and available patches. What it lacked was the disciplined management framework to make those elements work together.

That is the central lesson of ISO/IEC 27001: security is achieved not through technology alone but through governance, risk management, operational discipline, measurement and continual improvement.

Every major weakness identified after WannaCry maps to a requirement already present in the standard — the standard exists because organisations repeatedly suffered the consequences of unmanaged risk. The case transforms a patch-management story into a demonstration that an ISMS is a business-resilience framework, not a compliance exercise.

How Regulators Operationalise the Clauses

A strength of ISO/IEC 27001 is that it gives regulators a universal management framework to translate into sector-specific obligations. Increasingly regulators do not replace ISO 27001 — they operationalise it, turning management-system requirements into measurable compliance obligations.

India: CERT-In, SEBI and the SaaS Journey

CERT-In's Directions require specified cyber incidents to be reported within six hours of detection and logs retained for at least 180 days. What begins as an interested-party requirement under Clause 4.2 becomes an operational objective under Clause 6.2 ("100% of reportable incidents reported within six hours"), supported by incident-management and logging controls in Annex A (A.5.24–A.5.28, A.8.15). SEBI's Cyber Security and Cyber Resilience Framework extends the standard into finance by requiring board-level oversight, resilience testing, third-party risk management and formal incident reporting — mapping to Clause 5, Clause 9.3 and Annex A supplier and incident controls (A.5.19–A.5.23, A.5.24–A.5.28). For a growing Indian SaaS company the ISMS becomes the common foundation on which ISO 27001, SOC 2 Type II, GDPR, DPDPA and customer security reviews can all be built — one risk-management system serving many stakeholders rather than separate compliance programmes.

India: Lessons from Insider Threats and Phishing

Real incidents in India's IT-services sector show how operational controls translate into protection. Insider data-theft cases — employees copying confidential client information — exposed weaknesses in access management, segregation of duties, monitoring and awareness, prompting stronger RBAC, privileged-access management, DLP, user-behaviour analytics and insider-threat programmes. The 2019 phishing-led compromise at Wipro showed how one stolen credential can reach customer environments across an outsourcing ecosystem, accelerating adoption of MFA, EDR, advanced email security, threat hunting, supplier-risk governance and continuous awareness training. The recurring lesson: most incidents are failures of governance, awareness, access control, monitoring or operational discipline — mapping directly to Clause 7.3, Clause 8 and Annex A access, monitoring, incident and supplier controls.

Australia: Essential Eight and Supplier Assurance

The ASD Essential Eight maturity model maps cleanly onto the 2022 control set, giving a prioritised baseline that satisfies many Annex A controls at once:

Essential Eight control	ISO/IEC 27001:2022 control focus
1. Application control	A.8.19 (software on operational systems); A.8.7 (malware)

Essential Eight control	ISO/IEC 27001:2022 control focus
2. Patch applications & OS	A.8.8 (technical vulnerability management)
3. Multi-factor authentication	A.8.5 (secure authentication); A.5.17 (authentication information)
4. Restrict admin privileges	A.8.2 (privileged access rights)
5. Application hardening	A.8.27 (secure architecture); A.8.9 (configuration management)
6. Malware protection	A.8.7 (protection against malware)
7. Logging & monitoring	A.8.15 (logging); A.8.16 (monitoring activities)
8. Regular backups	A.8.13 (information backup)

Australia's government supplier-assurance models, shaped by the ACSC and Department of Home Affairs, address the same supply-chain risk seen in the Cosmos, Latitude and SolarWinds incidents — smaller vendors compromised to reach larger targets — so critical vendors must evidence controls and submit to ongoing assessment, enforcing Clause 8.3 and the A.5.19–23 supplier controls at national scale.

Key Takeaways

- ISO/IEC 27001:2022 organises the ISMS into Clauses 4–10, which map directly onto the seven steps of the S.T.E.P.S.™ staircase.
- The 2022 update consolidated controls into 93 across four categories and added eleven controls for

cloud, threat intelligence, data protection and secure development.

- Clause 6 is the heart of the system: risk assessment (DISCOVER) and risk treatment with the Statement of Applicability (DESIGN).
- Leadership (Clause 5) is the most-cited success factor; its absence the most common cause of failure.
- The standard mandates specific documented information — the audit trail that proves the system is real.
- WannaCry shows the consequence of skipping the clauses: a preventable, two-month-old vulnerability cost the NHS roughly £92 million.

Reflection Questions

1. Could your organisation produce a current, accurate Statement of Applicability today — and would it survive an auditor's scrutiny?
2. Which clause is weakest in your ISMS, and is the gap in leadership (5), planning (6), operation (8) or improvement (10)?
3. If WannaCry struck tomorrow, how quickly would your patch-management process have closed the vulnerability?
4. Do your security objectives (Clause 6.2) translate regulatory expectations — CERT-In timelines, sector frameworks — into measurable targets?
5. When did top management last conduct a genuine Clause 9.3 management review, with the full set of required inputs?

Action Deploy & Checklist

- Document or refresh your ISMS scope (4.3), policy (5.2) and Statement of Applicability (6.1.3), and confirm each is current.
- Run a clause-by-clause gap assessment of Clauses 4–10 and assign an owner to each gap.
- Establish a documented patch-management process with tracked SLAs against A.8.8 — the control WannaCry defeated.
- Translate every applicable regulatory expectation (CERT-In, SEBI, DPDPA, sector rules) into a measurable Clause 6.2 objective.
- Schedule impartial internal audits (9.2) and a full-input management review (9.3) at planned intervals.
- Implement the Essential Eight as a prioritised baseline and map your coverage to the 2022 control set.

CHAPTER

4

RISK-BASED SECURITY DECISION-MAKING

S.T.E.P.S.™ Engine — Operational Anchor: DISCOVER (Step 02)

Every executive step in this book is powered by the S.T.E.P.S.™ Governance Trust Cycle. The discipline of thinking like a risk leader is operationalised through DISCOVER — the systematic identification, analysis and evaluation of risk that turns the threat landscape of Step 1 into decisions the business can act on.

Chapter Overview

Information security delivers business value only when it is governed as risk. The leaders who endure replace the binary question of security with the continuous question of acceptable exposure — and insist their organisation answers it in a single, integrated language spanning enterprise strategy, security operations and privacy obligation.

That language is set at the top: the board defines appetite, management monitors tolerance, and a living risk register — sharpened where it matters by quantitative analysis

— connects every risk to a named owner and an explicit acceptance. Third-party and artificial-intelligence risk have moved from the margins to the centre of that picture, and regulators now hold individuals personally accountable for how risk is assessed, reported and treated.

Operationalised through the DISCOVER step of the S.T.E.P.S.™ cycle, risk leadership becomes a repeatable engine for decision-making — the foundation on which every later step toward Infosec Nirvana is built.

Chapter Objectives

By the end of this chapter, the reader will be able to:

- Explain why information security is fundamentally a risk discipline rather than a technology function, and why that changes who is accountable.
- Distinguish enterprise, security and privacy risk — and connect all three to a single board-level view of exposure.
- Define risk appetite and risk tolerance and articulate the board's non-delegable role in setting them.
- Compare qualitative and quantitative approaches and apply the FAIR model to express cyber risk in financial terms.
- Assess third-party, supply-chain and artificial-intelligence risk using structured, repeatable methods.
- Operate the DISCOVER step of the S.T.E.P.S.™ cycle to produce a defensible risk register and an executive risk dashboard.

The Boardroom Question Nobody Could Answer

In late 2013, in a war room at a Fortune 50 retailer, a simple question hung in the air: "How much risk were we actually carrying?" Nobody could answer it. The company had firewalls, intrusion-detection systems, a security team and a budget running into the hundreds of millions. What it lacked was a way to translate all that activity into a single, honest statement of exposure that a director could understand and a chief executive could own. Within weeks that company — Target — would become a case study taught in business schools worldwide, and its chief executive would lose his job.

The most consequential shift a leader can make is to stop asking "Are we secure?" and start asking "**How much risk are we carrying, is it within the limits we have chosen, and who has decided that it is acceptable?**" Framed this way, security is not a technical state to be achieved but *a continuous business decision about how much uncertainty an organisation is willing to live with in pursuit of its objectives.* The leaders who internalise this — who think like risk leaders rather than technology buyers — build organisations that endure.

Executive Insight

The wrong question — "Is our environment secure?" — invites a binary, technical and ultimately false answer. The right question — "Is our risk within appetite, and who owns the residual?" — forces ownership, prioritisation and honesty. The change in language is the change in leadership.

4.1 From Threats to Decisions: Security Is a Risk Discipline

Step 1 of this book mapped the threat landscape — ransomware crews, nation-state actors, supply-chain compromise, insider misuse and the new category of AI-enabled attack. Knowing the threats, however, is not the same as knowing what to do about them. An organisation cannot defend against everything; resources are finite, and every control carries a cost in money, friction and time. Risk management is the discipline that converts an unbounded list of threats into a bounded list of decisions.

The grammar of that discipline is consistent across every credible framework: a threat exploits a vulnerability affecting an asset, producing a consequence with some likelihood, and risk is the combination of that likelihood and consequence. Everything else — controls, budgets, certifications, dashboards — exists to move one of those variables. The leader's job is not to memorise the grammar but to insist the organisation speaks it consistently, so that a risk raised by an engineer and a risk discussed by the board are recognisably the same thing.

The Language of Risk: Enterprise, Security and Privacy

Three vocabularies of risk routinely collide inside organisations, and the collision is expensive. Enterprise risk management speaks the language of strategy, capital and shareholder value; security risk management speaks of threats, controls and incidents; privacy risk management speaks of individuals, rights and regulatory consequence. When the three operate in separate silos, the board receives three disconnected stories and no coherent picture of exposure.

The frameworks that matter knit these vocabularies together. ISO 31000:2018 provides universal principles and process for managing any risk; ISO/IEC 27005:2022 applies that process to information security; the COSO ERM framework links risk to strategy and performance at the enterprise level; and NIST IR 8286 was written precisely to connect cybersecurity risk to enterprise risk, so a CISO's register can be read in the same currency as a CFO's. The risk leader's task is integration: one process, three lenses, a single view.

Lens	Primary question	Owner	Typical measure
Enterprise (ERM)	Could this threaten our strategy or solvency?	Board / CEO / CFO	Impact on capital, revenue, strategy
Security	Could a threat compromise confidentiality, integrity or availability?	CISO / risk function	Likelihood × impact of a control failure
Privacy	Could processing harm an individual or breach a right?	DPO / Privacy Officer	Severity × likelihood of harm to data principals

Risk Attitude, Appetite and Tolerance: The Board's Job

Three terms are routinely confused, yet they operate at different levels of decision-making and form a hierarchy: risk attitude → risk appetite → risk tolerance, each more specific than the last.

Risk attitude is the organisation's general, cultural disposition toward uncertainty — risk-averse (preferring certainty), risk-neutral (balancing benefit and risk on objective analysis) or risk-seeking (accepting uncertainty for innovation or growth). It is shaped by culture, leadership philosophy, regulatory environment and market position, and provides the philosophical foundation for more specific decisions.

Risk appetite is the amount and type of risk the organisation is willing to pursue to achieve its objectives

— an explicit decision approved by the board and aligned with strategy. Crucially, information-security appetite should never be set in isolation by the security team; it is a subset of enterprise appetite, so security enables an approved digital-transformation strategy rather than imposing excessively restrictive limits that impede it.

Risk tolerance is the most operational level: the acceptable variation around a specific risk objective, defining measurable thresholds beyond which escalation and corrective action are triggered. Appetite is strategic and set by the board; tolerance is operational and monitored by management.

The distinction sounds academic until a real decision arrives — whether to delay a launch to remediate a vulnerability, accept a vendor with a weak posture, or run a legacy system one more year — at which point the absence of a stated appetite means the decision defaults, silently, to whoever shouts loudest or fears most. A usable appetite statement is specific, measurable and owned. "We take security seriously" is not an appetite statement; it is a slogan.

Risk category	Weak (slogan)	Strong (decision-ready) statement
Customer data	"We protect customer data."	"We will not retain customer data beyond defined purposes, and we accept zero tolerance for unencrypted storage of regulated personal data."
Third parties	"We vet our vendors."	"We will not grant network access to any third party that has not passed security due diligence and contractually accepted breach-notification within 24 hours."

Risk category	Weak (slogan)	Strong (decision-ready) statement
Availability	"We value uptime."	"For tier-1 services we accept no more than 4 hours of unplanned downtime per quarter; beyond that, executive escalation is mandatory."

Applied consistently, these concepts integrate the ISMS with enterprise risk management, so that security translates business strategy into proportionate objectives, controls and tolerances rather than operating as an isolated technical discipline.

Risk Ownership: Security Advises, Business Decides

Identifying and analysing risks is only half of DISCOVER. Every identified risk must have a clearly assigned owner — the individual with authority and accountability to decide about it. The security team may facilitate assessments, recommend controls and maintain the register, but it does not own business risk; ownership resides with the executive or manager responsible for the affected process, asset or service. Two owner duties are non-negotiable: approving the residual risk (confirming the remaining exposure after controls is acceptable within appetite, or requiring further treatment), and approving and signing the Risk Treatment Plan (turning a technical recommendation into a management commitment with actions, timelines and resources).

This reinforces the governance principle that security teams advise but business leaders decide and aligns with regulatory expectations — including Australia's prudential frameworks — that boards and executives demonstrate active oversight rather than delegating accountability to specialists. Documented approval of residual risk and the RTP is tangible evidence that management exercised informed judgement and accepted responsibility.

Cascading Consequences: "And Then What Happens Next?"

Risk analysis should never stop at the first observable consequence. Effective DISCOVER activity examines how a single failure can trigger a cascade across systems, processes, customers and the wider organisation — and a useful question for every assessment is simply "and then what happens next?" A compromised user account may appear to affect one employee, but if it holds privileged access an attacker can move laterally, compromise further systems, exfiltrate data, disrupt operations and ultimately trigger regulatory investigation and reputational damage.

The Equifax breach illustrates this: exploitation of a single unpatched web-application vulnerability evolved into extensive lateral movement and the exposure of millions of records. Realistic ratings therefore weigh not just the immediate operational impact but lateral movement, system dependencies, effects on confidentiality, integrity and availability, regulatory and contractual consequences, and the longer-term financial, reputational and strategic fallout.

Selecting the Treatment Strategy (DESIGN)

Once risks are analysed, management must decide how to treat them. ISO 27001 and ISO 31000 recognise four options, and the choice belongs to the risk owner — weighing approved appetite, resources, legal obligations and strategy — not to the security function alone:

- **Reduce (mitigate)** — lower the likelihood or impact by implementing appropriate controls.

- **Avoid** — eliminate the activity that gives rise to the risk altogether.
- **Transfer (or share)** — shift part of the financial or operational consequence through insurance, contract or outsourcing, while recognising that accountability cannot be transferred.
- **Accept** — formally accept the residual risk where further treatment is not cost-effective or the exposure falls within approved appetite.

The selected option should always be justified, documented and reflected in the Risk Treatment Plan — and the decision belongs to the business that ultimately bears the consequences.

Qualitative versus Quantitative Risk

Most organisations begin with qualitative assessment — the familiar red/amber/green heat map scoring likelihood and impact one to five. It is fast, intuitive and useful for triage, but on its own a poor basis for spending decisions, because it cannot answer the question a CFO truly cares about: "how much money are we talking about?"

Two risks both rated "high" may differ in expected loss by three orders of magnitude, and a colour cannot tell you which to fund first.

Quantitative assessment expresses risk in financial and probabilistic terms — not a colour but a distribution of likely losses — and integrates directly with budgeting, insurance and board reporting. Mature organisations use both: qualitative methods to triage breadth, quantitative methods to drive the decisions that matter most.

Dimension	Qualitative	Quantitative
Output	Ratings / heat map (High, Medium, Low)	Financial loss distribution (e.g. "10% chance of >₹20 crore loss/yr")
Speed	Fast — good for breadth and triage	Slower — reserved for material decisions
Best for	Initial screening, large registers	Budget allocation, insurance, board trade-offs
Main weakness	Subjective; cannot rank within a band	Needs data, skill and calibrated estimates

The FAIR Framework: Putting a Number on Cyber Risk

Factor Analysis of Information Risk (FAIR), maintained as the Open FAIR standard by The Open Group, is the most widely adopted method for quantifying cyber risk. Its power lies in decomposition: rather than guessing a single number, FAIR breaks risk into factors that subject-matter experts can each estimate with reasonable confidence, then combines them. The core taxonomy is simple enough to sketch on a whiteboard:

FAIR taxonomy (simplified)

- Risk = Loss Event Frequency × Loss Magnitude
- Loss Event Frequency = Threat Event Frequency × Vulnerability
- Threat Event Frequency = Contact Frequency × Probability of Action
- Loss Magnitude = Primary Loss + Secondary (stakeholder) Loss

Expressing a top risk as "a 15% annual probability of a loss event with a most-likely impact of ₹12 crore and a worst case of ₹45 crore" does something a heat map never can: it lets a board compare a security investment against any other use of capital, on equal terms. It also disciplines the conversation, because decomposition exposes which assumptions drive the number and forces estimates to be defended rather than asserted.

The goal is not false precision — FAIR works in ranges and distributions, not single points — but defensible, decision-grade quantification.

Third-Party and Supply-Chain Risk

Modern exposure no longer stops at an organisation's own perimeter; it extends to every vendor, contractor, managed-service provider and software dependency with access to its systems or data. The Verizon Data Breach Investigations Report has consistently found that a substantial and growing share of breaches involve a third party, and the most-taught breaches of the last decade — Target through an HVAC contractor, SolarWinds through a software-update channel — were third-party failures at heart.

Effective third-party risk management is a lifecycle, not a questionnaire: tier vendors by the access and data they touch, apply proportionate due diligence before onboarding, embed security and breach-notification obligations in the contract, monitor posture throughout the relationship rather than only at signing, and plan for secure offboarding.

The single most common failure is treating due diligence as a one-time gate — a form completed at procurement and never revisited — when the risk is continuous. In practice that means tiering by data sensitivity and system access rather than contract value, making breach-notification timelines (24–72 hours) a contractual obligation rather than a hope, re-assessing high-tier vendors on a defined cadence, and mapping fourth-party dependencies — your vendor's vendors — for your most critical services.

Artificial-Intelligence Risk: The New Frontier

Artificial intelligence introduces risks existing security and privacy frameworks were not designed to capture. Beyond confidentiality and availability, AI raises model bias, hallucination, data poisoning, prompt injection, opacity of decision-making, and the use of personal data for training without a clear lawful basis.

A risk leader cannot treat AI as just another application; it is a distinct risk surface crossing security, privacy, ethics and regulation simultaneously.

Two instruments now anchor the discipline:

1. the NIST AI Risk Management Framework organises AI risk around four functions — Govern, Map, Measure and Manage — giving a structured way to identify and treat it; and
2. ISO/IEC 42001:2023, the first certifiable AI management system standard, does for AI governance what ISO/IEC 27001 did for information security, providing an auditable system that boards can require and customers can trust.

For organisations already running an ISMS, integrating an AI management system is the natural next step and an emerging source of competitive differentiation.

Executive Insight

AI risk is where the security, privacy and ethics conversations finally merge. The organisations that build a single, integrated governance system across all three — rather than bolting an "AI policy" onto an unchanged security programme — will be the ones their customers and regulators trust to deploy AI at scale.

Operational Risk and the Risk Register

Operational risk — the risk of loss from failed processes, people and systems — is where security risk and enterprise risk meet most concretely, and the instrument that records and governs it is the risk register: the single, living source of truth for what the organisation is worried about, how much, who owns it and what is being done.

A neglected register is a filing exercise; a living register is the operating system of the risk programme.

Each entry should connect a specific risk to an owner, a current assessment, a treatment decision and a residual position that someone has explicitly accepted.

Field	Purpose	Example entry
Risk ID & description	Unambiguous statement of the risk	R-014: Unpatched internet-facing VPN appliance exploited for initial access
Owner	Named accountable individual	Head of Infrastructure
Inherent rating	Risk before controls	High (likely × severe)
Treatment	Mitigate / transfer / avoid / accept	Mitigate — patch SLA + MFA + monitoring

Field	Purpose	Example entry
Residual rating	Risk after controls	Medium
Acceptance	Who signed off the residual	CISO, accepted 02-2026, review 08-2026

The S.T.E.P.S.™ Engine in Practice: DISCOVER

Thinking like a risk leader becomes real only when operationalised. In the S.T.E.P.S.™ Governance Trust Cycle, DISCOVER is the engine room of risk-based decision-making: it takes the context and commitment established in DEFINE and produces the prioritised, owned, board-ready view of risk that every later step — DESIGN, DOCUMENT, DO — depends upon. Where the executive discipline of this chapter is the "why," DISCOVER is the repeatable "how."

DISCOVER activity	What it produces	ISO 27001:2022 anchor
Establish risk criteria	Agreed likelihood/impact scales and appetite	Clause 6.1.2
Identify risks	Asset-threat-vulnerability inventory	Clause 6.1.2 / 8.2
Analyse & evaluate	Rated, ranked risks (qual + quant on the material few)	Clause 8.2
Treatment decision	Mitigate / transfer / avoid / accept per risk	Clause 6.1.3 / 8.3
Record & assign	Risk register with named owners and residual sign-off	Clause 8.3 / 9.1

The Risk Leader's Dashboard

The final act of risk leadership is communication. A risk programme that cannot report itself clearly to the board is, for governance purposes, invisible. The executive risk dashboard translates the register into the handful of indicators a director needs — not a wall of technical metrics, but a concise answer to four questions: are we within appetite, what is changing, what needs a decision, and are our controls actually working?

Board question	Indicator	Why it matters
Are we within appetite?	Count of risks above tolerance, by category	Shows whether exposure exceeds the board's chosen limits
What is changing?	Trend in top risks vs. prior quarter	Distinguishes a deteriorating posture from a stable one
What needs a decision?	Risks awaiting acceptance or investment	Surfaces choices only the board can make
Are controls working?	Key control effectiveness + incident trend	Tests whether spending is buying real protection

Case Studies: Three Failures of Risk Leadership

Each of the following breaches is, on the surface, a technical story; read more carefully, each is a failure of risk leadership — of seeing, owning, prioritising or honestly reporting risk. Together they cover the three places where risk leadership most often breaks: at the perimeter of trust (third parties), inside the cloud (operational and configuration risk), and in the boardroom itself (governance and ethics).

Target (2013): Risk That Lived in a Vendor

Attackers stole network credentials from Fazio Mechanical, an HVAC contractor with remote access to Target's environment, and used them to pivot onto the retailer's point-of-sale systems, where RAM-scraping malware harvested payment data over roughly three weeks during the 2013 holiday season.

About 40 million payment cards and the personal records of around 70 million customers were exposed. Target's own tooling reportedly flagged the malware more than once, but the alerts were not acted upon.

The breach ultimately cost over USD 200 million, including an USD 18.5 million multi-state settlement in 2017, and both the CEO and CIO departed.

Lessons — Target

- Third-party access is your risk, wherever it originates; assess risk across the whole trust boundary, not just inside the corporate walls.
- Detection without response is theatre — alerts no one is accountable for triaging provide the comfort of monitoring without its protection.
- Network segmentation is a risk-treatment decision: a vendor billing portal should never have been a path to payment systems.

Capital One (2019): Risk That Was Written Down and Ignored

A former employee of the bank's cloud provider exploited a misconfigured web-application firewall to perform a server-side request forgery attack, reaching the cloud instance metadata service, obtaining credentials and reading more than a hundred storage buckets.

Personal information on roughly 100 million people in the United States and a further 6 million in Canada was exposed, including about 140,000 Social Security numbers and 80,000 linked bank-account numbers. Reporting indicated staff had warned about the firewall weakness before the attack.

The bank paid an USD 80 million regulatory penalty and later settled a class action for USD 190 million.

Lessons — Capital One

- A known, documented risk that is not treated is worse than an unknown one — it is a governance failure, not a surprise.
- Cloud migration changes the risk model: configuration is now a primary control surface, and assessing it must be continuous, not a one-time review.
- Regulators increasingly hold the board accountable for the risk-assessment process itself, not merely the technical outcome.

Uber (2016): Risk That Was Hidden from the Board

Attackers obtained credentials and accessed a cloud storage bucket containing data on approximately 57 million riders and drivers, including some 600,000 driver's-licence numbers. Rather than disclose the incident as required, the company paid the attackers USD 100,000 — routed through its bug-bounty programme and accompanied by non-disclosure agreements — and concealed the breach for roughly a year. The consequences were severe: a USD 148 million settlement with 50 US states and the District of Columbia in 2018 and, in 2022, the criminal conviction of the former chief security officer for obstruction and concealment. It remains the landmark case for personal accountability in security leadership.

Lessons — Uber

- Concealing a risk does not transfer it — it compounds it, adding legal and personal liability to the original loss.
- Risk governance includes the duty to report bad news upward and outward; a culture that punishes disclosure manufactures cover-ups.
- Accountability for security risk is now personal and criminal at the executive level, not merely organisational.

Key Takeaways

- Security is a risk discipline, not a technology state. The leadership question is not "Are we secure?" but "Is our risk within appetite, and who owns the residual?"
- Enterprise, security and privacy risk must be integrated into one view. Under regimes like India's DPDPA, a control failure is simultaneously a security, privacy and financial event.
- Risk appetite is the board's job and must be specific enough to drive real decisions; risk tolerance is management's to monitor.
- Qualitative methods triage breadth; quantitative methods like FAIR drive the decisions that matter by expressing risk in money.
- Third-party and AI risk are now first-order exposures requiring lifecycle management and, increasingly, certifiable governance (ISO/IEC 42001).

- The DISCOVER step turns these principles into a defensible risk register and a board-ready dashboard.

Chapter Overview

Information security delivers business value only when it is governed as risk.

The leaders who endure are those who replace the binary question of security with the continuous question of acceptable exposure — and who insist that their organisation answers it in a single, integrated language that spans enterprise strategy, security operations and privacy obligation.

That language is set at the top: the board defines appetite, management monitors tolerance, and a living risk register, sharpened where it matters by quantitative analysis, connects every risk to a named owner and an explicit acceptance.

Third-party and artificial-intelligence risk have moved from the margins to the centre of that picture, and regulators now hold individuals personally accountable for how risk is assessed, reported and treated.

Operationalised through the DISCOVER step of the S.T.E.P.S.™ cycle, risk leadership ceases to be a slogan and becomes a repeatable engine for decision-making — the foundation on which every later step of the journey to Infosec Nirvana is built.

Chapter Objectives

By the end of this chapter, the reader will be able to:

- Explain why information security is fundamentally a risk discipline rather than a technology function, and why that distinction changes who is accountable.
- Distinguish enterprise risk, security risk and privacy risk — and connect all three to a single, board-level view of exposure.

- Define risk appetite and risk tolerance, and articulate the board's non-delegable role in setting them.
- Compare qualitative and quantitative approaches to risk, and apply the FAIR model to express cyber risk in financial terms.
- Assess third-party, supply-chain and artificial-intelligence risk using structured, repeatable methods.
- Operate the DISCOVER step of the S.T.E.P.S.™ cycle to produce a defensible risk register and an executive risk dashboard.

The Boardroom Question Nobody Could Answer

In late 2013, in a war room at a Fortune 50 retailer, a simple question hung in the air: "How much risk were we actually carrying?" Nobody could answer it. The company had firewalls, intrusion-detection systems, a security team and a budget that ran into the hundreds of millions. What it did not have was a way to translate all of that activity into a single, honest statement of exposure that a director could understand, and a chief executive could own. Within weeks, that company — Target — would become a case study taught in business schools around the world, and its chief executive would lose his job.

- This chapter argues that the most consequential shift a leader can make is to stop asking "Are we secure?" and start asking "**How much risk are we carrying, is it within the limits we have chosen, and who has decided that it is acceptable?**" Security, framed this way, is not a technical state to be achieved. *It is a continuous business decision about how much uncertainty an organisation is willing to live with in pursuit of its objectives.* The leaders who internalise this — who think like risk leaders rather than technology buyers — are the ones who build organisations that endure.

Executive Insight

The wrong question — "Is our environment secure?" — invites a binary, technical, and ultimately false answer.

The right question — *"Is our risk within appetite, and who owns the residual?"* — forces ownership, prioritisation and honesty. The change in language is the change in leadership.

4.1 From Threats to Decisions: Security Is a Risk Discipline

Step 1 of this book mapped the threat landscape — ransomware crews, nation-state actors, supply-chain compromise, insider misuse, and the new category of AI-enabled attack. Knowing the threats, however, is not the same as knowing what to do about them. An organisation cannot defend against everything; resources are finite, and every control carries a cost in money, friction and time. Risk management is the discipline that converts an unbounded list of threats into a bounded list of decisions.

The grammar of that discipline is consistent across every credible framework. A **threat** exploits a **vulnerability** affecting an **asset**, producing a **consequence** with some **likelihood**. Risk is the combination of that likelihood and consequence. Everything else — controls, budgets, certifications, dashboards — exists to move one of those variables. The leader's job is not to memorise the grammar but to insist that the organisation speaks it consistently, so that a risk raised by an engineer and a risk discussed by the board are recognisably the same thing.

Risk Attitude, Risk Appetite, and Risk Tolerance: Understanding the Hierarchy

One of the most common sources of confusion in enterprise risk management and information security governance is the tendency to use the terms risk attitude, risk appetite, and risk tolerance interchangeably.

Although closely related, they describe three distinct concepts that operate at different levels of organizational decision-making. Understanding their relationship is essential because they influence strategy, investment, risk treatment decisions, and ultimately the design and operation of the Information Security Management System (ISMS).

The relationship can be viewed as a hierarchy:

Risk Attitude → Risk Appetite → Risk Tolerance

Each level becomes progressively more specific, translating organizational philosophy into practical operational limits.

Risk Attitude: The Organization's General Disposition Toward Risk

At the highest-level sits risk attitude, which reflects the organization's overall mindset or cultural disposition toward uncertainty. It describes how leadership generally perceives risk when making strategic decisions.

An organization may be:

- **Risk-averse**, preferring certainty and avoiding activities that could expose it to significant uncertainty.
- **Risk-neutral,** balancing potential benefits and risks based on objective analysis.
- **Risk-seeking,** deliberately accepting higher levels of uncertainty in pursuit of innovation, growth, or competitive advantage.

Risk attitude is largely shaped by factors such as organizational culture, leadership philosophy, regulatory environment, market position, stakeholder expectations, and industry characteristics.

Risk attitude provides the philosophical foundation upon which more specific risk decisions are built.

Risk Appetite: The Amount and Type of Risk the Organization Is Willing to Pursue

While risk attitude reflects an organization's general disposition, risk appetite defines the amount and type of risk that the organization is willing to accept or pursue in order to achieve its objectives.

Risk appetite is an explicit management decision approved by senior leadership or the board and should align with corporate strategy.

Unlike attitude, which is qualitative and cultural, appetite is intended to guide decision-making.

Examples include:

- A bank may have a very low appetite for customer data breaches but a moderate appetite for adopting innovative digital banking technologies.
- A healthcare provider may accept limited operational disruption during planned system upgrades but have virtually zero appetite for unauthorized disclosure of patient records.
- An e-commerce company may willingly invest in emerging technologies despite uncertainty but maintain a very low appetite for payment fraud.

Importantly, information security risk appetite should never be developed in isolation by the security team. It should be a clearly defined subset of the organization's overall enterprise risk appetite, ensuring that cybersecurity decisions support broader business strategy rather than conflict with it.

For example, if the board has approved an aggressive digital transformation strategy with moderate technology risk acceptance, the information security function should enable that strategy by defining controls consistent with the enterprise's approved risk appetite—not by independently imposing excessively restrictive limits that impede business objectives.

Risk Tolerance: Acceptable Variation Around a Specific Risk

The most operational level of the hierarchy is risk tolerance.

Risk tolerance defines the acceptable variation or deviation around a particular risk objective or performance measure. It establishes measurable boundaries beyond which management action is required.

Risk appetite expresses what the organization is willing to accept in principle; risk tolerance defines the operational limits within which individual risks may fluctuate.

When performance exceeds these thresholds, predefined escalation procedures and corrective actions are triggered.

Risk tolerances therefore translate board-level intentions into practical management criteria that can be monitored and measured.

Business leaders perceive security as an obstacle rather than an enabler.

Instead, security should operate within the enterprise's approved governance framework, translating business strategy into proportionate information security objectives, controls, and operational tolerances.

Aligning the ISMS with Enterprise Risk Management

ISO/IEC 27001 promotes a risk-based approach rather than a technology-driven approach. To achieve this effectively:

- Risk attitude should reflect the organization's overall philosophy toward uncertainty.
- Risk appetite should be established by top management as part of enterprise governance and communicated throughout the organization.
- Information security risk appetite should be derived from—and remain aligned with—the enterprise risk appetite.
- Risk tolerances should define measurable operational thresholds that guide implementation, monitoring, escalation, and continual improvement.

When these concepts are clearly distinguished and consistently applied, the ISMS becomes fully integrated with enterprise risk management, ensuring that security supports strategic objectives while maintaining acceptable levels of uncertainty. In this way, cybersecurity ceases to be an isolated technical discipline and becomes an integral component of business governance and value creation.

Enhancements to Step 02 (DISCOVER) and Step 03 (DESIGN)

Step 02 (DISCOVER): Make Risk Owner Duties Explicit

Identifying and analysing risks is only half of the DISCOVER phase.

Every identified risk must also have a clearly assigned risk owner—the individual with the authority and accountability to make decisions about that risk. The Information Security team may facilitate assessments, recommend controls, and maintain the risk register, but it does not own business risk. Ownership resides with the executive or manager responsible for the affected business process, asset, or service.

The role of the risk owner carries many responsibilities, but two are non-negotiable:

1. **Approve the Residual Risk.**

   After proposed controls have been implemented, the risk owner must determine whether the remaining (residual) risk is acceptable within the organization's approved risk appetite. If the residual risk exceeds acceptable levels, additional treatment or escalation is required.

2. **Approve and Sign the Risk Treatment Plan (RTP).**

   The risk owner must formally approve the selected treatment strategy, associated actions, timelines, and required resources. A Risk Treatment Plan without business ownership is simply a technical recommendation; once approved and signed, it becomes a management commitment.

This distinction reinforces a key governance principle: security teams advise, but business leaders decide.

It also aligns with increasing regulatory expectations, including those reflected in Australia's prudential frameworks, where boards and senior executives are expected to demonstrate active oversight of cyber and information security risks rather than delegating accountability entirely to technical specialists.

Documented approval of residual risk and the Risk Treatment Plan provide tangible evidence that management has exercised informed judgement and accepted responsibility.

Cascading Consequences: Looking Beyond the Immediate Impact

Risk analysis should never stop at the first observable consequence. Effective DISCOVER activities examine how a single failure can trigger a cascade of interconnected impacts across systems, processes, customers, and the wider organization.

A useful question for every risk assessment is:

"And then what happens next?"

This approach encourages analysts to move beyond isolated events and understand systemic effects.

For example, a compromised user account may initially appear to affect only one employee. However, if that account possesses privileged access, an attacker may move laterally across the network, compromise additional systems, exfiltrate sensitive information, disrupt operations, and ultimately trigger regulatory investigations and reputational damage.

The Equifax breach provides a compelling illustration. What began as exploitation of a single unpatched web application vulnerability evolved into extensive lateral movement within the environment, ultimately exposing the personal information of millions of individuals. The incident demonstrates that organizations must assess not only the initial event but also the chain reaction that may follow.

DISCOVER should therefore evaluate:

- Immediate operational impact.
- Potential lateral movement or privilege escalation.
- Dependencies on interconnected systems.
- Effects on confidentiality, integrity, and availability.
- Regulatory and contractual consequences.
- Financial losses.
- Reputational damage.
- Long-term strategic implications.

Understanding these cascading consequences produces more realistic risk ratings and more effective treatment decisions.

Step 03 (DESIGN): Selecting the Appropriate Risk Treatment Strategy

Once risks have been analysed, management must determine how they will be treated. ISO 27001 and ISO 31000 recognise four fundamental treatment options.

The choice is not made by the security team alone; it is a business decision made by the risk owner, considering the organization's approved risk appetite, available resources, legal obligations, and strategic objectives.

1. Risk Reduction (Mitigate)

Reduce either the likelihood or impact of the risk by implementing appropriate controls.

2. Risk Avoidance

Eliminate the activity that gives rise to the risk altogether.

3. Risk Transfer (or sharing)

Shift part of the financial or operational consequences of the risk to another party through insurance, contractual arrangements, or outsourcing, while recognising that accountability cannot be transferred.

4. Risk Acceptance

Formally accept the residual risk because further treatment would not be cost-effective or because the remaining exposure falls within the organization's approved risk appetite.

The selected treatment option should always be justified, documented, and reflected in the Risk Treatment Plan. Most importantly, the decision belongs to the risk owner, not to the information security function, because it is the business that ultimately bears the consequences of risk.

From Threats to Decisions: Security Is a Risk Discipline

Step 1 of this book mapped the threat landscape — ransomware crews, nation-state actors, supply-chain compromise, insider misuse, and the new category of AI-enabled attack. Knowing the threats, however, is not the same as knowing what to do about them.

An organisation cannot defend against everything; resources are finite, and every control carries a cost in money, friction and time. ***Risk management is the discipline that converts an unbounded list of threats into a bounded list of decisions.***

The grammar of that discipline is consistent across every credible framework. **A threat exploits a vulnerability affecting an asset, producing a consequence with some likelihood. Risk is the combination of that likelihood and consequence**.

Everything else — controls, budgets, certifications, dashboards — exists to move one of those variables. The leader's job is not to memorise the grammar but to insist that the organisation speaks it consistently, so that a risk raised by an engineer and a risk discussed by the board are recognisably the same thing.

The Language of Risk: Enterprise, Security and Privacy

Three vocabularies of risk routinely collide inside organisations, and the collision is expensive.

1. Enterprise risk management (ERM) speaks the language of strategy, capital and shareholder value.
2. Security risk management speaks the language of threats, controls and incidents.

3. Privacy risk management speaks the language of individuals, rights and regulatory consequence.

When these three operate in separate silos, the board receives three disconnected stories and no coherent picture of exposure.

The frameworks that matter are the ones that knit these vocabularies together. ISO 31000:2018 provides the universal principles and process for managing any risk. ISO/IEC 27005:2022 applies that process specifically to information security. The COSO ERM framework links risk to strategy and performance at the enterprise level. And NIST Interagency Report 8286 was written precisely to connect cybersecurity risk to enterprise risk so that a CISO's register can be read in the same currency as a CFO's.

The risk leader's task is integration: one process, three lenses, a single view.

Lens	Primary question	Owner	Typical measure
Enterprise risk (ERM)	Could this threaten our strategy or solvency?	Board / CEO / CFO	Impact on capital, revenue, strategy
Security risk	Could a threat compromise confidentiality, integrity or availability?	CISO / risk function	Likelihood × impact of a control failure
Privacy risk	Could processing harm an individual or breach a right?	DPO / Privacy Officer	Severity × likelihood of harm to data principals

Risk Appetite and Risk Tolerance:

The Board's Job

Risk appetite is the amount and type of risk an organisation is willing to pursue or retain in pursuit of its objectives. Risk tolerance is the acceptable variation around that appetite for a specific objective or risk category. Appetite is strategic and is set by the board; tolerance is operational and is monitored by management.

The distinction sounds academic until a real decision arrives — whether to delay a product launch to remediate a vulnerability, whether to accept a vendor with a weak security posture, whether to operate a legacy system one more year — at which point the absence of a stated appetite means the decision defaults, silently, to whoever shouts loudest or fears most.

A usable risk appetite statement is specific, measurable and owned. "We take security seriously" is not an appetite statement; it is a slogan. The examples below show the difference.

Risk category	Weak (slogan)	Strong (decision-ready) appetite statement
Customer data	"We protect customer data."	"We will not retain customer data beyond defined purposes, and we accept zero tolerance for unencrypted storage of regulated personal data."
Third parties	"We vet our vendors."	"We will not grant network access to any third party that has not passed security due diligence and contractually accepted breach-notification within 24 hours."

Risk category	Weak (slogan)	Strong (decision-ready) appetite statement
Availability	"We value uptime."	"For tier-1 services we accept no more than 4 hours of unplanned downtime per quarter; beyond that, executive escalation is mandatory."

Qualitative versus Quantitative Risk

Most organisations begin with qualitative risk assessment — the familiar red/amber/green heat map scoring likelihood and impact on a scale of one to five. It is fast, intuitive and useful for triage. It is also, on its own, a poor basis for spending decisions, because it cannot answer the only question a CFO truly cares about: "How much money are we talking about?"

Two risks both rated "high" may differ in expected loss by three orders of magnitude, and a colour cannot tell you which one to fund first.

Quantitative risk assessment expresses risk in financial and probabilistic terms — not a colour, but a distribution of likely losses. It is more demanding and requires data and discipline, but it produces outputs that integrate directly with budgeting, insurance and board reporting.

Mature organisations do not choose one over the other; they use qualitative methods to triage breadth and quantitative methods to drive the decisions that matter most.

Dimension	Qualitative	Quantitative
Output	Ratings / heat map (High, Medium, Low)	Financial loss distribution (e.g., "10% chance of >₹20 crore loss/yr")

Dimension	Qualitative	Quantitative
Speed	Fast — good for breadth and triage	Slower — reserved for material decisions
Best for	Initial screening, large registers	Budget allocation, insurance, board trade-offs
Main weakness	Subjective; cannot rank within a band	Needs data, skill and calibrated estimates

The FAIR Framework: Putting a Number on Cyber Risk

Factor Analysis of Information Risk (FAIR), maintained as the Open FAIR standard by The Open Group, is the most widely adopted method for quantifying cyber risk. Its power lies in decomposition: rather than guessing at a single number, FAIR breaks risk into factors that subject-matter experts can each estimate with reasonable confidence, then combines them. The core taxonomy is straightforward enough to sketch on a whiteboard:

FAIR taxonomy (simplified)

- Risk = Loss Event Frequency × Loss Magnitude
- Loss Event Frequency = Threat Event Frequency × Vulnerability
- Threat Event Frequency = Contact Frequency × Probability of Action
- Loss Magnitude = Primary Loss + Secondary (stakeholder) Loss

Expressing a top risk as "a 15% annual probability of a loss event with a most-likely impact of ₹12 crore and a worst case of ₹45 crore" does something a heat map never can: it lets a board compare a security investment against any other use of capital, on equal terms.

It also disciplines the conversation. Decomposition exposes which assumptions are driving the number, and forces estimates to be defended rather than asserted.

The goal is not false precision — FAIR works in ranges and distributions, not single points — but defensible, decision-grade quantification.

Third-Party and Supply-Chain Risk

The uncomfortable truth of modern risk is that an organisation's exposure no longer stops at its own perimeter. It extends to every vendor, contractor, managed-service provider and software dependency with access to its systems or data.

The Verizon Data Breach Investigations Report has consistently found that a substantial and growing share of breaches involve a third party, and the most-taught breaches of the last decade — Target through an HVAC contractor, SolarWinds through a software-update channel — were third-party failures at heart.

Effective third-party risk management is a lifecycle, not a questionnaire. It begins with tiering vendors by the access and data they touch, applies proportionate due diligence before onboarding, embeds security and breach-notification obligations in the contract, monitors posture during the relationship rather than only at signing, and plans for secure offboarding.

The single most common failure is treating due diligence as a one-time gate — a form completed at procurement and never revisited — when the risk is continuous.

Tier every third party by the sensitivity of data and the level of system access it holds — not by contract value.

- Make breach-notification timelines (e.g., 24–72 hours) a contractual obligation, not a hope.
- Re-assess high-tier vendors on a defined cadence; monitor for changes in their posture between assessments.
- Map fourth-party dependencies — your vendor's vendors — for your most critical services.

Artificial-Intelligence Risk: The New Frontier

Artificial intelligence introduces risks that existing security and privacy frameworks were not designed to capture. Beyond the familiar concerns of confidentiality and availability, AI systems raise questions of model bias, hallucination, data poisoning, prompt injection, opacity of decision-making, and the use of personal data for training without a clear lawful basis. A risk leader cannot treat AI as just another application; it is a distinct risk surface that crosses security, privacy, ethics and regulation simultaneously.

Two instruments now anchor the discipline.

The NIST AI Risk Management Framework organises AI risk around four functions — Govern, Map, Measure and Manage — giving organisations a structured way to identify and treat AI-specific risk.

ISO/IEC 42001:2023, the first certifiable AI management system standard, does for AI governance what ISO/IEC 27001 did for information security: it provides an auditable management system that boards can require and customers can trust.

For organisations already operating an ISMS, the integration of an AI management system is the natural next step — and an emerging source of competitive differentiation.

Executive Insight

AI risk is where the security, privacy and ethics conversations finally merge. The organisations that build a single, integrated governance system across all three — rather than bolting an "AI policy" onto an unchanged security programme — will be the ones their customers and regulators trust to deploy AI at scale.

Operational Risk and the Risk Register

Operational risk — the risk of loss from failed processes, people and systems — is where security risk and enterprise risk meet most concretely.

The instrument that records and governs it is the risk register: the single, living source of truth for what the organisation is worried about, how much, who owns it and what is being done.

A neglected register is a filing exercise; a living register is the operating system of the risk programme. Each entry should connect a specific risk to an owner, a current assessment, a treatment decision and a residual position that someone has explicitly accepted.

Field	Purpose	Example entry
Risk ID & description	Unambiguous statement of the risk	R-014: Unpatched internet-facing VPN appliance exploited for initial access
Owner	Named accountable individual	Head of Infrastructure
Inherent rating	Risk before controls	High (likely × severe)

Field	Purpose	Example entry
Treatment	Mitigate / transfer / avoid / accept	Mitigate — patch SLA + MFA + monitoring
Residual rating	Risk after controls	Medium
Acceptance	Who signed off the residual	CISO, accepted 02-2026, review 08-2026

The S.T.E.P.S.™ Engine in Practice: DISCOVER

Thinking like a risk leader becomes real only when it is operationalised. In the S.T.E.P.S.™ Governance Trust Cycle, the DISCOVER step is the engine room of risk-based decision-making. It takes the context and commitment established in DEFINE and produces the prioritised, owned, board-ready view of risk that every subsequent step — DESIGN, DOCUMENT, DO — depends upon. Where the executive discipline of this chapter is the "why," DISCOVER is the repeatable "how."

DISCOVER activity	What it produces	ISO 27001:2022 anchor
Establish risk criteria	Agreed likelihood/impact scales and appetite	Clause 6.1.2
Identify risks	Asset-threat-vulnerability inventory	Clause 6.1.2 / 8.2
Analyse & evaluate	Rated, ranked risks (qual + quant on the material few)	Clause 8.2
Treatment decision	Mitigate / transfer / avoid / accept per risk	Clause 6.1.3 / 8.3
Record & assign	Risk register with named owners and residual sign-off	Clause 8.3 / 9.1

The Risk Leader's Dashboard

The final act of risk leadership is communication.

A risk programme that cannot report itself clearly to the board is, for governance purposes, invisible. The executive risk dashboard translates the register into the handful of indicators a director needs to discharge oversight — not a wall of technical metrics, but a concise answer to four questions:

1. Are we within appetite?
2. What is changing?
3. What needs a decision?
4. Are our controls actually working?

Board question	Indicator	Why it matters
Are we within appetite?	Count of risks above tolerance, by category	Shows whether exposure exceeds the board's chosen limits
What is changing?	Trend in top risks vs. prior quarter	Distinguishes a deteriorating posture from a stable one
What needs a decision?	Risks awaiting acceptance or investment	Surfaces choices that only the board can make
Are controls working?	Key control effectiveness + incident trend	Tests whether spending is buying real protection

Case Studies: Three Failures of Risk Leadership

Each of the following breaches is, on the surface, a technical story. Read more carefully, each is a failure of risk leadership — of seeing, owning, prioritising or honestly reporting risk. Together they cover the three places where risk leadership most often breaks: at the perimeter of trust (third parties), inside the cloud (operational and configuration risk), and in the boardroom itself (governance and ethics).

Case Study 1 — Target (2013): Risk That Lived in a Vendor

Attackers stole network credentials from Fazio Mechanical, a heating-and-air-conditioning contractor with remote access to Target's environment, and used them to pivot onto the retailer's point-of-sale systems, where RAM-scraping malware harvested payment data over roughly three weeks during the 2013 holiday season. Approximately 40 million payment cards and the personal records of around 70 million customers were exposed. Target's own threat-detection tooling reportedly flagged the malware — more than once — but the alerts were not acted upon. The breach ultimately cost the company in excess of USD 200 million, including an USD 18.5 million multi-state settlement in 2017, and both the chief executive and chief information officer departed.

Lessons — Target

- Third-party access is your risk, wherever it originates. Risk must be assessed across the whole trust boundary, not just inside the corporate walls.
- Detection without response is theatre. Alerts that no one is accountable for triaging provide the comfort of monitoring without its protection.
- Network segmentation is a risk-treatment decision. A vendor billing portal should never have been a path to payment systems.

Case Study 2 — Capital One (2019): Risk That Was Written Down and Ignored

A former employee of the bank's cloud provider exploited a misconfigured web-application firewall to perform a server-side request forgery attack, reaching the cloud instance metadata service, obtaining credentials, and reading more than a hundred storage buckets.

Personal information on roughly 100 million people in the United States and a further 6 million in Canada was exposed, including approximately 140,000 Social Security numbers and 80,000 linked bank-account numbers. Reporting indicated that staff had warned about the firewall weakness before the attack. The bank paid an USD 80 million regulatory penalty to the Office of the Comptroller of the Currency and later settled a class action for USD 190 million.

Lessons — Capital One

- A known, documented risk that is not treated is worse than an unknown one — it is a governance failure, not a surprise.
- Cloud migration changes the risk model. Configuration is now a primary control surface, and assessing it must be continuous, not a one-time review.
- Regulators increasingly hold the board accountable for the risk-assessment process itself, not merely for the technical outcome.

Case Study 3 — Uber (2016): Risk That Was Hidden from the Board

Attackers obtained credentials and accessed a cloud storage bucket containing data on approximately 57 million riders and drivers, including some 600,000 driver's-licence numbers. Rather than disclose the incident as required, the company paid the attackers USD 100,000 — routed through its bug-bounty programme and accompanied by non-disclosure agreements — and concealed the breach for roughly a year.

The eventual consequences were severe: a USD 148 million settlement with 50 US states and the District of Columbia in 2018, and, in 2022, the criminal conviction of the former chief security officer for obstruction and concealment. It remains the landmark case for personal accountability in security leadership.

Lessons — Uber

- Concealing a risk does not transfer it — it compounds it, adding legal and personal liability to the original loss.
- Risk governance includes the duty to report bad news upward and outward. A culture that punishes disclosure manufactures cover-ups.
- Accountability for security risk is now personal and criminal at the executive level, not merely organisational.

Key Takeaways

- Security is a risk discipline, not a technology state. The leadership question is not "Are we secure?" but "Is our risk within appetite, and who owns the residual?"
- Enterprise, security and privacy risk must be integrated into one view. Under regimes like India's DPDPA, a control failure is simultaneously a security, privacy and financial event.

- Risk appetite is the board's job and must be specific enough to drive real decisions; risk tolerance is management's to monitor.
- Qualitative methods triage breadth; quantitative methods like FAIR drive the decisions that matter by expressing risk in money.
- Third-party and AI risk are now first-order exposures requiring lifecycle management and, increasingly, certifiable governance (ISO/IEC 42001).
- The DISCOVER step turns these principles into a defensible risk register and a board-ready dashboard.

Reflection Questions

- If a director asked you today, "How much cyber risk are we carrying, in rupees?" — could you answer, and how defensible would that answer be?
- Has your board issued a written risk appetite statement specific enough to settle a real trade-off, or only a slogan?
- Which of your third parties could become your Fazio Mechanical — and when were they last assessed?
- What known, documented risks are sitting in your register untreated, and who has formally accepted the residual?
- Does your culture make it safe and expected to report bad security news upward — or does it quietly incentivise the next Uber cover-up?
- Where does artificial intelligence already create exposure in your organisation, and which governance instrument covers it?

Action Deploy & Checklist

1. Convene the board to agree and document a risk appetite statement for your top three risk categories.
2. Stand up (or audit) a single integrated risk register that merges security, privacy and operational risk with named owners.
3. Select your three most material risks and run a quantitative (FAIR-style) analysis to express them in financial terms.
4. Tier all third parties by data sensitivity and access; re-assess every high-tier vendor and confirm contractual breach-notification timelines.
5. Inventory every use of AI and map each to the NIST AI RMF or ISO/IEC 42001; identify gaps in lawful basis and oversight.
6. Build a one-page executive risk dashboard answering the four board questions and present it at the next board meeting.
7. Establish and rehearse an escalation path that makes reporting bad security news the expected behaviour.

CHAPTER

5

THE 7-STEP FRAMEWORK DEFINED

Translating ISO 27001:2022 requirements into a practitioner's roadmap

Translating ISO/IEC 27001:2022 Requirements into a Practitioner's Roadmap

> **S.T.E.P.S.™ Engine — This Chapter Is the Engine**
>
> This is the keystone chapter: the full definition of the seven-step staircase that powers the rest of the book. Define → Discover → Design → Document → Do → Deploy & Check → Drive does not replace ISO/IEC 27001:2022 — it makes the standard navigable, mapping each step to specific clauses and to thirty years of implementation experience.

The S.T.E.P.S.™ Governance Trust Cycle — the engine beneath every chapter.

The PDCA cycle asks, "Are we improving?" The S.T.E.P.S.™ Framework asks, "Are we secure — and can we prove it?"

The difference between those two questions is the difference between operational efficiency and organisational trust. — **Seven Step Consulting**

Implementing an ISMS Using the Seven Step (7D) Framework: The Medicare Plus Journey

"A management system does not create trust because it exists. It creates trust because it consistently translates leadership intent into operational behaviour, measurable performance, and continual improvement."

Chapter Overview

ISO/IEC 27001:2022 tells organizations **what** an Information Security Management System (ISMS) must achieve, but it intentionally avoids prescribing **how** it should be implemented. This flexibility allows organizations of every size and sector to tailor the standard to their own business context. It also creates one of the greatest implementation challenges: many organizations understand the requirements of the standard but struggle to convert them into a practical, coordinated programme of work.

This chapter introduces the **Seven Step (7D) Framework**—a practical implementation methodology developed from more than three decades of consulting, auditing, and implementation experience across healthcare, banking, manufacturing, government, technology, and critical infrastructure. Rather than viewing ISO/IEC 27001 as a collection of clauses or documentation requirements, the framework presents it as a logical journey in which each stage builds upon the previous one.

The seven stages are:

	Step	What it does
01	**DEFINE**	Establish governance and context, ISMS scope, interested parties and risk criteria; secure top-management commitment

	Step	What it does
02	**DISCOVER**	Conduct the risk assessment: identify assets, threats and vulnerabilities; analyse and prioritise risk
03	**DESIGN**	Decide risk treatment; select controls; produce the Statement of Applicability; design policy and architecture
04	**DOCUMENT**	Convert governance decisions and produce the required and supporting documented information — policies, procedures, registers, records
05	**DO**	Implement controls across all four categories; train staff; integrate security into operations
06	**DEPLOY & CHECK**	Monitor, measure, audit and review: internal audit, management review, metrics, incident analysis
07	**DRIVE**	Continually improve correct nonconformities, refresh risk, respond to change, grow maturity through innovation, and organizational learning.

To demonstrate how the framework operates in practice, this chapter follows the journey of a fictional healthcare organization—**Medicare Plus**. Rather than introducing theory first and examples later, the entire chapter follows Medicare Plus as it plans, builds, operates, measures, and continually improves its Information Security Management System. Every concept is illustrated through the decisions, challenges, and governance practices of this organization.

By the end of the chapter, readers will understand not only what ISO/IEC 27001 requires, but also how successful organizations translate those requirements into an effective, business-aligned management system.

Learning Objectives

After studying this chapter, the reader will be able to:

- Explain the purpose and structure of the Seven Step (7D) Framework.
- Understand how each step aligns with ISO/IEC 27001:2022.
- Apply the framework to design and implement an effective ISMS.
- Appreciate the logical dependencies between implementation activities.
- Use the Medicare Plus case study as a practical implementation roadmap.
- Recognize how governance, risk management, controls, documentation, implementation, measurement, and continual improvement function as one integrated management system.

The Medicare Plus Journey Begins

Medicare Plus is a rapidly growing healthcare organization operating three hospitals, twenty outpatient clinics, diagnostic laboratories, and an expanding telemedicine platform serving more than one million patients.

Over the previous two years, the healthcare sector had become one of the world's most targeted industries for ransomware attacks, data theft, and business email compromise. Several well-known hospital networks suffered prolonged service disruptions, resulting in cancelled surgeries, inaccessible patient records, regulatory investigations, and significant reputational damage.

Although Medicare Plus had invested heavily in cybersecurity technologies—including firewalls, endpoint protection, cloud security, and backup systems—the Board recognised that technology alone did not guarantee resilience. Different departments managed security independently, supplier oversight varied considerably, policies were inconsistent, and risk decisions were often made without executive visibility.

During one Board meeting, the Chief Executive Officer posed a simple but fundamental question:

"If regulators, patients, or our Board asked us tomorrow whether we could demonstrate effective governance of information security, could we prove it?"

The silence that followed revealed the organization's real challenge.

The issue was not the absence of security tools. It was the absence of an integrated management system that aligned leadership, governance, risk management, operational controls, and continual improvement.

The Board therefore approved the implementation of an Information Security Management System based on **ISO/IEC 27001:2022**, adopting the **Seven Step (7D) Framework** as the implementation methodology.

Rather than approaching certification as a documentation exercise, Medicare Plus viewed the ISMS as a strategic business programme designed to achieve four objectives:

- Protect patient safety and confidentiality.
- Demonstrate regulatory compliance.

- Strengthen operational resilience.
- Build long-term trust among patients, regulators, partners, and shareholders.

Everything that follows in this chapter describes how Medicare Plus accomplished that journey.

The Seven Step (7D) Framework

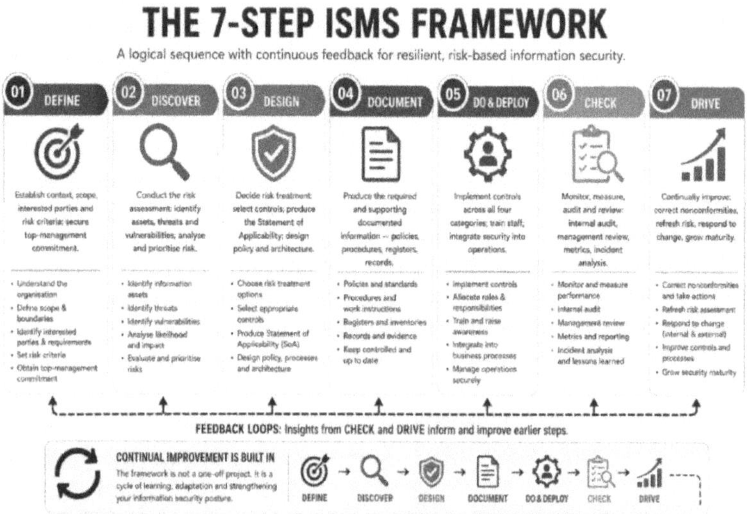

7Step Framework – Logical Dependency & Iteration Guide

Core principle

Steps are **named in logical order** (prerequisites first).

You can **iterate and loop** – but never skip a prerequisite.

The Seven Step Framework converts ISO/IEC 27001 from a collection of clauses into a logical implementation roadmap.

Unlike traditional compliance checklists, each stage produces tangible outputs that become essential inputs for the next stage.

Step	Purpose	Principal Outcome
Define	Understand the business and establish governance	Scope, leadership commitment, policy, risk criteria
Discover	Identify and assess risks	Prioritised risk register
Design	Select treatments and controls	Risk Treatment Plan and Statement of Applicability
Document	Produce controlled documentation	Policies, procedures, records
Do	Implement controls	Operational ISMS
Deploy & Deploy & Check	Measure effectiveness	Audit findings, metrics, management review
Drive	Continually improve	Mature, adaptive ISMS

Stepbystep dependencies

Step	What it does	Logical dependency
01 DEFINE	Establish context, scope, interested parties, risk criteria; secure topmanagement commitment	*Start here* – nothing before this
02 DISCOVER	Risk assessment: identify assets, threats, vulnerabilities; analyse and prioritise risk	**Depends on 01** – cannot discover risk without scope & criteria
03 DESIGN	Decide risk treatment; select controls; produce SoA; design policy & architecture	**Depends on 02** – cannot design controls before knowing which risks to treat

Step	What it does	Logical dependency
04 DOCUMENT	Produce required & supporting documented information: policies, procedures, registers, records	**Depends on 03** – cannot document what hasn't been designed
05 DO	Implement controls (all 4 categories); train staff; integrate security into operations	**Depends on 03 & 04** – cannot deploy what isn't designed or documented
06 DEPLOY & CHECK	Monitor, measure, audit, review: internal audit, management review, metrics, incident analysis	**Depends on 05** – cannot check what isn't deployed
07 DRIVE	Continually improve: correct nonconformities, refresh risk, respond to change, grow maturity	**Depends on 06** – cannot improve without measurement & review

Allowed loops (with logical integrity)

Loop	How it works
01 ↔ 02	Redefine scope after discovery; then rediscover. Never discover before current scope is defined.
06 → 03	Audit findings reveal control gap → return to Design (retreat risk) → Deploy again.
07 → 01	Organisation context evolves → update Define → reDiscover → reDesign ... (full cycle)

Do not skip

✗ Invalid (logical break)	☑ Correct approach
Discover before Define	Define → Discover
Design before Discover	Discover → Design

✕ Invalid (logical break)	☑ Correct approach
Deploy before Design	Design → Document → Deploy
Deploy & Check before Deploy	Deploy → Deploy & Check
Drive before Deploy & Check	Deploy & Check → Drive

Team cheat sheet (quick reference)

First time = follow 01→07 in order.

Every time after = loop freely but **never** skip a step that logically depends on a previous one.

If you need to ...	Return to ...	Then continue ...
Adjust scope	**01 DEFINE**	02 DISCOVER (then onward)
Treat a new risk	**03 DESIGN**	04 DOCUMENT → 05 DEPLOY
Fix a failed control	**03 DESIGN**	04 DOCUMENT → 05 DEPLOY → 06 DEPLOY & CHECK
Respond to change	**01 DEFINE**	full cycle 02–07

This dependency is fundamental.

Without clearly defining organizational context, meaningful risk assessment becomes impossible.

Without understanding risk, effective control design becomes guesswork.

Without documented guidance, implementation becomes inconsistent.

Without implementation, measurement has no value.

Without measurement, improvement becomes impossible.

Each step therefore creates the foundation for the next.

Stepbystep dependencies

Step	What it does	Logical dependency
01 DEFINE	Establish context, scope, interested parties, risk criteria; secure topmanagement commitment	*Start here* – nothing before this
02 DISCOVER	Risk assessment: identify assets, threats, vulnerabilities; analyse and prioritise risk	**Depends on 01** – cannot discover risk without scope & criteria
03 DESIGN	Decide risk treatment; select controls; produce SoA; design policy & architecture	**Depends on 02** – cannot design controls before knowing which risks to treat
04 DOCUMENT	Produce required & supporting documented information: policies, procedures, registers, records	**Depends on 03** – cannot document what hasn't been designed
05 DO	Implement controls (all 4 categories); train staff; integrate security into operations	**Depends on 03 & 04** – cannot deploy what isn't designed or documented
06 DEPLOY & CHECK	Monitor, measure, audit, review: internal audit, management review, metrics, incident analysis	**Depends on 05** – cannot check what isn't deployed
07 DRIVE	Continually improve: correct nonconformities, refresh risk, respond to change, grow maturity	**Depends on 06** – cannot improve without measurement & review

One of the most common misconceptions about implementation frameworks is that they imply a rigid, one-time sequence.

The Seven Step Framework is different.

Organizations normally complete the seven stages during initial implementation. Once operational, however, the framework becomes iterative. Audit findings may require redesigning controls. New business initiatives may require redefining scope. Emerging threats may trigger fresh risk assessments.

The sequence therefore represents **logical dependency**, not procedural rigidity.

Medicare Plus would experience this repeatedly throughout its implementation journey.

From Strategy to Trust

Before examining each stage in detail, it is useful to understand the philosophy underpinning the framework.

Many organizations view ISO/IEC 27001 primarily as a certification project.

Successful organizations view it differently.

They see the ISMS as an operating system for governance.

The Seven Step Framework ensures that every governance decision can be traced through a complete chain:

Business Objective → Risk → Control → Implementation → Evidence → Assurance → Improvement

This traceability creates something more valuable than certification.

It creates organizational trust.

Transition to Step 1

Having committed to implementing ISO/IEC 27001, Medicare Plus now faced its first challenge.

Before assessing risks or selecting controls, leadership first needed to answer a series of fundamental governance questions:

- What exactly are we protecting?
- Why are we protecting it?
- Who owns the risks?
- Which parts of the business are included?
- What level of risk are we prepared to accept?

Answering these questions marks the beginning of the first stage of the Seven Step Framework:

Step 1 — DEFINE: Establishing the Foundation

The **DEFINE** stage establishes the governance foundation for the entire Information Security Management System (ISMS). It is the point at which the organization decides **why** it is implementing the ISMS, **what** it intends to protect, **who** will be responsible, and **how** information security will support business objectives.

"A secure organisation is not built by deploying controls. It is built by making the right decisions before the first control is ever implemented."

When the Board of Medicare Plus approved the implementation of an Information Security Management System (ISMS), no new security technologies were purchased immediately. No firewalls were upgraded, no policies were rewritten, and no risk registers were created. Instead, the organisation began with governance.

This reflects one of the most important principles of the Seven Step (7D) Framework: before an organisation can protect information, it must first understand its business.

Many ISMS implementations fail because organisations begin with technology. They buy security tools, implement multi-factor authentication, conduct vulnerability scans, and produce policies without first establishing why the ISMS exists, what it is expected to protect, and how information security supports organisational objectives.

The DEFINE stage prevents this mistake. It establishes the strategic direction of the ISMS by ensuring that leadership, business strategy, risk appetite, regulatory obligations, and organisational priorities are aligned before operational work begins. Every decision made in subsequent stages depends upon the quality of the decisions made here.

An effective DEFINE phase therefore:

- Secures documented commitment from top management.
- Establishes an ISMS Steering Committee with clear governance responsibilities.
- Analyses the organization's external context (PESTLE).
- Examines the internal context (SWOT).
- Identifies interested parties and their requirements.
- Defines the ISMS scope, including its interfaces and dependencies.
- Establishes the Information Security Policy.
- Defines risk appetite, acceptance criteria, and governance principles.
- Commits the budget, resources, skills, and competencies needed for successful implementation.

The CEO decides to pursue ISO/IEC 27001 certification after several large hospitals experience ransomware attacks and major healthcare privacy breaches.

1. Securing Top Management Commitment

The implementation begins with a formal board meeting.

The CEO signs an Information Security Charter stating that:

- Information security is a strategic business priority.
- An ISMS will be implemented across critical healthcare services.
- Required financial and human resources will be allocated.
- Quarterly management reviews will monitor progress.

A cross-functional **ISMS Steering Committee** is established, including:

- CEO (Executive Sponsor)
- Chief Medical Officer
- Chief Information Officer
- Chief Information Security Officer
- Head of Legal and Compliance
- HR Director
- Operations Director

This committee becomes responsible for governance decisions throughout the programme.

2. Understanding the External Context (PESTLE)

The Steering Committee performs a PESTLE analysis.

Political

- New national cybersecurity reporting obligations for healthcare providers.

Economic

- Rising ransomware payments affecting healthcare organizations.

Social

- Patients increasingly expect secure digital consultations and privacy protection.

Technological

- Growing dependence on cloud-hosted Electronic Health Record (EHR) platforms and AI-assisted diagnostics.

Legal

- Health privacy legislation requires protection of patient information and timely breach notification.

Environmental

- Flood risks affecting one regional data centre.

Rather than simply recording these issues, the committee identifies resulting ISMS actions:

- Implement regulatory monitoring.
- Strengthen ransomware resilience.
- Review cloud supplier assurance.
- Enhance disaster recovery capabilities.

3. Understanding the Internal Context (SWOT)

The team next evaluates internal capabilities.

Strengths

- Mature IT infrastructure.
- Strong executive sponsorship.

- Experienced cybersecurity team.

Weaknesses

- Inconsistent supplier security reviews.
- Legacy patient databases.
- Limited employee security awareness.

Opportunities

- Build patient trust through ISO 27001 certification.
- Expand into international healthcare partnerships.

Threats

- Credential theft.
- Insider misuse.
- Third-party compromise.
- Cloud outages.

Again, the exercise moves beyond documentation into action planning.

4. Mapping Interested Parties

The organization identifies key stakeholders and converts expectations into ISMS requirements.

Interested Party	Expectation	ISMS Requirement
Patients	Confidentiality of medical records	Encryption, access control, privacy governance
Regulators	Compliance with health privacy laws	Compliance monitoring and audit programme

Interested Party	Expectation	ISMS Requirement
Shareholders	Protection of enterprise value	Enterprise risk management and board reporting
Doctors	Reliable system availability	Business continuity and disaster recovery
Cloud provider	Clear contractual responsibilities	Supplier governance and security clauses

This mapping ensures the ISMS reflects real business obligations.

5. Defining the Scope

The Steering Committee initially proposes the scope:

"Telemedicine platform operated from Head Office."

However, further analysis reveals that patient services also depend upon:

- Cloud infrastructure.
- Identity management provider.
- Laboratory integration APIs.
- Payment gateway.
- Outsourced Security Operations Centre (SOC).

The scope is revised to cover:

"The provision of telemedicine services, including supporting applications, patient data processing, cloud-hosted infrastructure, integrated healthcare services, and associated governance processes."

The committee deliberately avoids artificial exclusions simply to simplify certification.

6. Establishing Risk Appetite

Senior management agrees that:

- The organization has **very low appetite** for patient privacy breaches.
- **Low appetite** for service outages exceeding two hours.
- **Moderate appetite** for adopting innovative cloud technologies where risks can be managed.
- **Higher appetite** for investing in AI-assisted healthcare innovation.

These statements provide guidance for later risk treatment decisions.

7. Issuing the Information Security Policy

The CEO formally approves and signs the Information Security Policy.

The policy commits the organization to:

- Protect confidentiality, integrity, and availability.
- Meet legal and regulatory obligations.
- Continually improve the ISMS.
- Support patient trust and organizational resilience.

The signed policy is communicated to all employees and forms the cornerstone of governance.

8. Committing Resources

Management approves:

- Budget for Security Information and Event Management (SIEM).
- Multi-factor authentication deployment.

- Security awareness programme.
- External penetration testing.
- Additional security analysts.
- ISO 27001 implementation consultancy.
- Internal auditor training.

This demonstrates that leadership commitment is backed by tangible investment rather than statements alone.

Why DEFINE Comes First

Every successful management system begins by answering a small number of fundamental questions.

- Why are we implementing the ISMS?
- Which business objectives must it support?
- What information requires protection?
- Who owns the associated risks?
- Which legal and regulatory obligations apply?
- What level of risk is the Board willing to accept?
- How much investment is required?

Without clear answers to these questions, later activities become disconnected. Risk assessments lack context, controls address the wrong priorities, documentation becomes generic, and audits measure compliance rather than organisational effectiveness.

The DEFINE stage therefore creates the foundation upon which every other step depends.

At Medicare Plus, the Executive Committee recognised that the organisation was experiencing rapid growth.

Telemedicine services had expanded nationally, patient records were increasingly hosted in cloud environments, diagnostic laboratories exchanged information electronically with hospitals, and specialist clinicians frequently worked remotely. These developments created significant opportunities but also increased exposure to cyber threats, privacy breaches, supply chain risks, and operational disruption.

The Board understood that these risks could no longer be managed independently by individual departments. Information security required enterprise-wide governance.

- Leadership Makes Information Security a Strategic Objective
- The implementation officially commenced with a Board meeting chaired by the Chief Executive Officer.
- Rather than delegating responsibility entirely to the IT department, the Board adopted a formal Information Security Charter declaring that protecting information was essential to delivering safe healthcare, maintaining patient confidence, complying with regulatory obligations, and preserving organisational resilience.

The Charter committed Medicare Plus to:

- Establish an Information Security Management System aligned with ISO/IEC 27001:2022;
- Allocate sufficient financial and human resources;
- Integrate information security into organisational decision-making;
- Conduct regular management reviews; and
- Pursue continual improvement rather than one-time certification.

The Chief Executive Officer signed the Charter on behalf of the Board, signalling that information security was now a strategic business priority rather than simply a technical concern.

This visible leadership commitment reflects the intent of ISO/IEC 27001 Clauses 5.1 to 5.3, which require top management to demonstrate accountability, establish policy, assign responsibilities, and ensure that the ISMS supports organisational objectives.

Leadership commitment is demonstrated not by speeches or policy statements alone but by decisions. Budgets, priorities, governance structures, and executive oversight all become tangible evidence that information security matters.

Creating the ISMS Steering Committee

Recognising that information security affects every part of the organisation, Medicare Plus established an ISMS Steering Committee comprising senior executives representing business, clinical, legal, operational, and technical functions.

Membership included:

- Chief Executive Officer (Executive Sponsor)
- Chief Medical Officer
- Chief Information Officer
- Chief Information Security Officer
- Director of Clinical Operations
- Head of Legal and Compliance
- Human Resources Director
- Procurement Director
- Finance Director

Each member brought a different perspective. Clinical leaders focused on patient safety and service continuity. Legal representatives interpreted regulatory obligations. Human Resources addressed personnel security. Procurement considered supplier governance. Information technology managed technical implementation, while executive leadership ensured that information security remained aligned with organisational strategy.

This multidisciplinary approach reinforced an important governance principle: **cybersecurity is an organisational responsibility supported by technology—not an IT responsibility supported by the business.**

The Steering Committee became the principal decision-making body throughout the implementation journey, approving scope, risk criteria, treatment strategies, policies, investment decisions, and management reviews.

Understanding the Organisation's Context

With governance established, the Steering Committee turned its attention to understanding the environment in which Medicare Plus operated.

ISO/IEC 27001 begins with organisational context because every ISMS must reflect the business it serves. A hospital faces different risks from a manufacturing company. A financial institution operates under different regulatory obligations from a university. Even organisations within the same sector differ in size, geography, technology, culture, and risk tolerance.

Accordingly, the Steering Committee examined both the external environment and the organisation's internal capabilities.

External Context

The Committee conducted a structured PESTLE analysis to identify the external factors likely to influence the ISMS.

Political developments included increasingly stringent cybersecurity reporting obligations for healthcare providers. Governments were demanding faster notification of significant cyber incidents and greater accountability for protecting critical infrastructure.

Economic pressures were equally significant. Ransomware attacks were causing financial losses across the healthcare sector, while cyber insurance premiums continued to rise. Security investment could no longer be viewed solely as an operational cost; it had become a prerequisite for organisational resilience.

Social expectations were changing rapidly. Patients increasingly expected secure digital healthcare services and assumed that their medical information would remain confidential regardless of whether consultations occurred in hospitals or through telemedicine platforms.

Technological developments introduced both opportunity and risk. Cloud-hosted Electronic Health Record (EHR) systems, artificial intelligence-assisted diagnostics, connected medical devices, and mobile health applications improved patient care but simultaneously expanded the organisation's attack surface.

Legal obligations required compliance with healthcare privacy legislation, national cybersecurity regulations, contractual commitments, and emerging data protection laws governing personal information.

Environmental considerations also influenced planning. One regional data centre was located in an area vulnerable to seasonal flooding, highlighting the need for disaster recovery and resilient infrastructure.

Rather than documenting these issues as isolated observations, the Steering Committee converted each one into an actionable governance decision. Regulatory developments required continuous compliance monitoring. Growing ransomware threats justified stronger backup strategies and incident response capabilities. Increasing reliance on cloud services demanded enhanced supplier assurance. Environmental risks reinforced the need for geographically resilient recovery arrangements.

Context therefore became a driver of governance rather than an academic exercise.

Assessing Internal Capabilities

The Committee next examined the organisation itself.

The objective was not merely to identify weaknesses but to understand the capabilities available to support implementation.

Several strengths quickly became apparent. Medicare Plus enjoyed strong executive sponsorship, a mature IT infrastructure, experienced clinical leadership, and a culture committed to patient care. These strengths provided an excellent foundation for implementing an enterprise-wide ISMS.

However, the assessment also identified several weaknesses. Supplier security reviews lacked consistency. Some legacy systems remained unsupported. Security awareness training varied considerably across departments. Documentation standards differed between hospitals and outpatient facilities.

The organisation also recognised significant opportunities. Achieving ISO/IEC 27001 certification would strengthen patient confidence, improve relationships with insurance providers, support future international partnerships, and differentiate Medicare Plus within an increasingly competitive healthcare market.

At the same time, management acknowledged continuing threats including ransomware, credential theft, insider misuse, supply chain compromise, cloud service outages, and increasingly sophisticated social engineering attacks targeting healthcare professionals.

This balanced assessment ensured that implementation decisions reflected organisational reality rather than aspiration.

Identifying Interested Parties

The next task was to identify the individuals and organisations whose expectations would influence the ISMS.

- Patients expected confidentiality, integrity, and availability of their medical records.
- Clinicians required reliable access to Electronic Health Records to deliver safe patient care.
- Regulators demanded compliance with healthcare privacy legislation and cybersecurity reporting obligations.
- Shareholders expected effective governance that protected organisational value.
- Business partners required secure exchange of clinical information.
- Cloud service providers, laboratories, insurers, and technology vendors expected clearly defined contractual responsibilities.

Rather than treating these expectations as abstract stakeholder requirements, the Steering Committee translated each into specific ISMS obligations.

Interested Party	Expectation	ISMS Requirement
Patients	Confidentiality of medical records	Encryption, access control, privacy governance
Regulators	Compliance with health privacy laws	Compliance monitoring and audit programme
Shareholders	Protection of enterprise value	Enterprise risk management and board reporting
Doctors	Reliable system availability	Business continuity and disaster recovery
Cloud provider	Clear contractual responsibilities	Supplier governance and security clauses

For example, the expectation of patient confidentiality required encryption, robust access controls, identity management, and privacy governance. Regulatory expectations drove audit programmes, legal compliance monitoring, and documented evidence. Clinical requirements shaped availability objectives, business continuity planning, and disaster recovery capabilities.

In this way, stakeholder expectations became measurable management requirements rather than general aspirations.

Defining the Scope of the ISMS

One of the most significant decisions during DEFINE concerned the scope of the Information Security Management System.

The Steering Committee initially proposed limiting certification to the organisation's head office and telemedicine platform. Although attractive from a project management perspective, further analysis revealed that such a scope would exclude several systems essential to delivering healthcare services.

Patient consultations depended upon cloud-hosted applications. Diagnostic laboratories exchanged electronic information with hospitals. Identity management services authenticated clinicians across multiple facilities. External payment gateways processed billing transactions, while a managed Security Operations Centre monitored security events around the clock.

Excluding these dependencies would produce an artificial management system that failed to reflect operational reality.

Consequently, the Steering Committee adopted a much broader scope encompassing

"The provision of telemedicine services, including supporting applications, patient data processing, cloud-hosted infrastructure, integrated healthcare services, and associated governance processes."

The decision demonstrated a fundamental principle of ISO/IEC 27001: an ISMS should reflect how the business actually operates, not how the organisation wishes auditors to perceive it.

Defining Risk Appetite

Having established the organisational context and agreed upon the scope of the ISMS, the Steering Committee turned to a decision that would influence every subsequent stage of implementation: how much risk was the organisation prepared to accept?

No organisation can eliminate all information security risks. Attempting to do so would be prohibitively expensive, operationally restrictive, and ultimately counterproductive. The objective of an ISMS is therefore not to achieve absolute security but to ensure that risks are understood, evaluated, and managed within levels acceptable to the organisation.

Risk appetite provides this direction. It defines the boundaries within which management is prepared to operate and ensures that future decisions remain consistent with business objectives.

For Medicare Plus, these discussions were particularly important because healthcare organisations face competing priorities. On one hand, patient information must be rigorously protected. On the other, clinicians require immediate access to medical records, diagnostic systems, and telemedicine platforms. Excessive security can delay patient care, while inadequate security can compromise safety, privacy, and regulatory compliance.

After several workshops, the Board approved the following high-level risk appetite statements:

- Zero tolerance for deliberate unauthorised disclosure of patient information.
- Very low tolerance for prolonged disruption of critical clinical services.
- Low tolerance for non-compliance with healthcare and privacy regulations.
- Moderate tolerance for adopting innovative digital technologies where risks are appropriately managed.
- Higher tolerance for controlled experimentation within isolated research environments that do not process production patient data.

These statements became the benchmark against which every future risk would be evaluated. During the DISCOVER stage, identified risks would no longer be assessed in isolation but compared against the Board's approved appetite. Risks exceeding these limits would require treatment, while those falling within acceptable boundaries could be retained with documented justification.

In this way, risk appetite transformed risk management from subjective opinion into an executive governance decision.

Establishing the Information Security Policy

The next milestone was the development of the Information Security Policy.

Many organisations regard the policy as a compliance document prepared primarily for auditors. Medicare Plus adopted a different philosophy. The Steering Committee viewed the policy as the organisation's formal declaration of intent—a concise statement explaining why information security mattered and how it supported the organisation's mission.

Rather than attempting to include operational detail, the policy focused on strategic commitments. It affirmed that Medicare Plus would:

- protect the confidentiality, integrity, and availability of information;
- safeguard patient safety by ensuring secure and reliable healthcare services;
- comply with applicable legal, regulatory, and contractual obligations;
- manage information security risks systematically;
- provide adequate resources to operate the ISMS; and

- continually improve the effectiveness of the Information Security Management System.

Once approved by the Chief Executive Officer, the policy was communicated throughout the organisation. Every employee, contractor, and relevant supplier was expected to understand how their role contributed to these commitments.

Supporting policies covering access control, supplier security, incident management, acceptable use, cryptography, business continuity, and information classification would be developed later during the DOCUMENT stage. At DEFINE, however, the objective was simply to establish the overarching direction that would guide all subsequent governance decisions.

Committing Resources

An Information Security Management System cannot succeed through executive endorsement alone. Leadership commitment must be reflected in the allocation of people, budget, technology, and organisational attention.

Recognising this, the Board approved a comprehensive investment programme to support implementation.

Funding was allocated for:

- Security Information and Event Management (SIEM) capabilities.
- Multi-factor authentication across clinical and administrative systems.
- Security awareness and phishing simulation programmes.
- External vulnerability assessments and penetration testing.
- Enhanced backup and disaster recovery capabilities.

- Additional cybersecurity personnel.
- Internal auditor training.
- Specialist ISO/IEC 27001 implementation support.

Equally important, department heads were instructed to allocate staff time for risk assessments, policy development, process reviews, and implementation activities.

Information security was no longer treated as work to be completed "when time permitted"; it became part of normal organisational planning.

This visible commitment reinforced an important leadership message: information security was now recognised as an investment in organisational resilience rather than merely an operational expense.

The Outputs of DEFINE

Although no technical controls had yet been implemented, Medicare Plus had accomplished something far more significant. The organisation had created a shared understanding of what the ISMS was intended to achieve and how it would support business success.

By the conclusion of DEFINE, the organisation had produced:

- A clearly defined organisational context;
- Executive commitment and governance structures;
- An approved isms scope;
- Identified interested parties and their requirements;
- Board-approved risk appetite statements;
- The Information Security Policy;

- Defined roles and responsibilities; and
- Committed resources for implementation.
- Collectively, these outputs established the governance foundation upon which the remainder of the isms would be built.
- More importantly, they ensured that every subsequent activity would be aligned with organisational objectives rather than driven solely by technical considerations.

DEFINE- in a nutshell

Objective	**Establish the governance foundation for the ISMS**
Key Activities	Understand organisational context, identify interested parties, define scope, establish leadership commitment, approve risk appetite, issue Information Security Policy, allocate resources
Primary Deliverables	ISMS Scope, Information Security Policy, Governance Structure, Risk Criteria, Roles and Responsibilities
ISO/IEC 27001:2022 Alignment	Clauses 4.1–4.4 (Context), 5.1–5.3 (Leadership), 7.1–7.5 (Support)
Input to Next Step	A defined business environment within which information security risks can now be identified and assessed

Lessons from Medicare Plus

The DEFINE stage illustrates an important lesson that extends well beyond healthcare.

Successful organisations do not begin by asking, "Which security controls should we implement?" They begin by asking,

"What are we trying to achieve as a business, and how does information security enable that success?"

By answering this question first, Medicare Plus ensured that every later decision—whether selecting controls, approving budgets, responding to incidents, or measuring performance—could be traced back to the organisation's strategic objectives.

This traceability is one of the defining characteristics of a mature Information Security Management System. Governance decisions are no longer isolated activities; they become part of a coherent chain linking business strategy, risk management, operational controls, and continual improvement.

With the governance foundation firmly established, Medicare Plus was now ready to move from understanding its business to understanding its risks.

The Result

By the end of DEFINE, MediCarePlus has not yet implemented a single technical control, but it has created something even more valuable—a shared understanding of **why the ISMS exists, what it will protect, who is responsible, how much risk the organization is prepared to accept, and what resources are required to succeed.**

When the project moves into **DISCOVER** and begins identifying and assessing risks, it does so on a solid governance foundation rather than on assumptions.

This example illustrates why DEFINE is much more than an administrative starting point. It is the stage where strategy, governance, business objectives, stakeholder expectations, and executive commitment are translated into a coherent direction for the ISMS. Get DEFINE right, and every subsequent step becomes easier and more defensible. Get it wrong, and the organization risks building an elegant management system that protects the wrong assets, ignores critical dependencies, or fails to support the business it was intended to serve.

The Seven Step Framework therefore progresses naturally from DEFINE to DISCOVER.

In the next stage, the organisation identifies its critical information assets, analyses threats and vulnerabilities, evaluates business impact, assigns risk ownership, and develops a prioritised view of the risks that must be treated.

The outputs of DEFINE now become the inputs to DISCOVER, demonstrating the logical dependency that underpins the entire Seven Step Framework.

Step 2 — DISCOVER: Understanding Risk Before Selecting Controls

"You cannot protect what you do not understand, and you cannot manage risks that have never been identified."

With its governance foundation firmly established, Medicare Plus was ready to begin the second stage of the Seven Step (7D) Framework—DISCOVER.

If DEFINE answered the question, "What business are we protecting?", DISCOVER answers an equally important question:

"What could prevent us from achieving our business objectives?"

This distinction is fundamental.

Many organizations begin risk assessments by brainstorming cyber threats or compiling vulnerability lists. The Seven Step Framework takes a different approach. Risk assessment begins with understanding business value, because information security exists to protect the organization's ability to achieve its objectives—not simply to defend technology.

For Medicare Plus, the objective was never merely to prevent cyberattacks. It was to ensure that doctors could continue treating patients safely, that medical records remained accurate and available, that privacy obligations were fulfilled, and that public confidence in the organisation remained intact.

DISCOVER therefore transforms business understanding into informed decision-making by identifying, analysing, and prioritising the risks that threaten those objectives.

Risk Assessment: The Analytical Heart of the ISMS

Every subsequent decision in the Seven Step Framework depends upon the quality of the DISCOVER stage.

If risks are poorly identified, inappropriate controls will be selected.

If threats are misunderstood, investments will be misplaced.

If business impact is underestimated, management will accept risks it never intended to tolerate.

Conversely, when DISCOVER is performed thoroughly, the organisation gains a clear understanding of where its greatest exposures lie and where limited resources will have the greatest effect.

For this reason, ISO/IEC 27001 **places risk assessment at the centre of the management system**. Rather than prescribing a particular methodology, the standard requires organisations to ***establish a repeatable process that identifies, analyses, evaluates, and prioritises information security risks using criteria approved during the DEFINE stage.***

For Medicare Plus, the Board-approved risk appetite established in Step 1 now provided the benchmark against which every identified risk would be evaluated.

Beginning with Information Assets

The Steering Committee agreed that before discussing cyber threats, they first needed to identify what the organisation was trying to protect.

A common mistake is to regard servers, laptops, or databases as the primary assets. In reality, these are merely repositories or processing platforms. The true asset is information.

Without patient information, a hospital cannot diagnose illness, prescribe medication, process insurance claims, schedule surgery, or deliver telemedicine services. Information therefore represents the organisation's most valuable business resource.

Accordingly, Medicare Plus developed a comprehensive inventory of information assets.

These included:

Information Asset	Business Importance
Electronic Health Records (EHR)	Essential for diagnosis, treatment, and continuity of care
Patient Identity Database	Admissions, billing, insurance verification
Telemedicine Platform	Remote consultation and digital healthcare delivery
Clinical Imaging Archive	X-rays, MRI, CT scans and diagnostic images
Identity and Access Management System	Authentication and access control
Hospital Network Infrastructure	Enables communication between clinical systems

Information Asset	Business Importance
Cloud Backup Repository	Disaster recovery and business continuity
Medical Staff Credential Database	Regulatory compliance and HR management

Each asset was assigned a business owner responsible for ensuring that its associated risks would later be managed appropriately.

Ownership is an important governance principle. Information security cannot be delegated entirely to the Information Security team because the business—not IT—owns the risks.

Understanding Threats

Having identified its critical information assets, Medicare Plus next considered the events capable of compromising them.

Threats originate from many sources. Some are deliberate, such as cybercriminals deploying ransomware or insiders stealing confidential information. Others are accidental, including human error, software defects, equipment failure, or natural disasters.

The Steering Committee deliberately avoided focusing solely on cybersecurity. Information security risks are broader than malicious attacks.

Examples included:

Asset	Representative Threats
Electronic Health Records	Ransomware, data corruption, system failure
Telemedicine Platform	Distributed denial-of-service attacks, cloud outages

Asset	Representative Threats
Patient Database	Insider misuse, unauthorised disclosure
Identity Management System	Credential theft, privilege escalation
Clinical Imaging Archive	Data corruption, accidental deletion
Cloud Backups	Compromise of administrative credentials
Hospital Networks	Malware propagation, configuration errors

Rather than immediately estimating likelihood or selecting controls, the objective was simply to understand everything capable of affecting organisational objectives.

This comprehensive approach prevents organisations from overlooking less obvious but equally significant risks.

Looking Beyond Threats to Vulnerabilities

A threat alone does not create risk.

A ransomware group may target a hospital, but if systems are fully patched, access is tightly controlled, backups are protected, and network segmentation prevents lateral movement, the likelihood of successful compromise may be significantly reduced.

Conversely, even relatively unsophisticated attackers can succeed where vulnerabilities exist.

For each identified threat, Medicare Plus therefore asked a second question:

"What weaknesses could allow this threat to succeed?"

Examples quickly emerged.

Threat	Vulnerability
Ransomware	Unsupported operating systems and delayed patching
Credential Theft	Absence of multi-factor authentication
Insider Misuse	Excessive user privileges
Phishing	Limited employee awareness
Cloud Outage	Dependence upon a single cloud region
Malware	Weak endpoint protection
Privilege Escalation	Poor segregation of duties

One observation surprised the Steering Committee.

Most vulnerabilities were not technological.

Many reflected governance weaknesses, inconsistent processes, unclear responsibilities, inadequate training, or poor operational discipline.

The DISCOVER stage therefore reinforced an important lesson:

Technology rarely creates organisational risk on its own. Risk usually emerges when technology, people, and governance fail together.

Constructing Risk Scenarios

Rather than assessing threats or vulnerabilities independently, Medicare Plus combined them into complete business risk scenarios.

For example:

- Asset: Electronic Health Records
- Threat: Ransomware attack
- Vulnerability: Legacy servers remain unpatched.

This combination produces a meaningful business scenario:

Attackers exploit an unpatched vulnerability to encrypt the Electronic Health Record system, making patient information unavailable during clinical operations.

Unlike isolated technical findings, this scenario enables management to understand business consequences.

The Steering Committee then considered what would happen if this event actually occurred.

Immediate consequences included:

- Medical records unavailable during treatment.
- Emergency admissions delayed.
- Medication histories inaccessible.
- Laboratory results unavailable.
- Clinical workflows disrupted.

Secondary consequences soon became apparent.

- Patients might be transferred to other hospitals.
- Revenue could decline.
- Media attention could damage public confidence.
- Healthcare regulators might investigate.
- Civil litigation could follow.

The organisation's reputation—built over decades—could be affected within hours.

This exercise highlighted an important principle of effective risk assessment.

Business impact extends far beyond the initial technical incident.

Understanding Cascading Risk

One of the distinguishing features of mature risk assessment is recognising that security incidents rarely remain isolated.

The Steering Committee illustrated this using a realistic scenario.

A receptionist receives an apparently legitimate email requesting password verification.

Believing it to be genuine, the employee enters login credentials into a fraudulent website.

At first glance, this appears to be a relatively minor phishing incident.

However, DISCOVER requires the organisation to ask repeatedly:

"What happens next?"

The attacker now possesses valid credentials.

Using those credentials, the attacker accesses internal scheduling systems.

Privilege escalation techniques expose administrative accounts.

Electronic Health Records become accessible.

Malware spreads laterally throughout hospital networks.

Clinical systems become unavailable.

Surgeries are postponed.

Doctors revert to paper records.

Emergency departments experience delays.

Regulators are notified.

News media report a major cyber incident.

Patients begin questioning whether their personal information remains safe.

Within a matter of hours, a single phishing email has evolved into an enterprise-wide business crisis.

This phenomenon—known as cascading risk—is one of the defining characteristics of modern cyber incidents.

DISCOVER therefore examines not only immediate consequences but also dependency failures, regulatory implications, operational disruption, financial losses, reputational damage, and long-term strategic effects.

The objective is to understand the complete business impact rather than merely the initiating technical event.

Analysing and Prioritising Risks

Once risk scenarios had been identified, Medicare Plus evaluated each using the risk criteria approved during DEFINE.

Likelihood and business impact were assessed consistently across the organisation.

For example:

Risk Scenario	Likelihood	Business Impact	Overall Rating
Ransomware affecting Electronic Health Records	High	Very High	Critical
Insider misuse of patient data	Medium	High	High
Cloud outage disrupting telemedicine	Medium	High	High
Temporary failure of cafeteria booking application	Low	Low	Low

Not every identified risk required immediate treatment.

The Board's approved risk appetite now guided decision-making.

Critical risks exceeding organisational tolerance would require immediate action.

Lower-priority risks might be monitored or formally accepted.

Resources could therefore be directed towards the risks most likely to affect patient safety, regulatory compliance, and organisational resilience.

Risk	Selected Controls
Ransomware	Information backup, malware protection, secure authentication, logging and monitoring
Insider misuse	Access control, segregation of duties, privileged access management

Risk	Selected Controls
Phishing	Security awareness, email filtering, MFA
Cloud outage	Supplier management, business continuity, redundancy
Legacy infrastructure	Vulnerability management, patch management
Data leakage	Encryption, data masking, information deletion

Checking All 93 Annex A Controls

Even where risks appear well managed, Medicare Plus performs a structured review of **all 93 Annex A controls**.

This exercise answers four questions for every control:

- Is it applicable?
- If applicable, why?
- If excluded, why?
- Has implementation been completed?

This disciplined review prevents important controls from being overlooked.

For example:

Annex A Control	Decision
Information deletion	Applicable
Threat intelligence	Applicable
Secure coding	Applicable
Web filtering	Applicable
Information masking	Applicable
ICT readiness for business continuity	Applicable

Some controls may legitimately be excluded where no supporting business requirement exists, but every exclusion must be justified.

Considering Regulatory Requirements Beyond ISO 27001

ISO/IEC 27002 provides an excellent baseline, but healthcare organizations frequently face additional obligations.

Medicare Plus must also satisfy:

- Healthcare privacy legislation.
- National health regulations.
- Data protection laws.
- Payment card security requirements for billing systems.

Accordingly, additional controls are incorporated where necessary.

Examples include:

Regulation	Additional Design Requirement
HIPAA	Audit trails for patient record access
GDPR	Data subject rights processes
DPDPA	Consent management and purpose limitation
PCI DSS	Network isolation for payment systems

These controls complement—not replace—the Annex A framework.

Producing the Statement of Applicability (SoA)

The principal documentary output of DESIGN is the **Statement of Applicability (SoA).**

For every Annex A control, Medicare Plus records:

- Whether the control is applicable.
- Why it has been selected or excluded.

- The risks it addresses.
- Current implementation status.

Control	Applicable	Justification
Information Backup	Yes	Protects EHR availability against ransomware
Information Deletion	Yes	Supports patient privacy and retention obligations
Secure Authentication	Yes	Reduces credential compromise risk
Secure Coding	Yes	Telemedicine software development
Information Transfer	Yes	Protects patient referrals and laboratory data

The SoA therefore becomes the bridge between **risk assessment and control implementation**, demonstrating that every selected control has a business justification.

Designing the Technical Architecture

DESIGN extends beyond governance documentation into technical architecture.

Based on identified risks, Medicare Plus develops an integrated security design incorporating:

Network Segmentation

Clinical systems are isolated from administrative networks, guest Wi-Fi, and medical research environments to reduce lateral movement.

Identity and Access Management

Role-based access controls and multi-factor authentication restrict patient data access to authorized personnel only.

Encryption

Patient records are encrypted:

- At rest in databases.
- During transmission between hospitals.
- During cloud backup operations.

Incident Response

Automated detection integrates with a Security Operations Centre (SOC), enabling rapid containment of suspicious activity.

Backup and Recovery

Critical databases are backed up using immutable storage with regular restoration testing.

Supplier Integration

Cloud providers, laboratory partners, and telemedicine vendors are incorporated into supplier assurance and monitoring processes.

The result is a **layered defence architecture** rather than isolated technical controls.

DESIGN Produces Business-Aligned Security

By the end of Step 03, Medicare Plus has transformed a list of abstract risks into a structured control environment supported by governance, documented rationale, and technical architecture.

Most importantly, every design decision is traceable:

- **Business objective** → protect patient care.
- **Risk** → ransomware affecting Electronic Health Records.
- **Risk owner decision** → modify the risk.

- **Selected controls** → MFA, segmentation, immutable backups, EDR, patch management.
- **Statement of Applicability** → documents why those controls were selected.
- **Technical architecture** → implements them consistently across the enterprise.

This traceability is the hallmark of a mature ISMS. Controls are not implemented because a standard lists them; they are implemented because they enable the organization to achieve its objectives within its approved risk appetite. In this way, DESIGN transforms risk assessment into a coherent security architecture that supports patient safety, regulatory compliance, operational resilience, and long-term organizational trust.

By the end of DISCOVER, Medicare Plus no longer viewed cybersecurity as a collection of isolated technical problems. It possessed a structured understanding of its information assets, the threats they faced, the vulnerabilities that could be exploited, and the business consequences that might follow.

Most importantly, every significant risk had a clearly identified business owner and had been evaluated against the organisation's approved risk appetite.

The question was no longer "What risks do we have?"

It had become:

"How should we treat these risks in a way that supports our business objectives?"

Answering that question is the purpose of the third stage of the Seven Step Framework:

Step 3 — DESIGN: Transforming Risk into a Coherent Security Architecture

"Risk assessment tells us what could go wrong. Design determines what we will do about it."

By the completion of the DISCOVER stage, Medicare Plus possessed something many organizations never achieve—a clear understanding of its information assets, the risks threatening those assets, and the business consequences should those risks materialise.

However, identifying risks alone does not improve security.

Risk registers do not stop ransomware.

Asset inventories do not prevent insider misuse.

Threat assessments do not ensure patient care continues during a cyberattack.

Value is created only when risk information is translated into well-designed, business-aligned controls.

This is the purpose of DESIGN.

If DEFINE established governance and DISCOVER provided intelligence, DESIGN became the engineering discipline that transformed management decisions into an integrated security architecture.

Rather than asking,

"Which controls does ISO require?"

the Steering Committee asked a far more important question:

"What combination of governance, people, physical and technological controls will reduce our risks to an acceptable level while enabling our clinicians to deliver safe patient care?"

That subtle change in thinking distinguished Medicare Plus from organizations that implement controls simply to satisfy auditors.

Designing Before Deploying

One of the most common implementation mistakes is selecting controls directly from Annex A of ISO/IEC 27002 as though it were a shopping catalogue.

Organizations frequently decide that because ISO lists ninety-three controls, they should implement all ninety-three.

The Seven Step Framework deliberately avoids this approach.

Controls should never be selected because they appear in a standard.

They should be selected because they reduce identified business risks.

For Medicare Plus, every design decision followed a simple logic:

Business Objective → Risk → Treatment Decision → Control Selection → Implementation

This traceability ensured that every investment could be justified to executive management.

Selecting the Appropriate Risk Treatment

After reviewing the highest-priority risks identified during DISCOVER, the Steering Committee considered how each risk should be managed.

ISO 31000 and ISO/IEC 27001 recognise four fundamental treatment options.

An organization may:

- Modify the risk by reducing its likelihood or impact.
- Avoid the activity that creates the risk.
- Share part of the risk through contracts or insurance.
- Retain the residual risk when it falls within approved appetite.
- Importantly, these are business decisions.

The Chief Information Security Officer advises.

The business owner decides.

This distinction reinforces one of the central governance principles introduced in Chapter 2:

IT manages technology; management owns risk.

Modifying Risk

The Steering Committee first considered the organization's most critical exposure—ransomware affecting Electronic Health Records.

Because disruption of clinical services exceeded the Board's approved risk appetite, accepting the risk was not an option.

Instead, Medicare Plus chose to modify the risk by implementing multiple complementary controls.

No single technology could provide adequate protection.

Instead, the design combined preventive, detective, and recovery measures including:

- Multi-factor authentication for privileged users.
- Network segmentation separating clinical and administrative systems.

- Endpoint Detection and Response (EDR).
- Immutable offline backups.
- Continuous vulnerability management.
- Privileged Access Management (PAM).
- Security monitoring through the Security Operations Centre.

Collectively these measures substantially reduced both the likelihood and business impact of ransomware.

The objective was resilience rather than perfect prevention.

Management recognised that attacks might still occur, but they should no longer threaten patient safety or business continuity.

Sharing Risk

Some risks could not be eliminated entirely.

For example, despite extensive preventive measures, a significant cyber incident could still generate legal expenses, forensic investigation costs, patient notification obligations, and business interruption losses.

To address this exposure, Medicare Plus purchased comprehensive cyber insurance while simultaneously strengthening contractual obligations with cloud service providers, telemedicine partners, and outsourced service providers.

Service agreements now included:

- minimum security requirements;
- incident notification obligations;
- business continuity commitments;
- audit rights;

- breach reporting responsibilities; and
- data protection obligations.

Although accountability remained with Medicare Plus, certain financial consequences could now be shared with external parties.

Avoiding Risk

Not every proposed initiative deserved to proceed.

During implementation, the Marketing Department proposed introducing an experimental Artificial Intelligence platform hosted in a jurisdiction that lacked adequate healthcare privacy protections.

The proposed system promised valuable patient analytics but required transferring sensitive medical information outside approved regulatory boundaries.

Following assessment, the Steering Committee concluded that the privacy, regulatory, and reputational risks significantly exceeded the Board's approved appetite.

Rather than attempting to compensate with additional controls, management chose the simplest and most effective treatment:

The initiative was cancelled.

Sometimes the best control is deciding not to undertake an activity.

Avoidance removed the risk completely.

Retaining Risk

The Steering Committee also recognised that not every identified risk justified additional investment.

An internal cafeteria booking application processed no patient information and had little operational significance.

Although minor software vulnerabilities existed, their business impact was negligible.

After considering implementation costs, management formally accepted the residual risk.

The decision was documented, approved by the business owner, and scheduled for periodic review.

This illustrates another important governance principle.

Accepting risk does not mean ignoring it.

Accepted risks remain documented, monitored, and periodically reassessed to ensure that changing business conditions do not alter management's decision.

Designing an Integrated Control Architecture

Having agreed upon treatment strategies, Medicare Plus began designing the control environment.

Rather than implementing isolated technologies, the Steering Committee focused on creating defence in depth—multiple complementary layers of protection that together reduced organisational risk.

Governance controls established accountability.

People controls influenced behaviour.

Physical controls protected facilities.

Technology controls enforced security decisions.

These layers reinforced one another.

If one failed, others continued to provide protection.

This integrated architecture reflected one of the fundamental principles of ISO/IEC 27002: information security is most effective when organizational, human, physical, and technological controls operate as a coordinated system.

Mapping Risks to Controls

Each significant risk identified during DISCOVER was mapped directly to one or more security controls.

For example:

Business Risk	Principal Controls
Ransomware affecting Electronic Health Records	Backups, EDR, Patch Management, Network Segmentation, MFA
Insider misuse of patient records	Role-Based Access Control, Segregation of Duties, Privileged Access Management
Phishing	Security Awareness, Email Filtering, Multi-Factor Authentication
Cloud service disruption	Supplier Assurance, Redundant Cloud Architecture, Business Continuity Planning
Data leakage	Encryption, Information Classification, Secure Information Transfer
Unsupported infrastructure	Vulnerability Management, Secure Configuration, Asset Lifecycle Management

The Steering Committee deliberately avoided implementing controls simply because they appeared within Annex A.

Every selected control addressed an identified business risk.

This maintained clear traceability between business objectives and operational implementation.

Reviewing All 93 Annex A Controls

Although controls were selected through risk assessment, Medicare Plus also performed a systematic review of all 93 controls contained within ISO/IEC 27002:2022.

The objective was not to implement every control automatically.

Instead, each control was examined by asking four questions:

- Is the control applicable?
- Which identified risks justify its implementation?
- If excluded, what business rationale supports that decision?
- How will implementation be demonstrated?

This disciplined review prevented important controls from being overlooked while ensuring that exclusions remained transparent and defensible.

For example, controls relating to secure coding, information deletion, threat intelligence, web filtering, information masking, and ICT readiness for business continuity were all considered applicable because they supported Medicare Plus's identified business risks.

Where controls were deemed unnecessary, documented justification was recorded.

Looking Beyond ISO

The Steering Committee recognised that ISO/IEC 27001 established an excellent management framework, but healthcare organizations rarely operate under a single regulatory regime.

Medicare Plus also needed to comply with healthcare privacy legislation, national cybersecurity regulations, contractual obligations, payment card security requirements, and emerging data protection laws.

Accordingly, the control architecture incorporated additional requirements such as:

- detailed audit trails for patient record access;
- privacy rights management processes;
- consent management mechanisms;
- secure retention and deletion practices;
- network isolation for payment processing environments; and
- enhanced supplier due diligence for cloud service providers.

These measures complemented ISO rather than replacing it, demonstrating how the ISMS could integrate multiple regulatory obligations within a single governance framework.

Developing the Statement of Applicability

The principal documentary output of the DESIGN stage was the Statement of Applicability (SoA).

Often described as the blueprint of the ISMS, the SoA provides a direct link between identified risks and selected controls.

For every applicable control, Medicare Plus documented:

- whether the control applied;
- why it had been selected;
- which risks it addressed;
- who owned implementation; and
- its implementation status.

The Statement of Applicability therefore became far more than an audit document.

It became the organization's formal explanation of why its security architecture existed.

Every control could now be traced directly back to a business requirement identified during DISCOVER.

Designing the Technical Architecture

The final activity of the DESIGN stage involved translating governance decisions into an enterprise-wide security architecture.

Clinical systems were separated from administrative networks through network segmentation to minimise lateral movement during cyber incidents.

Identity and Access Management adopted role-based access supported by Multi-Factor Authentication to ensure that clinicians accessed only the information necessary for patient care.

Sensitive patient information was encrypted while stored, transmitted between healthcare facilities, and protected within cloud backups.

Automated monitoring integrated Security Information and Event Management (SIEM) with the Security Operations Centre, enabling rapid detection and response.

Immutable backups were incorporated into disaster recovery planning, while supplier assurance programmes extended governance beyond organisational boundaries to cloud providers, laboratories, and outsourced technology partners.

Rather than viewing these as isolated technologies, Medicare Plus regarded them as components of a single integrated control architecture designed to protect patient care, regulatory compliance, and organisational resilience.

Seven Step Deliverable – DESIGN

Objective	**Transform identified risks into an integrated, business-aligned control architecture**
Key Activities	Select treatment options, map risks to controls, review Annex A controls, design governance and technical architecture, develop the Statement of Applicability
Primary Deliverables	Risk Treatment Plan (RTP), Statement of Applicability (SoA), Security Architecture, Control Design
ISO/IEC 27001:2022 Alignment	Clauses 6.1.3, 6.2 and 6.3
Input to Next Step	Approved controls requiring formal documentation and operational implementation

Lessons from Medicare Plus

The DESIGN stage demonstrates that effective information security is never about implementing the greatest number of controls. It is about implementing the right controls for the right reasons.

Every design decision made by Medicare Plus could be traced through a logical chain:

Business Objective → Risk → Treatment Decision → Selected Control → Statement of Applicability

This traceability provided confidence not only to auditors but also to the Board, regulators, patients, and business partners.

Most importantly, the organisation had now answered a critical governance question:

"What controls should we implement?"

The next challenge was equally important.

Those carefully designed controls had to be translated into policies, procedures, standards, work instructions, and records that employees could understand and follow consistently.

This marks the beginning of the fourth stage of the Seven Step Framework:

Step 4 — DOCUMENT: Converting Design into Organisational Knowledge

"If DESIGN defines what the organisation intends to do, DOCUMENT ensures that everyone knows how to do it, every time, in the same way."

By the conclusion of the DESIGN stage, Medicare Plus had developed a robust security architecture. Risks had been evaluated, treatment decisions approved, and appropriate controls selected. Yet the Steering Committee recognised that even the best-designed control would fail if it remained only in the minds of a few specialists.

Policies that are not communicated become forgotten intentions. Procedures that are undocumented vary from one department to another. Controls that cannot be demonstrated cannot be audited, and improvements that are not recorded are eventually lost.

The organisation therefore entered the fourth stage of the Seven Step Framework—DOCUMENT.

Contrary to popular belief, this stage was not about creating paperwork to satisfy auditors. **It was about building**

organisational memory. Documentation would preserve management decisions, standardise operational practices, support training, provide evidence of implementation, and ensure that information security remained consistent even as personnel, technologies, and business priorities changed.

For Medicare Plus, documentation became the bridge between governance and daily operations.

Documentation Supports Governance—Not Bureaucracy

One of the misconceptions surrounding ISO/IEC 27001 is that it requires extensive documentation. In reality, the standard requires organisations to maintain only the documented information necessary for the effective operation of the ISMS.

The emphasis is therefore on quality rather than quantity.

Medicare Plus adopted four guiding principles for documentation:

- Every document should support a business process.
- Every document should have a clearly identified owner.
- Every document should be controlled throughout its lifecycle.
- Every document should contribute to consistent operational behaviour.

Whenever a proposed document failed to satisfy these principles, the Steering Committee challenged whether it was genuinely required.

Documentation was viewed as an operational asset rather than an administrative burden.

Building the Policy Framework

The first task involved establishing the organisation's policy hierarchy.

The Information Security Policy approved during DEFINE provided overall direction, but effective governance required supporting policies covering specific aspects of information security.

Rather than producing lengthy manuals, Medicare Plus developed concise, business-focused policies that clearly described management expectations.

The core policy suite included:

Policy	Purpose
Information Security Policy	Strategic direction and governance
Asset Management Policy	Ownership and classification of information assets
Access Control Policy	User access, authentication, and privilege management
Cryptography Policy	Encryption standards and key management
Acceptable Use Policy	Appropriate use of organisational systems
Supplier Security Policy	Security requirements for third parties
Physical Security Policy	Protection of facilities and equipment
Incident Management Policy	Reporting and responding to security incidents
Business Continuity Policy	Maintaining critical healthcare services
Information Retention and Disposal Policy	Managing information throughout its lifecycle

Each policy clearly identified its purpose, scope, responsibilities, and review cycle.

More importantly, every policy reflected decisions already taken during DEFINE and DESIGN. Nothing was written merely because ISO mentioned it. Every policy supported an identified business objective or mitigated an identified organisational risk.

Turning Policies into Operational Procedures

Policies describe what management expects.

Procedures explain how employees achieve those expectations.

Without documented procedures, identical situations are handled differently by different people, introducing inconsistency and increasing operational risk.

Accordingly, Medicare Plus developed procedures for every critical information security process.

Examples included:

Procedure	Operational Purpose
Risk Assessment Procedure	Standardise identification and evaluation of risks
Risk Treatment Procedure	Document approval and implementation of treatment decisions
User Access Management Procedure	Grant, modify, review, and revoke user access
Change Management Procedure	Secure implementation of technology changes
Incident Response Procedure	Coordinate detection, escalation, containment, and recovery
Backup and Restoration Procedure	Ensure recoverability of critical information

Procedure	Operational Purpose
Vulnerability Management Procedure	Identify, assess, and remediate vulnerabilities
Supplier Assessment Procedure	Evaluate third-party security capability
Internal Audit Procedure	Assess ISMS effectiveness
Management Review Procedure	Support executive oversight and continual improvement

These procedures established consistency across all hospitals, clinics, laboratories, and telemedicine operations.

For example, when a new clinician joined Medicare Plus, every location followed exactly the same onboarding process. Access rights were approved by authorised managers, identity verified, multi-factor authentication enabled, mandatory awareness training completed, and access reviewed periodically thereafter.

The process no longer depended upon individual judgement.

It became organisational practice.

Standards and Work Instructions

The Steering Committee recognised that some activities required greater technical precision than could reasonably be included within policies or procedures.

Accordingly, Medicare Plus introduced standards and work instructions.

Standards established mandatory technical requirements.

Examples included:

- Password Standard
- Encryption Standard

- Secure Configuration Standard
- Secure Software Development Standard
- Network Segmentation Standard

Work instructions, in contrast, described the detailed steps required to perform specific operational activities.

Examples included:

- Creating a clinician's Electronic Health Record account.
- Restoring patient data from backup.
- Registering medical devices on the network.
- Reporting suspected phishing emails.
- Performing vulnerability scans.

This layered documentation structure ensured that strategic policies remained stable while operational guidance could evolve as technology changed.

Creating Evidence Through Records

Policies and procedures explain what should happen.

Records demonstrate what actually happened.

One of the auditors involved in Medicare Plus's certification preparation summarised this principle succinctly:

"Say what you do. Do what you say. Prove that you did it."

Records provide that proof.

Throughout implementation, Medicare Plus established a structured records framework to capture objective evidence of ISMS operation.

Examples included:

Record	Evidence Provided
Risk Register	Identified and assessed information security risks
Risk Treatment Plan	Approved treatment decisions
Statement of Applicability	Justification for selected controls
Internal Audit Reports	Evaluation of ISMS effectiveness
Management Review Minutes	Executive oversight and governance
Incident Reports	Security event investigation and response
Access Review Records	Validation of user privileges
Security Awareness Records	Employee competence
Backup Restoration Tests	Recovery capability
Supplier Assessments	Third-party due diligence
Corrective Action Register	Continual improvement activities

These records demonstrated that information security was not simply documented but actively managed.

Documentation During a Real Incident

Several months into implementation, Medicare Plus experienced an attempted compromise of a clinical administrator's account.

Although the attack was detected and contained before patient information was exposed, the incident provided an opportunity to evaluate the documentation framework.

Because documentation had been standardised, investigators were able to retrieve immediately:

- the Access Control Policy;
- the User Access Management Procedure;
- the employee's approved access request;
- authentication logs;
- security monitoring alerts;
- incident response records;
- management notifications; and
- corrective actions approved following the investigation.

The organisation did not rely upon memory or verbal explanations.

Every significant decision and activity had been documented and preserved.

This enabled rapid investigation, transparent reporting, and effective organisational learning.

Managing Documents Throughout Their Lifecycle

Documentation rapidly loses value if outdated versions remain in circulation or unauthorised changes occur.

To address this risk, Medicare Plus implemented formal document control procedures.

Every controlled document included:

- unique document identification;
- version number;
- document owner;
- approval authority;

- issue date;
- review date;
- classification; and
- revision history.

Changes followed a defined approval process.

Superseded versions were archived but clearly marked as obsolete to prevent accidental use.

Only current, approved versions remained available for operational use.

This discipline proved particularly valuable during certification audits, where auditors frequently examined whether staff were working from current documentation.

Documentation Enables Continual Improvement

One of the greatest strengths of an ISMS lies in its ability to learn.

Every audit, every incident, every management review, and every corrective action generates new knowledge.

Documentation preserves that knowledge.

During one internal audit, Medicare Plus identified inconsistent backup testing between hospitals.

Rather than simply recording a nonconformity, the organisation updated its Backup and Restoration Procedure, revised technical standards, retrained administrators, repeated restoration testing, and documented the resulting improvements.

The documentation framework therefore became more than a compliance mechanism.

It became the organisation's learning system.

Each new experience strengthened future performance.

The Medicare Plus Documentation Architecture

By the conclusion of DOCUMENT, Medicare Plus had developed a coherent hierarchy of documented information.

Documentation Level	Medicare Plus Example
Policies	Information Security Policy, Access Control Policy
Standards	Password Standard, Encryption Standard
Procedures	Incident Response Procedure, Risk Assessment Procedure
Work Instructions	EHR User Creation Guide, Backup Restoration Guide
Records	Risk Register, Audit Reports, Incident Records, Training Records

Each level supported the one above it.

Policies established direction.

Standards defined mandatory requirements.

Procedures described repeatable processes.

Work instructions guided operational execution.

Records demonstrated effective implementation.

Together they transformed management decisions into organisational knowledge.

Seven Step Deliverable – DOCUMENT

Objective	**Convert governance decisions into controlled organisational knowledge**
Key Activities	Develop policies, standards, procedures, work instructions, records, and document control processes
Primary Deliverables	Policy Framework, Procedure Manual, Standards, Work Instructions, Controlled Records
ISO/IEC 27001:2022 Alignment	Clause 7.5 (Documented Information) and supporting documented information for applicable Annex A controls
Input to Next Step	Approved documentation required for operational implementation of controls

Lessons from Medicare Plus

The DOCUMENT stage illustrates that information security is sustained not by individual expertise but by organisational knowledge.

Policies communicate leadership intent.

Procedures create consistency.

Standards establish technical discipline.

Work instructions guide execution.

Records provide evidence and preserve organisational learning.

By the end of this stage, Medicare Plus had achieved far more than a collection of controlled documents. It had created a shared understanding of how information security should operate across every hospital, clinic, laboratory, and telemedicine service.

The ISMS now existed not merely in board decisions or architectural designs but within the everyday practices of the organisation.

The next challenge was to bring these documented decisions to life.

Policies had to become behaviour.

Procedures had to become routine.

Controls had to become operational.

This marks the fifth stage of the Seven Step Framework:

Step 4 — DOCUMENT: Converting Design into Organisational Knowledge

"Controls protect information only when people know what to do, how to do it, and can demonstrate that they have done it."

By the end of the DESIGN stage, Medicare Plus had developed a comprehensive control architecture. The Board had approved risk treatment decisions, control objectives had been defined, the Statement of Applicability had been completed, and the organisation knew exactly how it intended to reduce its information security risks.

Yet one important question remained.

How could these decisions be communicated consistently across three hospitals, twenty outpatient clinics, remote clinicians, cloud service providers, diagnostic laboratories, and more than two thousand employees?

The answer lay in the fourth stage of the Seven Step (7D) Framework—DOCUMENT.

This stage is often misunderstood. Many organisations believe ISO/IEC 27001 requires extensive paperwork and countless procedures. Consequently, they produce hundreds of pages of documentation that few people read and even fewer people follow.

The Seven Step Framework takes a different approach.

Documentation exists to support operations, not bureaucracy.

Its purpose is to preserve organisational knowledge, ensure consistent execution, demonstrate accountability, and provide objective evidence that governance decisions are being implemented throughout the enterprise.

For Medicare Plus, documentation became the bridge between strategy and day-to-day operations.

Documentation Is Organisational Memory

Healthcare organisations operate continuously.

Doctors change shifts.

Nurses rotate between departments.

IT personnel move to different projects.

Managers retire.

Suppliers change.

Without documented processes, knowledge leaves with people.

Documentation therefore performs two essential governance functions.

First, it ensures that critical activities are performed consistently regardless of who performs them.

Second, it provides evidence that those activities have actually taken place.

An auditor can verify documentation.

A regulator can review records.

Management can measure performance.

Without documentation, governance relies entirely upon individual memory and good intentions.

That is neither sustainable nor auditable.

Building the Documentation Architecture

Rather than writing policies at random, Medicare Plus adopted a structured documentation hierarchy.

Every document had a clear purpose within the management system.

The hierarchy consisted of five levels.

Level	Purpose	Medicare Plus Examples
Policies	Executive direction	Information Security Policy, Access Control Policy
Standards	Mandatory technical requirements	Password Standard, Cryptography Standard
Procedures	Defined business processes	Incident Response Procedure, Risk Assessment Procedure
Work Instructions	Detailed operational guidance	Creating EHR Accounts, Backup Restoration Steps
Records	Evidence of implementation	Audit reports, approvals, logs, training records

Each level supported the one above it.

Policies explained what management expected.

Standards established minimum requirements.

Procedures described how work should be performed.

Work instructions explained specific tasks.

Records demonstrated that the work had actually been completed.

Together they formed the organisational memory of the ISMS.

Developing the Policy Framework

The first priority was expanding the high-level Information Security Policy approved during DEFINE into a comprehensive policy framework.

Rather than producing lengthy legal documents, Medicare Plus developed concise, business-oriented policies that clearly communicated management's expectations.

The core policy suite included:

- Information Security Policy
- Asset Management Policy
- Information Classification Policy
- Access Control Policy
- Cryptography Policy
- Acceptable Use Policy
- Supplier Security Policy
- Physical Security Policy
- Incident Management Policy

- Business Continuity Policy
- Information Retention and Secure Deletion Policy

Each policy followed the same lifecycle.

Approve → Communicate → Make Aware → Review

The Chief Executive Officer approved the overarching Information Security Policy, while individual executive leaders approved policies within their areas of responsibility.

For example, the Human Resources Director approved personnel security requirements, the Procurement Director approved supplier security expectations, and the Chief Information Security Officer approved operational security policies.

This reinforced accountability across the organisation.

Policies were no longer viewed as documents owned solely by the Information Security Department.

They became management commitments owned by business leadership.

From Policies to Procedures

Policies establish principles.

Procedures explain how those principles are implemented.

For Medicare Plus, this distinction proved critical.

The Access Control Policy stated that access must be granted according to business need.

The User Access Management Procedure explained exactly how new accounts were requested, approved, created, reviewed, modified, suspended, and removed.

Similarly, the Incident Management Policy required all security incidents to be reported promptly.

The Incident Response Procedure described:

- how incidents were identified;
- who should be notified;
- escalation criteria;
- investigation responsibilities;
- communication requirements;
- recovery activities; and
- lessons learned following resolution.

This ensured that incidents were handled consistently regardless of which hospital or department experienced them.

- The organisation developed procedures for every critical ISMS process, including:
- Risk Assessment
- Risk Treatment
- User Access Management
- Change Management
- Vulnerability Management
- Backup and Recovery
- Incident Response
- Internal Audit
- Supplier Security Management
- Management Review
- Corrective Action

Because these procedures were standardised, implementation no longer depended upon individual interpretation.

Consistency became part of the management system.

Creating Records That Demonstrate Performance

Documentation alone cannot demonstrate that an ISMS is effective.

Evidence is equally important.

This evidence takes the form of records.

A useful principle frequently quoted during certification audits is:

"Say what you do. Do what you say. Prove that you did it."

The first statement refers to policies.

The second refers to procedures.

The third refers to records.

For Medicare Plus, records became the evidence that governance decisions were actually being implemented.

Examples included:

Record	Demonstrates
Risk Register	Risks have been identified and evaluated
Risk Treatment Plan	Management decisions have been approved
Statement of Applicability	Control selection is justified
Internal Audit Reports	Independent assessment of effectiveness
Management Review Minutes	Executive oversight
Security Incident Reports	Operational response capability

Record	Demonstrates
Training Records	Staff competence
Access Review Reports	User privilege validation
Backup Restoration Tests	Recovery capability
Supplier Assessments	Third-party assurance
Corrective Action Register	Continual improvement

Unlike policies, records are created continuously as the ISMS operates.

Each one provides objective evidence that organisational processes are functioning as intended.

Documentation in Practice

Several months after implementation began, Medicare Plus experienced an attempted unauthorised access to patient information.

Fortunately, the attack was detected before any records were compromised.

During the subsequent investigation, the Steering Committee reviewed the documentation produced by the ISMS.

Within minutes, investigators were able to retrieve:

- the Access Control Policy;
- the User Access Management Procedure;
- account approval records;
- authentication logs;
- quarterly access review reports;
- incident investigation records;

- corrective action documentation; and
- management review decisions.

The investigation proceeded efficiently because organisational knowledge had been documented before the incident occurred.

Nothing depended upon individual recollection.

Everything was supported by controlled information.

This illustrates an often-overlooked benefit of documentation.

Its greatest value is realised during periods of uncertainty, when organisations need reliable evidence rather than assumptions.

Controlling Documents Throughout Their Lifecycle

Documentation itself represents organisational information and therefore requires protection.

Medicare Plus implemented a formal document control process to ensure that employees always used current, authorised versions.

Every controlled document contained:

- unique document identification;
- version number;
- document owner;
- approval authority;
- effective date;
- review date;
- classification;
- revision history.

Supporting controls ensured that:

- only current versions were available for operational use;
- obsolete versions were archived appropriately;
- changes received formal approval before publication;
- distribution was controlled;
- retention periods were defined; and
- unauthorised modifications were prevented.

For example, when the Incident Response Procedure was revised following a national healthcare cyber exercise, Version 4.0 replaced Version 3.2.

The previous version remained archived for historical reference but was clearly marked as obsolete, preventing operational confusion during future incidents.

Document control therefore protected the integrity of the management system itself.

Documentation Supports Continual Improvement

One of the strengths of the Seven Step Framework is that every stage feeds the next.

Documentation illustrates this principle particularly well.

Every internal audit produces findings.

Every management review generates decisions.

Every incident investigation identifies lessons.

Every supplier assessment reveals improvement opportunities.

These outputs become new documented information that strengthens future governance.

For example, following an internal audit, Medicare Plus discovered that backup restoration testing differed between hospitals.

Rather than treating this as a simple audit finding, management updated the Backup and Recovery Procedure, standardised restoration testing, retrained technical teams, and documented the successful corrective actions.

Documentation therefore became both a historical record and a catalyst for continual improvement.

Seven Step Deliverable – DOCUMENT

Objective	Translate governance decisions into controlled organisational knowledge
Key Activities	Develop policies, standards, procedures, work instructions, records, and document control processes
Primary Deliverables	Policy Framework, Procedures, Standards, Records Framework, Controlled Documentation
ISO/IEC 27001:2022 Alignment	Clause 7.5 (Documented Information) and supporting documented information required throughout the standard
Input to Next Step	Controlled documentation enabling consistent operational implementation

Lessons from Medicare Plus

The DOCUMENT stage demonstrates that documentation is not created for auditors.

It is created for the organisation itself.

Policies communicate leadership intent.

Standards establish mandatory requirements.

Procedures ensure consistency.

Work instructions support operational execution.

Records provide evidence that governance is working.

Together they transform information security from individual knowledge into organisational capability.

By the conclusion of Step 4, Medicare Plus had converted every governance decision made during DEFINE, every risk identified during DISCOVER, and every control selected during DESIGN into documented information that employees could understand, follow, and demonstrate.

The organisation was now fully prepared for the next stage.

Until this point, the ISMS had existed primarily as governance decisions, documented processes, and carefully designed controls.

The next challenge was turning those plans into everyday operational reality.

That is the purpose of the fifth stage of the Seven Step Framework.

Step 5 — DO: Making Information Security Part of Everyday Business Operations

"A control has no value until it changes behaviour. Security becomes real only when policies become practices, designs become operations, and every employee understands their role in protecting the organisation."

By the end of the DOCUMENT stage, Medicare Plus had established a comprehensive Information Security Management System on paper. Governance structures were in place, risks had been assessed, controls had been designed, policies had been approved, procedures documented, and responsibilities clearly assigned.

Yet the Board recognised an uncomfortable truth.

Nothing had changed for a doctor beginning a morning clinic.

Nothing had changed for a nurse updating a patient's medication.

Nothing had changed for an IT administrator managing privileged accounts.

Nothing had changed for a supplier connecting to the hospital network.

Until people began working differently, the ISMS remained largely theoretical.

The fifth stage of the Seven Step (7D) Framework—DO — bridges this gap. It transforms carefully designed governance into everyday organisational behaviour. This is where the ISMS becomes operational and where information security ceases to be a project and becomes part of organisational culture.

For Medicare Plus, this represented the most resource-intensive stage of the entire implementation journey because it affected every employee, every department, every supplier, and every technology platform.

Bringing the ISMS to Life

Implementation is often misunderstood as the installation of security technologies. While technology is important, successful implementation requires much more.

Every control selected during DESIGN must now be embedded within:

- organisational governance;
- business processes;

- employee behaviour;
- physical environments;
- information systems; and
- supplier relationships.

Implementation therefore requires coordinated action across the entire enterprise.

The Steering Committee established a detailed implementation programme, assigning responsibilities, timelines, budgets, and success measures for each control. Department managers became accountable for implementation within their areas, while the Information Security Office coordinated progress and provided specialist guidance.

Rather than attempting to implement everything simultaneously, controls were prioritised according to business risk. Those protecting patient safety, clinical availability, and regulatory compliance were deployed first.

Deploying Organisational Controls

Implementation began with organisational controls because they provide the governance framework within which all other controls operate.

Policies approved during DOCUMENT were now formally communicated throughout Medicare Plus. Every department received guidance explaining how the policies affected its activities.

Managers were trained to understand their responsibilities for approving access requests, managing risks, reporting incidents, reviewing suppliers, and ensuring compliance within their teams.

Supplier agreements were also updated. Cloud providers, diagnostic laboratories, payment processors, managed service providers, and telemedicine partners all accepted revised contractual obligations covering information security, privacy, incident notification, audit rights, and business continuity.

Security governance was no longer confined within the organisation's boundaries. It now extended across the entire healthcare ecosystem supporting patient care.

At the same time, the Security Operations Centre (SOC) subscribed to healthcare-specific cyber threat intelligence services, enabling analysts to identify emerging ransomware campaigns, newly discovered vulnerabilities, and indicators of compromise relevant to hospitals.

Governance was becoming operational.

Deploying People Controls

The Steering Committee understood that people represent both the greatest source of organisational resilience and the greatest potential vulnerability.

Technology cannot prevent every mistake.

Employees therefore became the next priority.

A comprehensive security awareness programme was introduced across the organisation.

However, Medicare Plus deliberately avoided generic awareness presentations that employees would quickly forget.

Training became role-based.

Doctors and nurses learned:

- secure use of Electronic Health Records;
- patient confidentiality;

- recognising phishing attempts;
- protecting mobile devices;
- safe telemedicine practices.
- Administrative staff focused on:
- business email compromise;
- protecting financial information;
- handling confidential patient records;
- secure document disposal.

IT administrators received specialist training covering:

- privileged access management;
- secure configuration;
- vulnerability management;
- incident escalation;
- secure system administration.

Software developers responsible for the telemedicine platform completed additional training on secure coding, vulnerability management, and application security testing.

Each employee received training relevant to their responsibilities rather than generic cybersecurity advice.

Creating a Security Culture

Training alone does not change behaviour.

Consequently, Medicare Plus reinforced learning through continuous engagement.

Monthly awareness campaigns highlighted emerging cyber threats affecting healthcare organisations.

Simulated phishing exercises measured employee responses and identified departments requiring additional coaching.

Quarterly newsletters shared lessons from recent incidents within the healthcare sector.

Managers discussed information security during departmental meetings.

New employees completed security induction before receiving system access.

Information security gradually became part of everyday organisational conversation rather than an annual compliance event.

Employees no longer asked,

"Why do we have to do this?"

Instead, they increasingly understood,

"This is how we protect our patients."

The difference was cultural rather than technical.

Embedding Security into Human Resource Processes

People controls extended beyond awareness.

Human Resources incorporated information security throughout the employment lifecycle.

Before employment commenced, individuals handling sensitive patient information underwent:

- identity verification;
- professional qualification checks;
- background screening;

- reference verification; and
- confidentiality agreements.

During employment, role changes triggered automatic review of access rights.

When employees left the organisation, accounts were disabled immediately, identity cards collected, equipment returned, and privileged access revoked according to documented procedures.

Information security therefore became embedded within routine HR operations rather than existing as an independent security activity.

Deploying Physical Controls

Although cybersecurity receives significant attention, Medicare Plus recognised that patient information could be compromised just as easily through inadequate physical security.

Accordingly, hospitals strengthened protection of critical facilities.

Data centres received enhanced perimeter security, CCTV monitoring, environmental controls, intrusion detection systems, and controlled visitor access.

Server rooms required both smart-card authentication and biometric verification.

Medical records archives remained locked with monitored access.

Network equipment was relocated from publicly accessible areas into secure facilities.

Visitors were required to register, present identification, wear visitor badges, and remain escorted while within sensitive operational areas.

Clear desk and clear screen requirements were introduced throughout administrative departments, reducing opportunities for accidental disclosure of confidential information.

At the end of every shift, patient files were secured, workstations locked automatically, and confidential waste disposed of through approved destruction services.

Physical security became another layer supporting organisational resilience.

Deploying Technology Controls

Technology implementation represented the most visible aspect of DO , but it remained firmly aligned with business risks identified during DISCOVER.

Identity and Access Management was strengthened through role-based access control and Multi-Factor Authentication.

Doctors accessed only the clinical information required for patient care.

Administrative staff were prevented from viewing clinical records beyond their responsibilities.

Privileged accounts received additional monitoring and approval controls.

Network architecture was redesigned using segmentation principles established during DESIGN.

Clinical systems, medical devices, administrative applications, guest wireless networks, development environments, and research systems operated within separate security zones.

Should one environment become compromised, lateral movement would be significantly restricted.

Endpoint Detection and Response (EDR) software was deployed across servers, laptops, and clinical workstations.

Automated vulnerability scanning ensured that critical security patches were identified and applied according to defined service levels.

Encryption protected patient information while stored, transmitted, and backed up.

Security Information and Event Management (SIEM) consolidated logs from clinical systems, cloud services, firewalls, authentication systems, and endpoint protection into a single monitoring platform operated by the Security Operations Centre.

Backup processes were redesigned around immutable storage with routine restoration testing.

Backups were no longer regarded as successful merely because they completed.

Success was measured by the organisation's ability to restore patient services within approved Recovery Time Objectives.

Technology implementation therefore reflected operational resilience rather than technical compliance.

Measuring Implementation Success

The Steering Committee recognised that implementation should be measured objectively rather than assumed.

Accordingly, progress was reviewed against clearly defined indicators.

Examples included:

Control Area	Evidence of Successful Deployment
Governance	Policies approved and communicated; Steering Committee operational

Control Area	Evidence of Successful Deployment
People	Security awareness completion rates; phishing simulation results; screening records
Physical Security	Visitor logs; CCTV monitoring; access control reports
Technology	MFA enabled; EDR deployment; vulnerability remediation; SIEM operational; successful backup restoration tests
Suppliers	Security clauses incorporated into contracts; supplier assurance reviews completed

These measures demonstrated that implementation extended well beyond technology. Governance, people, facilities, suppliers, and operational processes all contributed to organisational security.

Security as an Organisational Capability

Several months after implementation, Medicare Plus experienced a targeted phishing campaign aimed at clinical staff.

A nurse recognised the suspicious message during routine patient administration and reported it using the organisation's one-click reporting mechanism introduced during awareness training.

Within minutes, the Security Operations Centre isolated similar emails, blocked malicious domains, and prevented further compromise.

No patient information was exposed.

No clinical systems were disrupted.

The incident was successfully managed not because of one security product but because multiple controls worked together.

Leadership had established governance.

Training had influenced employee behaviour.

Technology detected malicious activity.

Documented procedures guided response.

Monitoring enabled rapid containment.

This demonstrated the true purpose of DO .

The organisation had not merely implemented controls.

It had built capability.

Seven Step Deliverable – DO

Objective	**Implement approved controls and integrate them into everyday organisational operations**
Key Activities	Deploy organisational, people, physical, and technological controls; train employees; integrate suppliers; operationalise governance
Primary Deliverables	Operational ISMS, Implemented Controls, Awareness Programme, Supplier Security, Technical Security Architecture
ISO/IEC 27001:2022 Alignment	Clause 8.1 (Operational Planning and Control), Clause 8.3 and implementation of ISO/IEC 27002:2022 controls
Input to Next Step	Operational evidence, performance data, security events, audit trails, and measurable control performance

Lessons from Medicare Plus

DO represents the point at which information security becomes visible throughout the organisation.

Policies become behaviour.

Procedures become routine business processes.

Technology reinforces governance.

Employees become active participants in protecting information.

Most importantly, security evolves from being an IT initiative into an organisational capability embedded within everyday healthcare delivery.

By the conclusion of Step 5, Medicare Plus had transformed its ISMS from a carefully designed management system into an operational business capability supporting patient safety, regulatory compliance, and organisational resilience.

However, implementation alone does not guarantee effectiveness.

Controls may deteriorate.

New threats may emerge.

Business priorities may change.

The organisation therefore needed a disciplined process for asking a critical question:

«Is our ISMS actually working as intended?"

Answering that question is the purpose of the sixth stage of the Seven Step Framework.

Step 6 — DEPLOY & CHECK: Measuring Performance, Providing Assurance, and Verifying Effectiveness

"Implementation is not the end of the journey. It is the beginning of evidence. An ISMS creates confidence only when it can demonstrate that it is working today—not that it worked when it was certified."

After nearly eighteen months of planning and implementation, Medicare Plus had transformed its approach to information security. Governance structures were functioning, risks had been assessed, controls deployed, employees trained, suppliers integrated, and clinical systems protected by multiple layers of defence.

The Board could have declared the project complete.

Many organisations do.

Unfortunately, this is where many certified Information Security Management Systems begin to deteriorate.

Threats evolve.

Technology changes.

Employees join and leave.

Business priorities shift.

Controls that were effective twelve months ago may no longer provide adequate protection today.

Recognising this reality, Medicare Plus entered the sixth stage of the Seven Step (7D) Framework—DEPLOY & CHECK.

If DO answers the question,

"Have we implemented our controls?"

DEPLOY & CHECK asks the more important question:

"Are those controls actually achieving the outcomes we intended?"

This distinction transforms an ISMS from a compliance programme into a living management system.

Measuring What Matters

One of the first discussions held by the Steering Committee concerned measurement.

The Chief Executive Officer asked a deceptively simple question.

"How will we know whether our investment in information security has improved organisational resilience?"

The question exposed a common weakness in many organisations.

They collect large quantities of technical statistics but very little management information.

Reports may contain thousands of firewall events, malware detections, authentication logs, and vulnerability scan results without answering the questions senior leadership actually needs answered.

Following the principles advocated by security measurement expert David Brotby, Medicare Plus adopted a simple philosophy:

Every metric must support a management decision.

If a measurement did not influence action, it would not be collected.

The organisation therefore designed its measurement programme around three complementary levels.

Operational Metrics

Operational metrics enabled technical teams to manage day-to-day security activities.

Examples included:

- percentage of critical vulnerabilities remediated within agreed timeframes;
- multi-factor authentication coverage;
- endpoint protection deployment rates;

- backup success and restoration performance;
- incident response times;
- phishing simulation results.

These indicators helped operational teams understand whether individual controls continued to function effectively.

Management Metrics

Department managers required different information.

Rather than technical detail, they focused on organisational performance.

Examples included:

- completion of mandatory awareness training;
- overdue corrective actions;
- supplier assessment status;
- privileged access review completion;
- unresolved audit findings;
- business continuity exercise performance.

These measures enabled managers to identify weaknesses requiring corrective action before they developed into larger problems.

Executive Metrics

The Board required a broader perspective.

Executive reporting therefore concentrated on strategic indicators demonstrating organisational resilience.

Quarterly reports included:

- overall information security risk profile;
- trends in significant incidents;

- regulatory compliance status;
- internal audit results;
- progress against ISMS objectives;
- supplier risk exposure;
- maturity improvements;
- major investment requirements.

Rather than presenting hundreds of technical charts, reports focused on answering four questions.

1. Are organisational risks increasing or decreasing?
2. Are controls achieving their intended outcomes?
3. Are we complying with our obligations?
4. What decisions require executive attention?

The Board now received information that supported governance rather than technical administration.

Monitoring Control Effectiveness

Performance measurement alone could not provide complete assurance.

Medicare Plus therefore established continuous monitoring across operational activities.

The Security Operations Centre monitored authentication events, privileged account activity, malware detections, network anomalies, cloud services, endpoint protection, and critical infrastructure.

Automated alerts identified unusual behaviour requiring investigation.

Patch compliance was reviewed weekly.

Backup restoration tests were performed quarterly.

Access rights were reviewed regularly by business managers.

Supplier performance was monitored through agreed service levels and security reviews.

Monitoring ensured that control failures were detected before they developed into significant business incidents.

Internal Audit: Independent Assurance

The Steering Committee regarded internal audit as one of the most valuable components of the ISMS.

Unfortunately, audits are often misunderstood.

Many organisations view internal audits as inspections designed to identify nonconformities.

Medicare Plus adopted a different philosophy.

Internal audits were intended to answer one fundamental question:

"Is the management system achieving its intended purpose?"

The audit programme was risk-based rather than calendar-based.

Areas presenting greater organisational risk received more frequent attention.

Clinical systems handling patient information, supplier governance, incident management, identity management, and backup arrangements were therefore audited more regularly than lower-risk activities.

Auditors remained independent of the activities they reviewed and evaluated not only documentation but also operational effectiveness.

Typical audit questions included:

Are policies being followed consistently?

Do employees understand their responsibilities?

Are controls operating as designed?

Are risks being managed within approved appetite?

Are previous corrective actions effective?

Findings were classified according to significance and assigned to responsible managers with agreed completion dates.

The objective was continual improvement—not fault finding.

Learning from Security Incidents

Several months after certification, Medicare Plus experienced an attempted ransomware attack targeting one of its regional hospitals.

Fortunately, endpoint detection technology identified suspicious activity before malware could spread beyond the initial workstation.

Patient services continued without interruption.

From an operational perspective, the incident had been successfully contained.

From a governance perspective, however, the Steering Committee asked a different question.

"What can this incident teach us?"

The investigation identified several valuable lessons.

Although technical controls performed effectively, one affected employee hesitated before reporting suspicious activity because they were uncertain whether the event represented a genuine incident.

Awareness training was therefore updated.

Incident reporting guidance was simplified.

Managers reinforced the message that rapid reporting was more important than perfect judgement.

The organisation viewed every incident—even successfully managed ones—as evidence for improving the ISMS.

Failures became opportunities for learning.

Successes became opportunities for validation.

Management Review: Governance in Action

Twice each year, the Executive Committee conducted formal Management Reviews in accordance with ISO/IEC 27001 requirements.

Unlike operational meetings, these reviews focused on strategic governance.

The agenda included:

- progress against ISMS objectives;
- changes affecting organisational context;
- significant information security risks;
- audit findings;
- incident trends;
- supplier performance;
- legal and regulatory developments;
- resource requirements;
- opportunities for improvement.

During one review, the Chief Medical Officer highlighted increasing reliance on connected medical devices.

Although no significant incidents had occurred, management recognised that expanding digital healthcare created new risks not fully considered during the original implementation.

The Board therefore directed the Steering Committee to initiate a fresh risk assessment covering Internet of Medical Things (IoMT) technologies.

This decision illustrates an important principle.

Management Review does not merely evaluate past performance.

It prepares the organisation for future change.

Testing Organisational Resilience

Medicare Plus recognised that some controls cannot be evaluated through routine operations alone.

Business continuity arrangements, disaster recovery capabilities, and incident response plans required practical testing.

Accordingly, the organisation conducted regular exercises.

Tabletop simulations allowed executives to rehearse strategic decision-making during cyber incidents.

Technical recovery exercises tested restoration of Electronic Health Records from immutable backups.

Business continuity exercises examined the ability of hospitals to continue providing patient care during extended technology outages.

Supplier participation ensured that external dependencies were incorporated into organisational planning.

Each exercise generated observations, improvement opportunities, revised procedures, and additional evidence supporting continual improvement.

Testing therefore became an integral component of organisational assurance.

Corrective Actions

Every audit finding, incident investigation, monitoring activity, and management review produced opportunities for improvement.

Rather than implementing isolated fixes, Medicare Plus maintained a central Corrective Action Register linking each issue to:

- identified cause;
- agreed corrective action;
- responsible manager;
- target completion date;
- implementation status;
- effectiveness review.

Importantly, corrective actions addressed root causes rather than symptoms.

For example, repeated delays in applying security patches were initially attributed to technical workload.

Further investigation revealed that maintenance windows were inconsistently scheduled across hospitals.

Management standardised change management processes, improving patch performance throughout the organisation.

The corrective action therefore strengthened the management system rather than merely resolving an isolated issue.

Seven Step Deliverable – DEPLOY

Objective	**Verify that the ISMS is effective, compliant, and continually improving**
Key Activities	Performance measurement, monitoring, internal audit, management review, incident analysis, resilience testing, corrective actions
Primary Deliverables	Audit Reports, Management Review Minutes, KPI Dashboards, Corrective Action Register, Improvement Recommendations
ISO/IEC 27001:2022 Alignment	Clauses 9.1 (Monitoring and Measurement), 9.2 (Internal Audit), 9.3 (Management Review)
Input to Next Step	Evidence-based improvement opportunities, updated risks, management decisions, and organisational learning

Lessons from Medicare Plus

The DEPLOY & CHECK stage demonstrates that confidence in an ISMS comes from evidence, not assumption.

Controls are measured rather than presumed effective.

Audits evaluate performance rather than documentation alone.

Management Reviews drive strategic decisions rather than simply recording compliance.

Incidents become opportunities for organisational learning rather than sources of blame.

By the conclusion of Step 6, Medicare Plus possessed something far more valuable than certification.

It had developed a culture of verification.

Leadership no longer relied on optimism or anecdotal reassurance.

Instead, every important governance decision was supported by objective evidence.

The Board could now answer a critical question with confidence:

"Yes, our Information Security Management System is working—and we can prove it."

Yet one final stage remained.

No organisation operates in a static environment.

Business strategies evolve.

Technologies advance.

Threats become more sophisticated.

Regulations change.

An ISMS that fails to adapt inevitably becomes obsolete.

The final stage of the Seven Step Framework therefore focuses on ensuring that improvement never stops.

Step 7 — DRIVE: Embedding Continual Improvement and Building Organisational Trust

"Certification demonstrates that an organisation has reached a destination. Continual improvement ensures it never stops moving."

After two years of disciplined implementation, Medicare Plus had achieved ISO/IEC 27001 certification. Independent auditors confirmed that its Information Security Management System conformed to the requirements of the standard. The Board celebrated an important milestone.

Yet during the first Management Review following certification, the Chief Executive Officer reminded the leadership team:

"Certification was never our destination. It is simply evidence that we are travelling in the right direction."

That statement captures the philosophy of the seventh and final stage of the Seven Step (7D) Framework—DRIVE.

If DEPLOY & CHECK asks,

"Is our ISMS working?"

DRIVE asks,

"How do we make it even better?"

This is where an Information Security Management System evolves from a compliance programme into a strategic business capability. Organisations that neglect this stage gradually become less secure despite remaining certified. Those that embrace continual improvement become increasingly resilient, adaptive, and trusted.

For Medicare Plus, DRIVE was not an annual activity. It became part of organisational culture.

Continual Improvement Is a Leadership Responsibility

One of the most common misconceptions is that continual improvement belongs exclusively to the Information Security team.

In reality, improvement begins with leadership.

The Board recognised that information security is affected by changing business strategies, emerging technologies, evolving regulations, and increasingly sophisticated cyber threats. Consequently, every significant organisational change required management to reconsider whether the ISMS remained appropriate.

Each quarterly Board meeting therefore included a standing agenda item:

"What has changed since our last review?"

This simple question ensured that the ISMS evolved alongside the business rather than remaining fixed while the organisation changed around it.

Responding to a Changing Business

Only six months after certification, Medicare Plus announced an ambitious expansion strategy.

The organisation planned to:

- open two new specialist hospitals;
- acquire a regional diagnostic laboratory;
- introduce AI-assisted radiology services;
- expand telemedicine into neighbouring countries; and
- deploy Internet of Medical Things (IoMT) devices throughout critical care facilities.

These initiatives promised significant clinical and commercial benefits.

They also fundamentally altered the organisation's risk profile.

Rather than attempting to bolt security onto completed projects, the Steering Committee returned to the beginning of the Seven Step Framework.

The organisation revisited:

- organisational context;
- interested parties;

- ISMS scope;
- regulatory obligations;
- business objectives;
- risk appetite.
- New risks were assessed.
- Additional controls were designed.
- Policies were updated.
- Training programmes expanded.
- Supplier assessments repeated.
- Implementation plans revised.

This illustrates an essential principle of the Seven Step Framework.

DRIVE naturally reconnects with DEFINE.

Continual improvement is therefore not a straight line.

It is a continuous cycle of learning and adaptation.

Learning from Experience

Throughout implementation, Medicare Plus accumulated valuable operational experience.

Internal audits identified recurring themes.

Security incidents highlighted opportunities for improvement.

Employees suggested simpler procedures.

Suppliers introduced more secure technologies.

Regulators issued new guidance.

Rather than treating these as isolated events, the Steering Committee looked for patterns.

For example, several audit findings revealed that although access reviews were completed on time, different hospitals applied inconsistent criteria when removing dormant user accounts.

Instead of issuing another reminder, management redesigned the entire access review process.

Automated workflows were introduced.

Standard approval criteria were established.

Managers received additional guidance.

The improvement addressed the underlying process rather than repeatedly correcting individual findings.

The organisation therefore shifted its focus from fixing problems to improving systems.

Innovation as Part of the ISMS

Continual improvement is not limited to correcting weaknesses.

It also includes identifying opportunities to strengthen organisational capability.

As artificial intelligence matured, Medicare Plus evaluated how automation could improve information security operations.

After careful risk assessment, the organisation introduced AI-assisted security analytics capable of:

- identifying unusual user behaviour;
- prioritising security alerts;
- detecting anomalous network activity;
- accelerating incident investigations;
- supporting vulnerability prioritisation.

Importantly, these technologies complemented rather than replaced human judgement.

Clinical decisions remained under medical supervision.

Security decisions remained accountable to management.

Innovation therefore strengthened governance instead of bypassing it.

Developing Organisational Maturity

Certification demonstrates conformity.

Maturity reflects capability.

Recognising this distinction, the Steering Committee introduced an annual ISMS maturity assessment based on the Seven Step Framework.

Rather than asking simply whether controls existed, management evaluated how effectively each stage was operating.

Questions included:

DEFINE

Does leadership actively review changing organisational context?

Are business objectives driving security decisions?

DISCOVER

Are emerging risks identified before they become incidents?

Is risk ownership clearly understood?

DESIGN

Do control decisions remain aligned with business priorities?

Are new technologies evaluated systematically?

DOCUMENT

Is documentation concise, current, and widely understood?

Are procedures regularly reviewed?

DO

Are controls consistently implemented across all locations?

Do employees demonstrate secure behaviours?

DEPLOY & CHECK

Do performance indicators support management decisions?

Are audits driving meaningful improvements?

DRIVE

Are lessons from incidents translated into organisational learning?

Does the ISMS evolve alongside the business?

This broader perspective shifted organisational attention from maintaining certification to developing long-term resilience.

Building Trust Beyond Compliance

As the ISMS matured, Medicare Plus began noticing benefits extending well beyond cybersecurity.

Patients increasingly selected Medicare Plus because they trusted the organisation with sensitive health information.

Insurance providers recognised its disciplined governance.

Regulators observed consistent compliance.

Business partners viewed the organisation as a lower-risk healthcare provider.

Employees became more confident reporting incidents because leadership treated mistakes as learning opportunities rather than reasons for blame.

The organisation discovered something important.

Information security had become a competitive advantage.

Trust, once difficult to quantify, had become a measurable business asset.

This reinforces one of the central themes of this book.

Technology protects information.

Governance creates trust.

The Seven Step Framework Comes Full Circle

At the conclusion of the first three-year certification cycle, the Steering Committee reviewed the entire implementation journey.

The organisation recognised that every stage had depended upon the one before it.

DEFINE had established strategic direction.

DISCOVER had identified business risks.

DESIGN had translated those risks into coherent controls.

DOCUMENT had preserved organisational knowledge.

DO had embedded security into daily operations.

DEPLOY & CHECK had provided evidence that the system was working.

DRIVE had ensured that the ISMS remained relevant as the organisation evolved.

The framework had never been intended as a linear project.

It functioned as a continuous governance cycle.

Each improvement initiated another journey through the Seven Steps.

This relationship can be visualised simply:

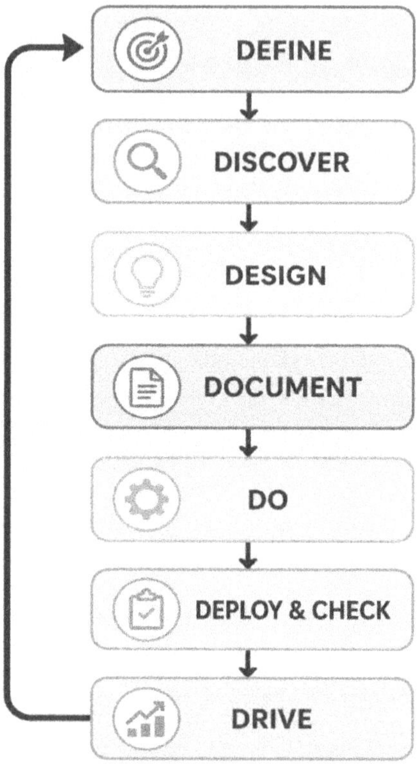

Every cycle increased organisational maturity, strengthened resilience, and enhanced stakeholder confidence.

Seven Step Deliverable – DRIVE

Objective	**Ensure the ISMS continually evolves with organisational needs, emerging risks, and changing business priorities**

Key Activities	Analyse lessons learned, implement corrective actions, reassess risks, improve processes, adopt innovation, review organisational maturity
Primary Deliverables	Improvement Plans, Updated Risk Assessments, Revised Policies, Maturity Assessments, Enhanced ISMS
ISO/IEC 27001:2022 Alignment	Clause 10.1 (Continual Improvement) and Clause 10.2 (Nonconformity and Corrective Action)
Output	A resilient, adaptive, and continually improving Information Security Management System

Lessons from Medicare Plus

The Medicare Plus journey demonstrates that implementing ISO/IEC 27001 is not about collecting policies, deploying technology, or passing certification audits.

It is about creating an organisation capable of learning, adapting, and improving.

Each stage of the Seven Step Framework builds logically upon the previous one:

1. DEFINE establishes purpose and governance.
2. DISCOVER identifies what threatens organisational objectives.
3. DESIGN selects the most appropriate controls.
4. DOCUMENT transforms decisions into organisational knowledge.
5. DO embeds security into everyday operations.
6. DEPLOY & CHECK verifies that controls are effective.
7. DRIVE ensures that improvement never stops.

Together, these seven stages convert ISO/IEC 27001 from a set of requirements into a practical implementation methodology that leaders, managers, auditors, and practitioners can apply regardless of organisational size or industry.

For Medicare Plus, the outcome was more than certification.

The organisation became demonstrably more resilient, better governed, and more trusted by patients, regulators, employees, and business partners.

That is the ultimate purpose of an Information Security Management System.

Chapter Summary

This chapter introduced the Seven Step (7D) Framework as a practical roadmap for implementing an Information Security Management System aligned with ISO/IEC 27001:2022. Through the continuous case study of Medicare Plus, the chapter demonstrated how governance, risk management, control design, documentation, implementation, assurance, and continual improvement are interconnected stages within a single management system.

The journey began with defining organisational context and leadership commitment before identifying and evaluating business risks. Those risks were translated into an integrated control architecture, supported by controlled documentation and implemented across governance, people, physical, and technological domains. Continuous monitoring, internal audit, management review, and corrective actions ensured that the ISMS remained effective, while continual improvement enabled the organisation to adapt to changing technologies, regulations, and business priorities.

The key lesson is that ISO/IEC 27001 is not fundamentally about compliance—it is about governance, resilience, and trust. The

Seven Step Framework provides organisations with a practical methodology for transforming the standard's requirements into an operational management system that continuously protects information, supports business objectives, and strengthens stakeholder confidence.

The chapters that follow build upon this foundation by examining the implementation of the 93 controls of ISO/IEC 27002:2022 in greater depth, showing how each control contributes to the successful operation of the Seven Step Framework.

References

Mind Your S.T.E.P.S.™: From Compliance to Trust. (2025). Mind Your S.T.E.P.S.™: From Compliance to Trust. Notion Press.

International Organization for Standardization & International Electrotechnical Commission. (2022). ISO/IEC 27001:2022 — Information Security, Cybersecurity and Privacy Protection — Information Security Management Systems — Requirements. Geneva: ISO.

International Organization for Standardization & International Electrotechnical Commission. (2022). ISO/IEC 27002:2022 — Information Security, Cybersecurity and Privacy Protection — Information Security Controls. Geneva: ISO.

International Organization for Standardization. (2018). ISO 31000:2018 — Risk Management — Guidelines. Geneva: ISO.

National Institute of Standards and Technology. (2024). Cybersecurity Framework (CSF) 2.0. Gaithersburg, MD: U.S. Department of Commerce.

David G. Brotby. (2009). Information Security Metrics: A Practical Framework for Measuring Security & Protecting Data. CRC Press.

James P. Womack & Daniel T. Jones. (2003). Lean Thinking. Free Press.

W. Edwards Deming. (1986). Out of the Crisis. MIT Press.

Peter F. Drucker. (2007 edition). Management Challenges for the 21st Century. HarperBusiness.

George A. Miller. (1956). The Magical Number Seven, Plus or Minus Two: Some Limits on Our Capacity for Processing Information. Psychological Review, 63(2), 81–97.

Australian Signals Directorate. (2025). Information Security Manual (ISM). Australian Government.

National Institute of Standards and Technology. (2012). NIST Special Publication 800-61 Revision 2: Computer Security Incident Handling Guide.

National Institute of Standards and Technology. (2020). NIST Special Publication 800-53 Revision 5: Security and Privacy Controls for Information Systems and Organizations.

Further Reading

Beyond Firewalls: Rethinking Cybersecurity and Privacy in the Digital Age. (Forthcoming).

The Seven Pillars of Responsible AI Governance. (Forthcoming).

The 9P Paradigm for Business Growth. (Forthcoming).

Why this reference list works

This collection is academically sound and aligns directly with the chapter:

- **ISO/IEC 27001:2022** and **ISO/IEC 27002:2022** provide the normative foundation.
- **ISO 31000** underpins the risk management concepts used throughout the DISCOVER and DESIGN stages.

- **NIST CSF 2.0** and **NIST SP 800-53** provide internationally recognised governance and control guidance.
- **David Brotby** supports the DEPLOY & CHECK stage's discussion of meaningful security metrics.
- **Deming** provides the conceptual basis for continual improvement and PDCA.
- **George Miller** supports the rationale for the Seven Step Framework as a cognitively manageable implementation model.
- **Mind Your S.T.E.P.S.™** appropriately cites your previously published work, from which the governance philosophy and S.T.E.P.S.™ concepts evolved into the Seven Step (7D) Framework presented in this chapter. This establishes continuity without over-citing your own work.

Key Takeaways

- The S.T.E.P.S.™ Framework — Define, Discover, Design, Document, Do, Deploy & Check, Drive — is a practitioner roadmap that makes ISO/IEC 27001:2022 navigable.
- Seven steps is a deliberate choice: it is the number a leader can hold in working memory and use in practice.
- Each step maps to specific ISO clauses, to PDCA, and to the ASD ISM's six functions — one framework, three languages.
- The framework is iterative, not strictly linear: Define and Discover loop, and Drive feeds back into Define.
- Equifax shows the steps interlock: a failure at any one step propagates through all that follow.
- Chapters 5–8 expand the DO step across all 93 controls of ISO/IEC 27002:2022.

Reflection Questions

1. If you scored your organisation 1–5 at each of the seven steps today, which would be lowest — and is that where your last incident originated?
2. Could a failure like Equifax's expired monitoring certificate go undetected in your environment right now?
3. Does your framework live as an operational dashboard, or only as a project that ended at certification?
4. Which regulatory expectations — NSE-style governance, UPI-style ecosystem fraud, ASIC-style board reporting — are not yet reflected in your steps?
5. When Drive last fed back into Define, what changed — or has the loop never actually closed?

Action Deploy & Checklist

- Run a S.T.E.P.S.™ maturity self-assessment within 30 days, scoring each step 1–5; your lowest step is your priority.
- If no formal risk assessment has been done in 12 months, execute DISCOVER immediately — a stale risk register is the most dangerous ISMS weakness.
- Establish a monthly 'S.T.E.P.S. review' treating the framework as a living dashboard against defined milestones.
- Put automated compliance monitoring on at least three controls — certificate validity, patch status and privileged-account activity first.

- Train at least two internal auditors against ISO/IEC 27001 — the single most cost-effective improvement mechanism in the standard.
- Map your ISMS to the ASD ISM's six functions for dual-framework client assurance.

Part II

PRACTICAL IMPLEMENTATION OF ISO/IEC 27002:2022 CONTROLS AND THE FUTURE OF INFORMATION SECURITY

Overview

Part II of this book transitions from strategic planning and governance concepts into the practical implementation of security controls. It serves as the operational heart of the Information Security Management System (ISMS), providing readers with detailed guidance on how to implement, manage, monitor, and continually improve the 93 controls defined in ISO/IEC 27002:2022.

Unlike earlier editions of the standard, ISO/IEC 27002:2022 organizes controls into four logical categories—Organizational Controls, People Controls, Physical Controls, and Technological Controls—reflecting a holistic approach to protecting information assets. This section examines each category in depth, explaining not only what each control requires but also how organizations can successfully implement it in real-world environments.

Each chapter combines theory with practical application through implementation roadmaps, governance models, policy recommendations, procedures, roles and responsibilities, key performance indicators (KPIs), examples, and common pitfalls. Readers will gain a comprehensive understanding of how individual controls work together to create a resilient and adaptive security ecosystem.

Beyond the implementation of controls, Part II also explores methods for measuring effectiveness, integrating security into business operations, fostering a culture of continual improvement, and preparing organizations for emerging challenges such as artificial intelligence, quantum computing, supply chain risks, and evolving regulatory requirements.

Ultimately, this part demonstrates that successful information security is not achieved by deploying isolated technical safeguards but by establishing an integrated system of governance, people, processes, technology, and continuous learning.

CHAPTER

5

ORGANIZATIONAL CONTROLS

ISO/IEC 27002:2022 A.5 — Thirty-Seven Controls for Governance and Policy

ISO/IEC 27002:2022 A.5 — Thirty-Seven Controls for Governance and Policy

> **S.T.E.P.S.™ Engine — Operational Anchor: DO (the Governance Layer)**
>
> This is the first of four chapters expanding the DO step across all 93 controls of ISO/IEC 27002:2022. The 37 organizational controls of A.5 are the governance backbone — designed in DESIGN and DOCUMENT, operated in DO — that make every people, physical and technological control coherent.

Chapter Overview

If technical controls are the locks, organizational controls are the walls, the floor plan and the people who decide where the locks go. The 37 controls of ISO/IEC 27002:2022 Annex A.5 establish the policy, roles, asset governance, access rules, supplier assurance, incident response, continuity and legal compliance on which every other control depends. The 2022 edition added the three controls the modern threat landscape demanded — threat intelligence, ICT supply-chain security and cloud governance — and the largest breaches of the era confirm why: SolarWinds, Target and Cosmos were defeats of supplier assurance, intelligence and detection, not of technology. For Indian organisations the privacy and legal controls now carry ₹250 crore consequences under the DPDPA, and in Australia the same governance and supplier disciplines are enforced as national practice. Mastering A.5 is therefore not a compliance chore but the act of building the management architecture that makes security real.

Chapter Objectives

By the end of this chapter, the reader will be able to:

- Explain why organizational controls are the management architecture on which all other controls depend.
- Navigate the seven natural clusters of the 37 A.5 controls and the intent of each.
- Identify the three new A.5 controls in the 2022 edition and why they were added.
- Apply meaningful metrics to governance, supplier, incident and compliance controls.
- Draw the supply-chain lessons of SolarWinds for threat intelligence, supplier assurance and incident detection.

The Architecture Behind the Architecture

Technical controls get the attention; organizational controls do the work. A firewall is only as good as the policy that configures it, the role that owns it, the supplier process that vets the vendor who supplied it, and the incident process that responds when it fails.

The 37 organizational controls of A.5 — the largest of the four categories — are the governance infrastructure that gives every other control its meaning. They are where the ASD ISM's Govern and Identify principles find their operational expression: executive accountability (GOV-01), CISO leadership (GOV-02), risk embedding (GOV-03) and supplier assurance (GOV-11) are all delivered through A.5. This chapter presents the 37 controls in seven natural clusters rather than as an undifferentiated list, because that is how they are actually governed.

Annex A as a System of Controls, not a Deploy & Checklist

Many organizations approach **Annex A of ISO/IEC 27001:2022** as a checklist of individual controls to be implemented one by one. This is a fundamental misunderstanding. Annex A is **not a collection of disconnected safeguards,** but a **system of interdependent controls** designed to work together in support of the organization's Information Security Management System (ISMS) and risk treatment objectives.

Think of the controls as the components of a living organism rather than the parts of a machine. Each control has value in its own right, but its greatest effectiveness emerges from its relationship with the others. Governance influences people, people operate processes, processes protect technology, and technology safeguards information. Weakness in one area inevitably affects the strength of the whole system.

This is precisely why **Category A.5 – Organizational Controls** appears first. It provides the **governance framework and connective tissue** that binds the remaining control themes together.

Before an organization can effectively manage people (A.6), physical security (A.7), or technology (A.8), it must establish clear policies, responsibilities, decision-making structures, supplier governance, asset ownership, risk management processes, and accountability mechanisms.

Without governance, technical controls become isolated technical measures. With governance, they become part of a coordinated management system aligned with business objectives and risk appetite.

In this sense:

- A.5 defines direction.
- A.6 enables people to act consistently.
- A.7 protects the physical environment in which information resides.
- A.8 safeguards the technological infrastructure that processes and stores information.

Together they form a coherent architecture in which each category reinforces the others.

The Policy Lifecycle: From Document to Daily Practice

Policies are among the most visible organizational controls, yet many fail because they are treated as static documents rather than living governance instruments. An information security policy locked away in a document repository cannot influence behaviour or reduce risk.

Throughout this book, a simple four-stage **Policy Lifecycle** provides a practical model for understanding how policies create organizational value:

Approve → Communicate → Make Aware → Review

1. Approve

Every policy should be formally approved by appropriate management authority, demonstrating leadership commitment and ensuring alignment with organizational strategy and risk appetite.

2. Communicate

Approved policies must be distributed to relevant employees, contractors, suppliers, and other stakeholders through suitable communication channels.

3. Make Aware

Communication alone does not guarantee understanding. Organizations must ensure that people comprehend the policy, understand how it applies to their role, and know what actions are expected of them through training, awareness programmes, and ongoing reinforcement.

4. Review

Business environments, technologies, regulations, and threats continually evolve. Policies must therefore be reviewed periodically and updated whenever significant organizational or external changes occur.

This lifecycle transforms policies from administrative documents into active governance mechanisms. The same motif will recur throughout Chapters 6 to 8 when discussing human resources, physical security, technology controls, supplier management, and operational procedures.

Derive First, Benchmark Second: The Proper Role of Annex A and the Statement of Applicability

One of the most common implementation mistakes is to begin with Annex A and work backwards, selecting controls from a checklist before understanding the organization's actual risks.

ISO/IEC 27001 adopts the opposite philosophy.

The correct sequence is:

Business Context → Risk Assessment → Risk Treatment Decisions → Control Selection → Statement of Applicability (SoA)

In other words, organizations should **derive** their control requirements from their own business objectives, legal obligations, stakeholder expectations, and risk assessments before they **benchmark** those decisions against Annex A.

Annex A serves as a comprehensive reference catalogue of controls and provides an internationally recognized baseline for comparison, but it is **not intended to replace organizational judgement**. Controls should be selected because they address identified risks—not merely because they appear in a predefined list.

The **Statement of Applicability (SoA)** documents this reasoning. It records:

- Which Annex A controls have been selected.
- Which controls have been excluded.
- The justification for each decision.
- The implementation status of applicable controls.

The SoA therefore demonstrates that control selection is the outcome of a deliberate, risk-based process rather than a mechanical checklist exercise.

A useful principle for practitioners is:

Derive your controls from risk. Benchmark them against Annex A. Document the rationale in the Statement of Applicability.

This order reinforces one of the central themes introduced in Chapter 4: **the ISMS is designed around the organization's unique objectives and risks, with Annex A providing guidance and validation rather than dictating implement**

Executive Insight

- The most expensive breaches of the last decade — SolarWinds, Target, Cosmos — were not defeats of technology.
- They were failures of organizational controls: supplier assurance, threat intelligence, incident detection.
- Boards that fund only the technical layer are buying locks for a house with no walls.

5.1 Cluster A — Policy, Roles and Governance (A.5.1–A.5.8)

This cluster sets management direction. It establishes the information-security policy and topic-specific policies (A.5.1), allocates roles and responsibilities (A.5.2), segregates conflicting duties (A.5.3), commits management to active support (A.5.4), maintains contact with authorities and special-interest groups (A.5.5–6), institutes threat intelligence as a discipline (A.5.7, new in 2022), and embeds security into project management so it is designed in rather than bolted on (A.5.8).

Control	Intent	Representative metric
A.5.1 Policies	Documented, approved, communicated, reviewed security policies	Policy coverage & acknowledgement rates
A.5.2 Roles & responsibilities	Every policy, process and control has a named owner	RACI completeness; role-vacancy rate

Control	Intent	Representative metric
A.5.3 Segregation of duties	No single person controls a high-risk activity end-to-end	SoD violations found in access reviews
A.5.4 Management responsibilities	Management actively requires and models security	Security items on leadership agendas/quarter
A.5.5 Contact with authorities	Pre-established lines to regulators, CERTs, law enforcement	Time-to-notification compliance
A.5.6 Special-interest groups	Engagement with ISACs and security forums	Active intelligence sources monitored
A.5.7 Threat intelligence [NEW]	Collect and analyse threat data to inform risk decisions	Control changes made per quarter from intel
A.5.8 Security in project management	Security designed into projects from initiation	% projects with security assessment at start

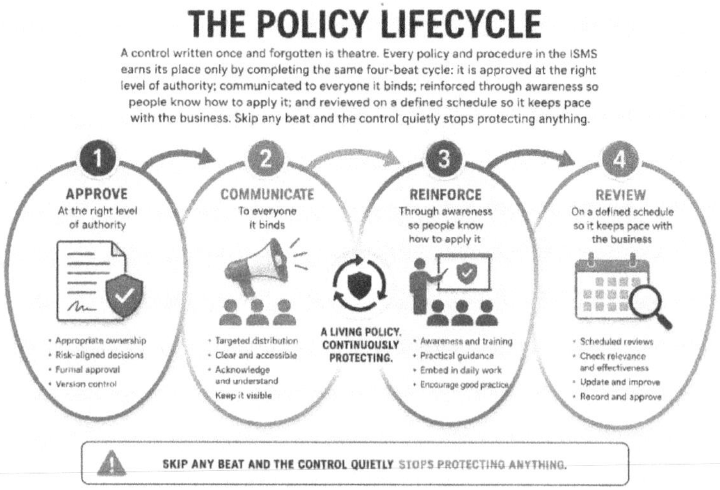

5.2 Cluster B — Asset Management and Classification (A.5.9–A.5.14)

You cannot protect what you have not inventoried or classified. This cluster builds and maintains the asset inventory with owners (A.5.9) — the foundation of the entire risk assessment — defines acceptable use (A.5.10) and asset return on exit (A.5.11), classifies information by value and sensitivity (A.5.12), labels it accordingly (A.5.13), and secures its transfer inside and outside the organisation (A.5.14).

Control	Intent	Representative metric
A.5.9 Asset inventory	Documented inventory of information and associated assets with owners	Inventory completeness; owner-assignment rate
A.5.10 Acceptable use	Documented rules for using and handling assets (BYOD, cloud, email)	AUP acknowledgement; violations per period
A.5.11 Return of assets	Assets recovered on employment/contract end	Asset-return compliance at off-boarding
A.5.12 Classification	Information classified by value, criticality, sensitivity	% assets with assigned classification
A.5.13 Labelling	Classification labels applied to documents and data	% correctly labelled in sample audit
A.5.14 Information transfer	Secure rules for all transfer channels (encryption, DLP, agreements)	% confidential transfers via approved channels

5.3 Cluster C — Access Control and Identity (A.5.15–A.5.18)

These four controls govern who can reach what. Access control rules enforce least privilege and need-to-know (A.5.15); identity management ensures every user and system has a unique, lifecycle-managed identity (A.5.16); authentication-information management protects credentials and mandates MFA for privileged and remote access (A.5.17); and access-rights management provisions, reviews and — critically — revokes access promptly on role change or termination (A.5.18).

Control	Intent	Representative metric
A.5.15 Access control	Least-privilege, need-to-know access, regularly reviewed	Privilege-creep index; dormant-account rate
A.5.16 Identity management	Unique, lifecycle-managed identities; no shared accounts	Orphaned accounts; time-to-deactivate
A.5.17 Authentication information	Controlled credentials; MFA for privileged/remote access	MFA adoption for privileged accounts

Control	Intent	Representative metric
A.5.18 Access rights	Provision, review, modify, revoke access in a timely way	On-schedule access-review completion

5.4 Cluster D — Supplier and Cloud Security (A.5.19–A.5.23)

The cluster the modern threat landscape has made decisive. It manages supplier security risk across the relationship (A.5.19), embeds security requirements in supplier agreements (A.5.20), governs the ICT supply chain including build integrity and component provenance (A.5.21, new in 2022), monitors and change-manages supplier services over time (A.5.22), and governs the full lifecycle of cloud-service use from acquisition to exit (A.5.23, new in 2022).

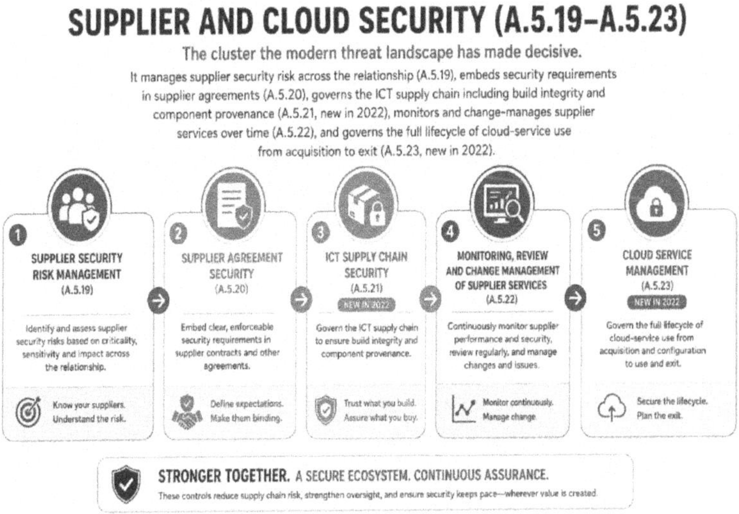

SolarWinds, Target, Cosmos and Latitude all entered through this cluster.

Control	Intent	Representative metric
A.5.19 Supplier relationships	Manage security risk from supplier products and services	% suppliers with security assessment on file
A.5.20 Supplier agreements	Security requirements agreed and contractual	% contracts with security clauses
A.5.21 ICT supply chain [NEW]	Manage risk in the ICT product/service supply chain	% ICT products integrity-verified pre-deployment
A.5.22 Monitoring suppliers	Regularly review, audit and change-manage supplier services	% suppliers under annual security review
A.5.23 Cloud services [NEW]	Govern cloud acquisition, use, management and exit	% cloud services with completed assessment

5.5 Cluster E — Incident Management (A.5.24–A.5.28)

Incident management is a proactive discipline, not a reactive scramble. This cluster plans and prepares the incident-response capability before it is needed (A.5.24), establishes triage to decide which events are incidents (A.5.25), drives consistent response — containment, eradication, recovery, communication (A.5.26), captures lessons to prevent recurrence (A.5.27), and preserves admissible evidence with chain of custody (A.5.28). The recurring failure across major breaches is detection latency — measured in months at SolarWinds, Marriott and Equifax.

Control	Intent	Representative metric
A.5.24 IR planning & preparation	Documented, approved, tested incident-response plan	Date of last IRP test; MTTD; MTTR
A.5.25 Assessment & decision	Triage criteria to classify events as incidents	Event-to-incident classification accuracy
A.5.26 Incident response	Consistent containment, eradication, recovery, comms	% incidents handled within SLA
A.5.27 Learning from incidents	Root-cause analysis feeds back into controls	% significant incidents with completed RCA
A.5.28 Collection of evidence	Admissible evidence with maintained chain of custody	% investigations with documented custody

5.6 Cluster F — Security Through Disruption (A.5.29–A.5.30)

Two controls ensure security and availability survive a crisis. Information security during disruption (A.5.29) requires that critical controls — or documented manual workarounds — remain operational when systems fail, and that security is built into the business-continuity plan. ICT readiness for business continuity (A.5.30, new in 2022) requires defined and tested Recovery Time and Recovery Point Objectives for critical systems. This cluster is the bridge to the dedicated treatment of resilience later in the book.

Control	Intent	Representative metric
A.5.29 Security during disruption	Maintain critical security controls (or workarounds) in a crisis	Critical controls with continuity provisions
A.5.30 ICT readiness for BC [NEW]	Plan, implement and test RTOs/RPOs for critical systems	RTO/RPO achievement rate in tests

5.7 Cluster G — Legal, Privacy and Compliance (A.5.31–A.5.37)

The final cluster ties the ISMS to the law and to itself. It maintains a legal and regulatory register (A.5.31), manages intellectual-property obligations (A.5.32), protects records against loss and falsification (A.5.33), protects personal data in line with privacy law (A.5.34) — the direct link to ISO/IEC 27701, GDPR and India's DPDPA — secures independent review of the security programme (A.5.35), checks compliance with the organisation's own policies (A.5.36), and documents operating procedures (A.5.37).

Control	Intent	Representative metric
A.5.31 Legal & regulatory requirements	Maintained register of applicable law and obligations	Register completeness & currency
A.5.32 Intellectual property	Compliance with licensing and IP obligations	Software-licence compliance rate
A.5.33 Protection of records	Records protected and retained per schedule	Records-retention compliance rate

Control	Intent	Representative metric
A.5.34 Privacy & PII protection	Meet privacy-law requirements (GDPR, DPDPA, links to 27701)	DPIA completion; DSR response within SLA
A.5.35 Independent review	Independent review of the security approach at intervals	Audit frequency; findings closed on time
A.5.36 Compliance with policies	Managers verify compliance in their areas	Internal compliance-audit pass rate
A.5.37 Documented operating procedures	Operating procedures documented and available	% procedures reviewed within 12 months

Case Study: SolarWinds (2020) — Organizational Controls Under Siege

In December 2020, the security firm FireEye disclosed that it had been compromised through a malicious update to SolarWinds Orion, a widely used IT-management platform. Investigation revealed that a trojanised Orion update — carrying the SUNBURST backdoor — had been distributed to as many as 18,000 SolarWinds customers, including US federal agencies and numerous large enterprises. The attackers, attributed by the US government to Russia's SVR foreign-intelligence service, had first breached SolarWinds' software build environment around September 2019, more than a year before discovery, and pushed the tainted updates between March and June 2020. Of the 18,000 who received the backdoor, a smaller subset — around nine US federal agencies and roughly a hundred private organisations — saw active follow-on intrusion.

CISA issued Emergency Directive 21-01 — one of the rare emergency directives in its history — ordering federal agencies to disconnect affected systems. The episode reset global expectations for software supply-chain security.

Organizational-control failures

A.5.7 (threat intelligence): few affected organisations had intelligence capable of recognising a trusted-update attack vector.

A.5.19–A.5.21 (supplier & ICT supply chain): neither SolarWinds nor its customers required verification of software build integrity.

A.5.8 (security in project management): the build pipeline lacked the security gates that would have caught the code insertion.

A.5.24–A.5.25 (incident management): detection took more than a year — an extraordinary mean-time-to-detect failure.

Lessons — SolarWinds

Trust in a vendor's update channel is itself an attack surface; supply-chain integrity (A.5.21) must be verified, not assumed.

Organizational controls are not overhead — they are the governance infrastructure that makes every technical control coherent.

The attack succeeded through gaps in supplier assurance, threat intelligence and detection — every one of them an organizational control.

Regional Lens: Governance and Supply Chain in India and Australia

India — DPDPA as the A.5.31/A.5.34 Driver

For Indian organisations, the legal and privacy controls of Cluster G have acquired sharp financial teeth. The Digital Personal Data Protection Act, 2023 turns A.5.31 (legal register) and A.5.34 (PII protection) from documentation exercises into board-level obligations, with penalties of up to ₹250 crore for failing to take reasonable security safeguards. The Air India passenger-data breach — which entered through a passenger-service-system provider rather than the airline itself — is a direct A.5.19–A.5.21 supplier-chain lesson, reinforcing that an Indian enterprise's legal exposure now extends through every processor that touches its customers' data.

Australia — Supplier Assurance as National Practice

Australia's government supplier-assurance models, shaped by the ASD, ACSC and Department of Home Affairs, operationalise A.5.19–A.5.22 at national scale: critical vendors must evidence controls and submit to independent verification (GOV-11), precisely the discipline whose absence enabled SolarWinds. APRA's CPS 234, met in Chapter 2, enforces the governance cluster (A.5.1–A.5.4) by mandating board accountability and clear security roles for regulated entities. Together they show A.5 not as paperwork but as enforceable, supervised practice.

Key Takeaways

- Organizational controls (A.5) are the governance and policy architecture that make all other controls coherent — the largest of the four categories at 37 controls.
- They group into seven natural clusters: policy/ roles, asset management, access/identity, supplier/ cloud, incident management, disruption, and legal/ compliance.
- Three controls are new in 2022: threat intelligence (A.5.7), ICT supply-chain security (A.5.21) and cloud-service security (A.5.23).
- Supplier and supply-chain controls (A.5.19–A.5.23) are now decisive: the era's biggest breaches entered through this cluster.
- Incident management (A.5.24–A.5.28) is a proactive discipline; detection latency is the recurring failure across major breaches.
- SolarWinds was a failure of organizational, not technical, controls — supplier assurance, threat intelligence and detection.

Reflection Questions

1. Does every policy, process and control in your ISMS have a named owner — or are some simply assumed to belong to 'IT'?

2. Could a SolarWinds-style trusted-update attack be detected in your environment, and do you verify supplier build integrity?

3. How long would it take you to detect an intruder who entered through a vendor and moved quietly — days, or the months it took the biggest victims?

4. Under the DPDPA, is your legal register (A.5.31) current and your PII protection (A.5.34) defensible to ₹250 crore?

5. When did an independent party last review your security programme (A.5.35), and were the findings actually closed?

Action Deploy & Checklist

- Tier all suppliers by security impact within 60 days and apply enhanced due diligence to those with access to sensitive data or systems (A.5.19).
- Stand up a software-bill-of-materials process for critical commercial and open-source software (A.5.21).
- Subscribe to at least two authoritative threat-intelligence feeds and assign a named reviewer within a 48-hour SLA (A.5.7).
- Test your incident-response plan against a trusted-software-update scenario; update it if that vector is not covered (A.5.24).
- Make ISO 27001, SOC 2 Type II or a completed security questionnaire a condition of every new or renewed supplier contract (A.5.20).
- Confirm your DPDPA legal register and PII-protection controls are current and owned (A.5.31, A.5.34).

Controls in Brief

A.5.1 | Policies for Information Security	
Purpose	To provide management direction and support for information security in accordance with business requirements and relevant laws and regulations.
Implementation Guidance	An information security policy, and topic-specific policies, shall be defined, approved by management, published, communicated to, and acknowledged by relevant personnel and relevant interested parties, and reviewed at planned intervals and if significant changes occur. Topic-specific policies should address access control; physical and environmental security; asset management; information transfer; use of cryptography; information security in supplier relationships; incident management; and business continuity.
Key Metrics	• Policy coverage rate (% of required controls covered by approved policies); • Policy review compliance rate (% of policies reviewed within schedule); • Policy acknowledgement rate (% of staff who have acknowledged security policies).
ASD ISM 2026	All cyber security policies must be documented, approved by an appropriate authority, and communicated to all relevant personnel. Policies must be reviewed at defined intervals.

A.5.2 | Information Security Roles and Responsibilities	
Purpose	To establish a defined, approved, and understood information security responsibilities framework.
Implementation Guidance	All information security responsibilities shall be defined and allocated. An information security role owner should be assigned for each policy, process, and control. The CISO (or equivalent) should have clearly defined authority, resources, and reporting lines. Segregation of duties should be considered when assigning roles.
Key Metrics	• RACI matrix completeness (% of ISMS processes with documented role assignments); • Role vacancy rate (% of security roles unfilled or unactioned for >30 days).
ASD ISM 2026	GOV-02: A CISO provides leadership and oversight of cyber security activities and delivers regular and timely risk-based reporting to the board.

A.5.3 | Segregation of Duties	
Purpose	To reduce risks of fraud, error, or bypass of information security controls by preventing any single individual from having complete authority over high-risk activities.

A.5.3 | Segregation of Duties	
Implementation Guidance	Conflicting duties and conflicting areas of responsibility shall be segregated. Where segregation is not possible due to the size of the organisation, compensating controls such as monitoring, audit trails, and management supervision should be applied. Key examples include separation of development and production environments; separation of IT operations from security audit; separation of authorisation and execution in financial processes.
Key Metrics	• Segregation of duties violations identified in access reviews (count per period); • Compensating control coverage rate for areas where full segregation is impractical.
ASD ISM 2026	GOV-12: Only personnel whose suitability and trustworthiness have been established are granted access to systems.

A.5.4 | Management Responsibilities	
Purpose	To ensure that management actively supports information security within the organisation.
Implementation Guidance	Management should require all personnel to apply information security in accordance with the established policies. Responsibilities include directing, communicating, and promoting compliance; supporting staff who report security concerns; leading by example in security behaviour; and allocating appropriate security resources.

A.5.4 | Management Responsibilities	
Key Metrics	Management security training completion rate; number of security agenda items raised at leadership forums per quarter.

A.5.5 | Contact with Authorities	
Purpose	To maintain appropriate contacts with relevant authorities to address information security issues.
Implementation Guidance	Appropriate contacts with relevant authorities (law enforcement, regulators, emergency services, national CERTs) shall be maintained. Contacts should be established before incidents occur. The organisation should know when and how to notify authorities of incidents — including mandatory breach notification timelines under GDPR (72 hours), DPDP Act, HIPAA, and similar regulations.
Key Metrics	• Number of regulatory reporting obligations documented; • Time-to-notification compliance rate for mandatory incident reports.

A.5.6 | Contact with Special Interest Groups	
Purpose	To maintain appropriate contacts with special interest groups or specialist security forums to stay current on security developments.
Implementation Guidance	Appropriate contacts with special interest groups — including information security associations, ISAC communities, vendor security advisory forums, and research groups — shall be maintained. Memberships should be reviewed periodically for continued relevance.

A.5.6 | Contact with Special Interest Groups	
Key Metrics	Number of active threat intelligence sources monitored; percentage of threat advisories reviewed within 48 hours of publication.

A.5.7 | Threat Intelligence	
Purpose	To provide awareness of the organisation's threat environment to enable informed risk management decisions. [NEW in ISO 27002:2022]
Implementation Guidance	Information relating to information security threats shall be collected and analysed to produce threat intelligence. This intelligence should be used in the risk assessment process and to inform control selection and monitoring priorities. Sources include: open-source threat feeds; CERT advisories; vendor security bulletins; sector-specific ISACs; dark web monitoring; and information sharing with trusted peers.
Key Metrics	Number of threat intelligence sources actively monitored; number of control adjustments made in response to new threat intelligence per quarter; mean time from threat alert to risk assessment update.
ASD ISM 2026	IDE-06: The organisation actively monitors and responds to cyber threats. ISM requires that threat intelligence is incorporated into security risk management activities.

A.5.8 | Information Security in Project Management	
Purpose	To ensure that information security is addressed throughout the project lifecycle and is not bolted on after delivery.
Implementation Guidance	Information security shall be integrated into project management regardless of the type of project. Security requirements should be identified during project initiation; risk assessments should be performed as part of project planning; security reviews should be conducted at key project milestones; and security acceptance testing should be completed before go-live. Security should be a standing agenda item in project governance forums.
Key Metrics	• Percentage of projects with security assessment at initiation; • Number of security defects identified at go-live versus during development (earlier is better).

A.5.9 | Inventory of Information and Other Associated Assets	
Purpose	To identify the organisation's information assets and define appropriate ownership and protection responsibilities.
Implementation Guidance	An inventory of information and other associated assets, including owners, shall be developed and maintained. The inventory should include: information assets (databases, files, contracts, personal data); software assets (applications, tools, licences); physical assets (servers, endpoints, network equipment); service assets; people assets (knowledge, expertise). The asset inventory is the foundation for the risk assessment.

A.5.9 | Inventory of Information and Other Associated Assets	
Key Metrics	• Asset inventory completeness rate (% of information assets documented); • Asset owner assignment rate (% of assets with named owner); • Asset review frequency compliance.
ASD ISM 2026	IDE: Identify assets and associated security risks. The ISM 2026 emphasises that asset identification is a prerequisite for all subsequent security activities.

A.5.10 | Acceptable Use of Information and Other Associated Assets	
Purpose	To ensure information and associated assets are used, protected, and disposed of appropriately.
Implementation Guidance	Rules for the acceptable use and procedures for handling information and associated assets shall be identified, documented, and implemented. The Acceptable Use Policy should address use of personal devices (BYOD); use of internet and social media; email and communications; use of cloud services; handling of confidential information; and consequences of policy violations.
Key Metrics	• AUP acknowledgement rate; • Number of AUP violations reported per period; • Percentage of endpoint devices enrolled in mobile device management.

A.5.11 | Return of Assets	
Purpose	To ensure that assets are returned when employment or contracts end, and to protect against data leakage.
Implementation Guidance	All personnel and external party users shall return all organisational assets in their possession upon change or termination of employment, contract, or agreement. The return process should be documented in the off-boarding procedure and verified by HR and IT before final payment or contract closeout.
Key Metrics	• Asset return compliance rate at off boarding (% of leavers completing asset return checklist); • Days-to-account-deactivation after termination.

A.5.12 | Classification of Information	
Purpose	To ensure that information receives an appropriate level of protection in accordance with its importance to the organisation.
Implementation Guidance	Information shall be classified in accordance with legal requirements, value, criticality, and sensitivity to unauthorised disclosure or modification. A classification scheme — typically with levels such as Public, Internal, Confidential, and Restricted — should be defined, documented, and applied consistently. The classification must be based on the information's business value and the impact of compromise.

A.5.12 | Classification of Information	
Key Metrics	• Percentage of information assets with assigned classification; • Classification accuracy rate (% of classifications confirmed correct in sample audits).

A.5.13 | Labelling of Information	
Purpose	To ensure that information is labelled in accordance with its classification to facilitate handling.
Implementation Guidance	An appropriate set of procedures for information labelling shall be developed and implemented in accordance with the information classification scheme. Physical documents should be marked with their classification. Electronic files, emails, and reports should include classification labels. Staff should be trained on labelling requirements.
Key Metrics	• Percentage of documents and emails correctly labelled during sample audit; • Number of mislabelling incidents per quarter.

A.5.14 | Information Transfer	
Purpose	To maintain the security of information transferred within an organisation and with any external entity.

A.5.14 | Information Transfer	
Implementation Guidance	Rules, procedures, or agreements shall be in place for the transfer of information for all types of transfer facilities. Transfers may be via email, file transfer, physical media, voice, or video. Requirements include: use of encryption for confidential transfers; DLP controls for outbound email; secure destruction of physical media; formal data transfer agreements with external parties.
Key Metrics	• Percentage of external confidential transfers using approved secure channels; • Number of data leakage events detected per period.

A.5.15 | Access Control	
Purpose	To ensure that access to information and other associated assets is defined and restricted according to business and information security requirements.
Implementation Guidance	Rules to control physical and logical access to information and other associated assets shall be established and implemented based on business and information security requirements. Access should be granted on the principle of least privilege and need-to-know. Access rights should be reviewed at regular intervals and on change of role or employment status.
Key Metrics	• Privilege creep index (growth in number of privileged accounts over time); • Access review completion rate; • Percentage of accounts with no activity in past 90 days.

A.5.16 | Identity Management	
Purpose	To allow unique identification of individuals and systems accessing the organisation's information and systems.
Implementation Guidance	The full lifecycle of digital identities shall be managed: creation, provisioning, modification, suspension, and deletion. Every user should have a unique identity. Shared or generic accounts should be avoided. Service accounts should be managed with the same rigour as user accounts. Identity management should be integrated with HR processes.
Key Metrics	• Percentage of users with unique identities; number of orphaned accounts (accounts without active user); • Mean time to deactivate accounts after termination.

A.5.17 | Authentication Information	
Purpose	To ensure proper management of authentication information to prevent unauthorised access.
Implementation Guidance	The allocation and management of authentication information shall be controlled by a management process, including advising personnel on proper handling of authentication information. Passwords should meet complexity and length requirements. Multi-factor authentication (MFA) should be required for privileged access and remote access. Password managers should be used. Default passwords on devices and systems should be changed before deployment.

A.5.17 | Authentication Information	
Key Metrics	• MFA adoption rate for privileged accounts; • Percentage of systems with default credentials changed; • Mean time between password compromises (from threat intelligence).

A.5.18 | Access Rights	
Purpose	To ensure that access rights to information and systems are provisioned, reviewed, modified, and removed in a timely manner.
Implementation Guidance	Access rights to information and other associated assets shall be provisioned, reviewed, modified, and removed following the organisation's access control policy and rules for managing access rights. Provisioning should be based on business justification and approved by the information owner. De-provisioning should occur immediately upon termination or role change. Access reviews should be conducted quarterly for privileged access.
Key Metrics	• Access provisioning cycle time; access review completion rate on schedule; • Number of access rights found inappropriate in access review.

A.5.19 | Information Security in Supplier Relationships	
Purpose	To maintain an agreed level of information security and service delivery in line with supplier agreements.
Implementation Guidance	Processes and procedures shall be defined and implemented to manage the information security risks associated with the use of supplier products or services. This includes: supplier risk assessment before engagement; security requirements in contracts; security clauses in all supplier agreements; right-to-audit provisions; and regular monitoring of supplier security performance.
Key Metrics	• Percentage of suppliers with security assessment on file; • Percentage of contracts with security clauses; • Number of supplier security incidents per period.
ASD ISM 2026	GOV-09: Security risk management responsibilities for suppliers and partners are documented and communicated. GOV-11: Systems are delivered and supported by trustworthy suppliers whose cyber security practices are independently verified.

A.5.20 | Addressing Information Security within Supplier Agreements	
Purpose	To ensure that suppliers and partners meet and maintain the agreed information security requirements.

A.5.20 | Addressing Information Security within Supplier Agreements	
Implementation Guidance	Relevant information security requirements shall be established and agreed with each supplier that may access, process, store, communicate, or provide IT infrastructure components for the organisation's information. Agreements should address: data handling and confidentiality; access controls; incident reporting obligations; audit rights; sub-contractor requirements; data return and destruction on contract end; business continuity obligations.
Key Metrics	• Percentage of supplier agreements reviewed and updated within last 12 months; • Number of supplier incidents involving contractual breaches.

A.5.21 | Managing Information Security in the ICT Supply Chain	
Purpose	To maintain an agreed level of information security and service delivery in line with ICT supply chain requirements. [NEW in ISO 27002:2022]
Implementation Guidance	Processes and procedures shall be defined and implemented to manage the information security risks associated with the ICT products and services supply chain. The organisation must understand its supply chain dependencies, identify critical components and their origins, assess the risk of tampering or substitution, and require security verification of ICT products before deployment.

<table>
<tr><th colspan="2">A.5.21 | Managing Information Security in the ICT Supply Chain</th></tr>
<tr><td>Key Metrics</td><td>• Number of critical ICT suppliers with verified security posture;
• Percentage of ICT products subject to integrity verification before deployment;
• Number of supply chain security incidents per period.</td></tr>
<tr><td>ASD ISM 2026</td><td>GOV-11: Systems delivered and supported by trustworthy suppliers with independently verified cyber security practices. The ISM 2026 specifically addresses technology supply chain security as a priority concern.</td></tr>
</table>

<table>
<tr><th colspan="2">A.5.22 | Monitoring, Review and Change Management of Supplier Services</th></tr>
<tr><td>Purpose</td><td>To maintain an agreed level of information security and service delivery consistent with supplier agreements.</td></tr>
<tr><td>Implementation Guidance</td><td>The organisation shall regularly monitor, review and audit supplier service delivery. Supplier performance reviews should cover: compliance with security requirements; incident reports; changes affecting the organisation's information; and evidence of continuous improvement. Changes to supplier services must be assessed for security impact.</td></tr>
<tr><td>Key Metrics</td><td>• Percentage of suppliers subject to annual security review;
• Number of unmanaged supplier changes affecting security per period.</td></tr>
</table>

A.5.23 | Information Security for Use of Cloud Services	
Purpose	To specify and manage information security for the use of cloud services. [NEW in ISO 27002:2022]
Implementation Guidance	Processes for acquisition, use, management, and exit from cloud services shall be established in accordance with the organisation's information security requirements. The organisation must: assess the security posture of cloud service providers; understand the shared responsibility model; implement appropriate access controls; ensure data is encrypted in transit and at rest; maintain visibility of data location; and plan for exit from cloud services.
Key Metrics	• Cloud service inventory completeness; percentage of cloud services with completed security assessment; • Data residency compliance rate for regulated data.
ASD ISM 2026	PRO-08 (ISM 2026): Controls are implemented for cloud services consistent with data sensitivity and regulatory requirements.

A.5.24 | Information Security Incident Management Planning and Preparation	
Purpose	To ensure quick, effective, and orderly response to information security incidents.
Implementation Guidance	The organisation shall plan and prepare for managing information security incidents by defining, establishing, and communicating information security incident management processes, roles, and responsibilities. An Incident Response Plan (IRP) must be documented, approved, and tested. Incident categories, escalation paths, communications protocols, and evidence preservation procedures must be defined.
Key Metrics	• Incident response plan currency (date of last test); • Mean time to detect (MTTD); • Mean time to respond (MTTR); Percentage of incident types covered by documented procedures.
ASD ISM 2026	DET/RES (ISM 2026): Cyber security incidents must be detected, analysed, and responded to through documented plans that have been tested.

A.5.25 | Assessment and Decision on Information Security Events	
Purpose	To enable effective decisions to be made about information security events, including whether they constitute incidents.

A.5.25 | Assessment and Decision on Information Security Events	
Implementation Guidance	The organisation shall establish the ability to assess information security events and decide if they are to be classified as information security incidents. Triage criteria — event severity thresholds, classification criteria, escalation triggers — must be defined. Security Operations Centre (SOC) or equivalent function must have the tools and authority to make these determinations in real time.
Key Metrics	• Event-to-incident classification accuracy rate; • False positive rate in SIEM alerting; • Mean time from event detection to incident classification.

A.5.26 | Response to Information Security Incidents	
Purpose	To ensure a consistent and effective approach to responding to information security incidents.
Implementation Guidance	Information security incidents shall be responded to in accordance with documented procedures. The response process must include: incident containment; eradication of threats; recovery of systems and data; documentation of all actions taken; evidence preservation; and communication with affected parties and authorities. Post-incident reviews must capture lessons learned.

A.5.26 | Response to Information Security Incidents	
Key Metrics	Percentage of incidents responded to within SLA; Percentage of incidents with post-incident review completed within 5 working days; Number of repeat incidents (same root cause).
ASD ISM 2026	RES (ISM 2026): Respond to cyber security incidents. DET-09: Conduct cyber security exercises to test incident response capabilities.

A.5.27 | Learning from Information Security Incidents	
Purpose	To reduce the likelihood or impact of future incidents by applying lessons learned.
Implementation Guidance	Knowledge gained from analysing and resolving information security incidents shall be used to reduce the likelihood or impact of future incidents. Root cause analysis should be conducted for all significant incidents. Findings should be fed back into the risk assessment process, control design, and awareness training. Incident trend analysis should be presented at management reviews.
Key Metrics	Percentage of significant incidents with root cause analysis completed; number of control improvements implemented as a result of incident analysis per quarter.

A.5.28 | Collection of Evidence	
Purpose	To ensure that the organisation's ability to collect, preserve, and present evidence in support of disciplinary or legal action is maintained.
Implementation Guidance	The organisation shall define and apply procedures for the identification, collection, acquisition, and preservation of information which can serve as evidence. Evidence must be collected in a way that is admissible in legal proceedings and disciplinary processes. Chain of custody must be maintained. Forensic readiness planning should address how evidence will be collected and preserved before an incident occurs.
Key Metrics	• Percentage of incident investigations with documented chain of custody; • Forensic readiness assessment score.

A.5.29 | Information Security during Disruption	
Purpose	To protect information and other associated assets during disruption.
Implementation Guidance	The organisation shall plan how to maintain information security at an appropriate level during disruption. This includes: identifying critical information security controls that must remain operational during a disruption; documenting manual workarounds if automated controls are unavailable; integrating information security requirements into the Business Continuity Plan.

A.5.29 | Information Security during Disruption	
Key Metrics	• Number of critical security controls with documented continuity provisions; • BCP test results covering security control continuity.

A.5.30 | ICT Readiness for Business Continuity	
Purpose	To ensure the availability of the organisation's information and other associated assets during disruption.
Implementation Guidance	ICT readiness for business continuity shall be planned, implemented, maintained, and tested based on business continuity objectives and ICT continuity requirements. Recovery Time Objectives (RTOs) and Recovery Point Objectives (RPOs) must be defined for critical systems and tested through regular exercises.
Key Metrics	• RTO/RPO achievement rate in tests; • BCM test frequency; • Percentage of critical systems with tested recovery procedures.
ASD ISM 2026	REC (ISM 2026): Resume normal business operations following cyber security incidents.

A.5.31 | Legal, Statutory, Regulatory and Contractual Requirements	
Purpose	To ensure compliance with applicable legal, statutory, regulatory, and contractual requirements.

A.5.31 | Legal, Statutory, Regulatory and Contractual Requirements	
Implementation Guidance	Relevant legislative, statutory, regulatory, and contractual requirements and the organisation's approach to meeting these requirements shall be explicitly identified, documented, and kept up to date for each information system and the organisation. The Legal and Regulatory Register should identify applicable laws, assigned owners, compliance status, and review dates.
Key Metrics	• Legal register completeness and currency; • Compliance assessment pass rate; • Number of regulatory breaches reported per period.

A.5.32 | Intellectual Property Rights	
Purpose	To ensure compliance with legal, regulatory, and contractual requirements related to intellectual property.
Implementation Guidance	The organisation shall implement appropriate procedures to ensure compliance with legislative, regulatory, and contractual requirements related to intellectual property. This includes: licence management for software; controls on duplication and use of copyrighted material; protection of the organisation's own intellectual property; and staff awareness of intellectual property obligations.
Key Metrics	• Software licence compliance rate; • Number of intellectual property incidents per period.

A.5.33 | Protection of Records	
Purpose	To protect records from loss, destruction, falsification, unauthorised access, and unauthorised release.
Implementation Guidance	Records shall be protected from loss, destruction, falsification, unauthorised access, and unauthorised release. Retention schedules must be defined for all categories of records. Records must be stored securely, backed up, and disposed of at end of retention period in a manner that prevents reconstruction.
Key Metrics	• Records retention compliance rate; • Percentage of records with defined and applied retention schedules; • Number of records incidents per period.

A.5.34 | Privacy and Protection of Personal Identifiable Information (PII)	
Purpose	To ensure privacy and protection of PII as required by relevant legislation and regulations where applicable.
Implementation Guidance	The organisation shall identify and meet the requirements for privacy and protection of PII. This control links directly to ISO 27701 (Privacy Information Management) and applicable privacy regulations (GDPR, DPDP Act, CCPA, HIPAA). Requirements include: lawful basis for processing; data subject rights (access, erasure, portability); privacy notices; consent management; DPIA processes; and breach notification.

A.5.34 | Privacy and Protection of Personal Identifiable Information (PII)	
Key Metrics	• DPIA completion rate for high-risk processing activities; • Data subject request response rate within statutory timeframes; • Number of privacy breaches per period.

A.5.35 | Independent Review of Information Security	
Purpose	To ensure the continued suitability, adequacy, and effectiveness of the organisation's approach to managing information security.
Implementation Guidance	The organisation's approach to managing information security and its implementation shall be reviewed independently at planned intervals, or when significant changes occur. Independent review may be conducted by internal audit, external consultants, or certification bodies. Review findings must be reported to management and acted upon.
Key Metrics	• Independent audit frequency; number of findings from independent reviews; • Percentage of findings closed within agreed timelines.

A.5.36 | Compliance with Policies, Rules and Standards for Information Security	
Purpose	To ensure information security is implemented and operated in accordance with the organisational information security policies, rules, and standards.

A.5.36 | Compliance with Policies, Rules and Standards for Information Security	
Implementation Guidance	The manager shall regularly review the compliance of information processing and procedures within their area of responsibility with the appropriate security policies, standards, and any other security requirements. Non-compliance should be documented and reported.
Key Metrics	• Internal compliance audit pass rate; • Number of confirmed policy violations per period; • Mean time to resolve identified non-compliance.

A.5.37 | Documented Operating Procedures	
Purpose	To ensure correct and secure operation of information processing facilities.
Implementation Guidance	Operating procedures for information processing activities shall be documented and made available to all users who need them. Procedures should address: start-up and close-down of computers and systems; backup procedures; equipment maintenance; incident handling; use of utilities and special technical functions; and restart and recovery procedures for system failure.
Key Metrics	• Procedure currency rate (% of operating procedures reviewed within last 12 months); • Percentage of critical procedures with evidence of staff training.

Key Takeaways

- Organizational controls (A.5) establish the governance, policy, and risk management framework for the entire ISMS — they are the management architecture that makes all other controls coherent.
- Key additions in ISO 27002:2022 include Threat Intelligence (A.5.7), ICT Supply Chain Security (A.5.21), and Cloud Services Security (A.5.23) — reflecting the contemporary threat landscape.
- The ASD ISM 2026's Govern principles (GOV-01 through GOV-14) are largely operationalized through the A.5 organizational control set.
- Supplier security management (A.5.19-A.5.22) has become significantly more important as organizations become more dependent on cloud services and third-party ICT supply chains.
- Incident management planning (A.5.24-A.5.28) must be treated as a proactive discipline, not a reactive emergency response — forensic readiness, pre-defined escalation paths, and tested procedures are essential.

CHAPTER

6

PEOPLE CONTROLS

ISO/IEC 27002:2022 A.6 — Eight Controls Addressing the Human Element

ISO/IEC 27002:2022 A.6 — Eight Controls Addressing the Human Element

S.T.E.P.S.™ Engine — Operational Anchor: DO (the Human Layer)

The second of the four control chapters. The eight people controls of A.6 manage information security across the entire employment lifecycle — before, during and after — because the human element is involved in the majority of significant security incidents, and culture is the control that no technology can replace.

Chapter Overview

Technology can be bought; a security culture must be built, and the eight people controls of ISO/IEC 27002:2022 Annex A.6 are how it is built. They run the full length of the employment relationship — establishing trust through screening and contractual obligation before a person joins, sustaining secure behaviour through measured awareness training, fair discipline, remote-working controls and blame-free event reporting during employment, and protecting the organisation through disciplined off-boarding when they leave. The human element is involved in most significant incidents, but the lesson of the Twitter attack is not that people are the problem; it is that the organisation had not governed the human dimension with the seriousness it gave the technical one. For India's outsourcing sector a demonstrable security culture has become a market differentiator, and Australia's Medibank breach shows that the human perimeter now extends to every contractor with a credential. Mastering A.6 is the work of turning an organisation's largest risk surface into its largest sensor network.

Chapter Objectives

By the end of this chapter, the reader will be able to:

- Explain why the human element is the most significant and most frequently exploited source of security risk.
- Map the eight A.6 controls across the before, during and after phases of the employment lifecycle.
- Design a security-awareness programme that measures behaviour change, not just course completion.
- Treat off-boarding, remote working and event reporting as first-order controls rather than afterthoughts.
- Draw the lessons of the Twitter social-engineering attack for awareness, least privilege and monitoring.

The Control No Firewall Provides

People controls address what is consistently identified as the most significant source of information security risk: human behaviour. Whether through malice, negligence, social engineering, or simple error, the human element is involved in the majority of significant security incidents. These eight controls create the framework for managing information security throughout the employment lifecycle and for every category of worker.

The ASD ISM 2026 GOV-12 principle — "Only personnel whose suitability and trustworthiness have been established, and are subject to ongoing assurance, are granted access to systems" — captures the essence of people controls. The ISM also emphasises that a positive cyber security culture (GOV-01 requirement for the board) begins with the people controls that shape that culture.

Every serious study of security incidents reaches the same conclusion: the human element — through malice, negligence, social engineering or simple error — is involved in the majority of them. This is not a reason to mistrust people; it is a reason to govern the human dimension as deliberately as the technical one. The eight people controls of A.6 do exactly that, creating a framework that runs the full length of the employment relationship and covers every category of worker, from permanent staff to contractors.

The ASD ISM captures their essence in a single principle (GOV-12): only personnel whose suitability and trustworthiness have been established, and are subject to ongoing assurance, are granted access to systems — and a positive security culture, which the board is expected to foster, begins here.

Executive Insight

Security-awareness training is among the highest-return investments an organisation can make — and among the most commonly mis-measured. Counting who finished the e-learning module tells you nothing; measuring whether the phishing click-rate fell tells you everything. Behaviour, not completion, is the metric that matters.

6.1 The Eight Controls Across the Employment Lifecycle

People controls are best understood not as a list but as a lifecycle. Some controls establish trust before a person joins; others sustain secure behaviour during employment; one governs the obligations that survive a departure. The table below maps all eight controls to that arc.

Phase	Control	Intent & representative metric
Before	A.6.1 Screening	Proportionate background verification before and during employment — screening completion rate
Before	A.6.2 Terms & conditions	Security responsibilities written into employment contracts — % contracts with security clauses

Phase	Control	Intent & representative metric
Before / ongoing	A.6.6 Confidentiality / NDAs	Reviewed, enforceable NDAs covering post-employment — NDA coverage rate
During	A.6.3 Awareness, education & training	Role-relevant training that changes behaviour — phishing click-through rate (lower is better)
During	A.6.4 Disciplinary process	Fair, consistent, communicated response to violations — consistency across similar cases
During	A.6.7 Remote working	Security for off-premises work — remote-access MFA & endpoint-enrolment rates
During	A.6.8 Event reporting	Easy, blame-free reporting of suspected events — events reported per month; time-to-report
After	A.6.5 Responsibilities after termination/ change	Surviving obligations, prompt deactivation, asset return — time-to-deactivate after exit

6.2 The High-Leverage Controls

A.6.3 — Awareness, Education and Training

This is the control with the widest reach and the most commonly squandered potential. A programme that covers the security policy, individual responsibilities, information handling, event reporting, phishing and social-engineering recognition, acceptable use and password hygiene will reduce the organisation's largest risk surface — but only if its effect is measured. Best practice tracks the phishing-simulation click-rate over time, knowledge-assessment scores before and after training, and the incidence of social-engineering events. The aim is a measurable fall in susceptibility, not a wall of completion certificates.

A.6.5 — Responsibilities After Termination or Change

Off boarding is the most underestimated risk in the people domain. Every day between a person's departure and the deactivation of their access is a day of unnecessary insider-threat exposure, and the risk applies equally to contractors and temporary staff. A disciplined off-boarding checklist — covering continuing confidentiality obligations, asset return, immediate account deactivation and an exit interview — closes a gap that attackers and disgruntled leavers both exploit. The single most telling metric is the mean time to deactivate access after termination; anything beyond 24 hours is a live exposure.

A.6.7 — Remote Working

Once an exception, remote working is now a permanent feature of the operating model, and with it the organisation's perimeter has dissolved into thousands of homes and cafes. The minimum controls are VPN with multi-factor authentication, managed endpoint protection, cloud-based document handling to avoid local storage of sensitive data, and guidance on the home environment — screen privacy, secure Wi-Fi and monitored remote access. Remote working is not a relaxation of security standards; it is the same standards applied to a far larger surface.

A.6.8 — Information Security Event Reporting

An organisation's people are its largest sensor network — if they will report what they see. The reporting mechanism must be easy (a one-click 'report phishing' button is best practice), well-publicised, confidential on request, and genuinely responsive, with acknowledgement and feedback. Above all it must be blame-free for good-faith reports: a culture that punishes the messenger manufactures silence, and silence is what lets an incident become a catastrophe. The volume and speed of reporting is a leading indicator of ISMS maturity.

Case Study: The Twitter Social-Engineering Attack (2020)

On 15 July 2020, attackers seized control of 130 high-profile Twitter accounts — among them those of Barack Obama, Joe Biden, Elon Musk, Bill Gates, Apple and Uber — tweeting from 45 of them to promote a cryptocurrency scam that netted roughly US$120,000 in Bitcoin within hours. The attack required almost no technical sophistication. Using a phone-based spear-phishing ('vishing') campaign, the attackers convinced Twitter employees to surrender credentials, then used staff with access to internal admin tools to take over the accounts. The alleged mastermind, a 17-year-old, was arrested in Tampa, Florida and prosecuted as an adult (later sentenced to three years); co-conspirators were charged in the United Kingdom and elsewhere.

People-control failures

A.6.3 (awareness): training had not prepared employees to recognise and resist a real-time social-engineering attack by phone.

A.5.18 / least privilege: internal tools granted far more reach than individual roles required, so a single compromise cascaded.

Monitoring: there was no real-time anomaly detection for unusual use of powerful internal admin tools.

Lessons — Twitter

People controls are not 'soft': they are often the hardest to implement and the most frequently exploited.

Awareness training must include realistic social-engineering and voice-phishing simulations, not just e-learning.

Even a technology-native company with strong technical controls can be defeated by a convincing phone call — unless least privilege and monitoring contain the blast radius.

Regional Lens: The Human Element in India and Australia

India — Insider Risk and Awareness Culture

India's large IT and outsourcing sector has made the people controls a competitive necessity. The insider-misuse and phishing incidents examined earlier — employees copying client data to unauthorised devices, or surrendering credentials to socially engineered emails — prompted sector-wide investment in exactly the A.6 disciplines: screening (A.6.1), contractual obligations and NDAs (A.6.2, A.6.6), continuous awareness with phishing simulation (A.6.3), and behavioural monitoring tied to a fair disciplinary process (A.6.4). For firms handling global clients' regulated data under the DPDPA, a demonstrable security culture is now part of the value proposition, not merely an internal control.

Australia — The Credential at the Edge

Australia's Medibank breach is, at root, a people-and-access story: initial access was obtained through stolen credentials belonging to a third-party contractor, which then unlocked sensitive health data. It is a vivid reminder that screening, least privilege and MFA must extend to every contractor and remote worker (A.6.1, A.6.7), and that the human perimeter now includes everyone with a credential, not just employees. Australia's ISM reinforces the point, requiring MFA for remote access and ongoing suitability assurance for all who can reach systems.

Key Takeaways

- People controls (A.6) govern the human element — the most significant source of security risk — across the entire employment lifecycle.
- The eight controls span before (screening, terms, NDAs), during (awareness, discipline, remote working, event reporting) and after (post-termination responsibilities).
- Awareness training (A.6.3) is high-ROI only when it measures behaviour change, not course completion.
- Off-boarding (A.6.5) is a frequently underestimated insider-threat exposure; time-to-deactivate is the key metric.
- Remote working (A.6.7) made MFA and managed endpoints minimum controls across a dissolved perimeter.
- Twitter shows that even sophisticated technical defences fall to a phone call when awareness, least privilege and monitoring are weak.

Reflection Questions

1. Does your awareness programme measure whether behaviour changed — a falling phishing click-rate — or merely who completed the module?

2. What is your mean time to deactivate access after an employee or contractor departs, and who is accountable for it?
3. Could your employees recognise and resist a convincing phone call asking for credentials, as Twitter's could not?
4. Do your screening, MFA and least-privilege controls extend to every contractor and remote worker, or stop at permanent staff?
5. Is reporting a suspected security event genuinely easy and blame-free in your organisation — or quietly discouraged?

Action Deploy & Checklist

- Run a simulated phishing and voice-phishing (vishing) campaign within 60 days to learn your true social-engineering exposure (A.6.3).
- Implement just-in-time, second-approver access for any internal tool that can affect many accounts or systems (least privilege).
- Measure mean time from departure notification to full account deactivation; drive it under 24 hours (A.6.5).
- Add 'social-engineering resistance' as an explicit requirement for roles with sensitive access (A.6.2).
- Deploy a one-click 'report phishing' button and a single, well-publicised channel for security concerns (A.6.8).
- Extend screening, MFA and managed endpoints to all contractors and remote workers (A.6.1, A.6.7).

Controls in Brief

A.6.1 | Screening	
Purpose	To ensure that all personnel are eligible and suitable for the roles for which they are considered and remain suitable throughout their employment.
Implementation Guidance	Background verification checks on all candidates for employment shall be carried out prior to joining the organisation and on an ongoing basis, taking into account applicable laws and regulations and proportionate to the business requirements, the classification of the information to be accessed, and the perceived risks. Pre-employment screening should include: identity verification; right to work; criminal record check (where legally permissible); employment history verification; educational qualification verification; reference checks; and credit check for roles with financial responsibility.
Key Metrics	Pre-employment screening completion rate; percentage of roles with defined screening requirements; number of screening failures resulting in withdrawal of offer per period.
ASD ISM 2026	GOV-12: Only personnel whose suitability and trustworthiness have been established are granted access.

A.6.2 | Terms and Conditions of Employment	
Purpose	To ensure that personnel understand their information security responsibilities as a condition of employment.

A.6.2 | Terms and Conditions of Employment	
Implementation Guidance	The contractual agreements with personnel shall state their and the organisation's responsibilities for information security. Employment contracts should include: obligation to comply with information security policies; confidentiality obligations extending beyond employment; responsibilities for handling information assets; obligations regarding personal devices and remote working; and consequences of violation. These terms should be reviewed when policies or regulatory requirements change.
Key Metrics	Percentage of employment contracts with security obligations clause; percentage of contractor agreements with information security requirements.

A.6.3 | Information Security Awareness, Education and Training	
Purpose	To ensure that personnel and relevant interested parties are aware of and fulfil their information security responsibilities.
Implementation Guidance	All personnel of the organisation and relevant interested parties shall receive appropriate information security awareness education and training, and regular updates on organisational policies and procedures, as relevant for their job function. The awareness programme should cover: the organisation's information security policy; individual responsibilities; classification and handling of information; how to report security events; phishing awareness and social engineering; acceptable use of IT resources; and password hygiene. Training effectiveness should be measured — not just completion.

A.6.3 | Information Security Awareness, Education and Training	
Key Metrics	Security awareness training completion rate; phishing simulation click-through rate (lower is better); security knowledge assessment scores before and after training; number of social engineering incidents per period.
ASD ISM 2026	GOV-12 requires ongoing suitability assurance. The ISM 2026 emphasises that cyber security awareness training must be provided to all personnel and contractors.

A.6.4 | Disciplinary Process	
Purpose	To ensure that personnel and other interested parties are aware of consequences of information security policy violations, to deter and deal with violations.
Implementation Guidance	A formal and communicated disciplinary process shall exist and shall be used to take action against personnel who have committed an information security policy violation. The process should: be applied consistently and fairly; address a range of violations from minor to serious; include graduated responses (warning, formal warning, dismissal, referral to law enforcement); be communicated to all personnel as part of the awareness programme; and be integrated with HR policy.
Key Metrics	Number of disciplinary actions taken for security violations per period; consistency of disciplinary response across similar violations.

A.6.5 | Responsibilities after Termination or Change of Employment	
Purpose	To protect the organisation's interests as part of the process of changing or terminating employment.
Implementation Guidance	Information security responsibilities and duties that remain valid after termination or change of employment shall be defined, communicated to the individual, and enforced. This includes: continuing confidentiality obligations; restrictions on future employment (non-compete); return of assets; account deactivation; exit interviews. The off-boarding checklist must be followed for every departure, including temporary staff and contractors.
Key Metrics	Mean time to account deactivation after termination; off-boarding checklist completion rate; number of post-termination security incidents.

A.6.6 | Confidentiality or Non-Disclosure Agreements	
Purpose	To maintain confidentiality of information accessible to personnel and external parties.
Implementation Guidance	Requirements for confidentiality or non-disclosure agreements reflecting the organisation's needs for the protection of information shall be identified, documented, regularly reviewed, and signed by personnel and other relevant interested parties. NDAs should: cover all categories of confidential information; specify the duration of obligations (including post-employment); address permitted disclosures; include consequences of breach; and be reviewed for legal enforceability.

A.6.6 | Confidentiality or Non-Disclosure Agreements	
Key Metrics	NDA coverage rate (% of personnel with current NDA); percentage of NDAs reviewed for enforceability in past 24 months.

A.6.7 | Remote Working	
Purpose	To ensure the security of information accessed, processed, or stored at remote working locations.
Implementation Guidance	Security measures shall be implemented when personnel are working remotely to protect information accessed, processed, or stored outside the organisation's premises. Measures should include: VPN with MFA for all remote access; endpoint protection on remote devices; screen privacy filters; secure Wi-Fi use requirements; home environment security guidance; cloud-based document management to avoid storing sensitive data locally; and monitoring of remote access activity.
Key Metrics	Remote access MFA adoption rate; percentage of remote workers enrolled in endpoint management; number of remote working policy violations per period.
ASD ISM 2026	The ISM 2026 addresses remote access security explicitly in its People control guidelines, requiring MFA for all remote access and managed devices where practicable.

A.6.8 | Information Security Event Reporting	
Purpose	To support timely, consistent, and effective reporting of information security events that can be identified by personnel.
Implementation Guidance	The organisation shall provide a mechanism for personnel to report observed or suspected information security events in a timely manner through appropriate channels. The reporting mechanism should be: easy to use (one-click reporting for phishing is best practice); well-publicised across the organisation; confidential where the reporter requests it; and responsive — all reports should receive acknowledgement and, where appropriate, feedback. Reporting should be encouraged: a "no blame" culture for good-faith reports is essential.
Key Metrics	Number of security events reported by personnel per month; mean time from event occurrence to report; percentage of reported events that result in identified incidents.
ASD ISM 2026	The ISM 2026 DET principles require that all personnel are able and encouraged to report cyber security events promptly.

CHAPTER

7

PHYSICAL CONTROLS

ISO/IEC 27002:2022 A.7 — Fourteen Controls for the Physical Environment

S.T.E.P.S.™ Engine — Operational Anchor: DO (the Physical Layer)

The third of the four control chapters. The fourteen physical controls of A.7 create the environmental protection that every technical control depends upon — because physical access to an unprotected server, an unattended workstation or a discarded hard drive can defeat the most sophisticated logical defence.

Chapter Overview

Physical security is the oldest discipline in information protection and, in the Internet-of-Things era, a newly urgent one. The fourteen controls of ISO/IEC 27002:2022 Annex A.7 secure the environment in which information lives — layered perimeters and monitored entry, protection against fire, flood and power failure, and the disciplined management of equipment and media from siting through to verified destruction at end of life. The 2022 edition's addition of continuous physical monitoring reflects a world in which deterrence is no longer enough. The recurring lesson, made vivid by a casino breached through a fish-tank thermometer, is that physical and technical controls are now a single fabric: every connected device is both a physical asset and an attack surface, and the path of least resistance is usually the one nobody classified as a computer. For India's data-centre and critical-infrastructure operators, A.7 is where availability is decided; for Australia's regulated entities, sanitisation and coordinated physical-logical security are expected practice. Mastering the physical layer is what keeps the digital layer honest.

Chapter Objectives

By the end of this chapter, the reader will be able to:

- Explain why physical controls are the foundation on which logical controls depend, especially in the IoT era.
- Navigate the fourteen A.7 controls across perimeters, environment and equipment lifecycle.
- Identify the new physical-monitoring control in the 2022 edition and why it was added.
- Apply secure-disposal and off-premises controls to prevent data leakage from physical assets.
- Draw the lessons of the casino IoT breach for the integration of physical and technical security.

The Original Information Security

Physical security is the original form of information security: the ancient archive, the locked safe, the guarded vault. In the digital age, it may seem less important than technical controls — but physical access to an unprotected server, unattended workstation, or improperly disposed hard drive can defeat the most sophisticated logical security architecture. Physical controls create the environmental protection that technical controls depend upon.

The ASD ISM 2026 PRO (Protect) principles include explicit physical security requirements, recognising that logical security controls cannot fully compensate for physical access vulnerabilities. The ASD also emphasises that physical and logical security must be coordinated — not managed as separate, siloed disciplines.

Physical security is the oldest form of information security: the ancient archive, the locked safe, the guarded vault. In a digital age it can seem secondary to firewalls and encryption — until one remembers that an attacker with physical access to a server, an unattended logged-in workstation or an improperly disposed disk can bypass the entire logical architecture.

Physical controls are not a lesser discipline; they are the environmental foundation that gives logical controls something solid to stand on. The ASD ISM treats them as such, requiring physical access controls for systems holding sensitive data and — crucially — insisting that physical and logical security be coordinated rather than run as separate silos.

Executive Insight

- In the Internet-of-Things era the line between physical and technical security has dissolved.
- Every device physically installed and network-connected — a camera, a sensor, a building-management controller — is simultaneously a physical asset and a technical attack surface.
- The most poorly defended device on a well-protected network is often the one nobody thought of as a computer.

7.1 Cluster A — Perimeters, Entry and Secure Areas (A.7.1–A.7.4, A.7.6, A.7.7)

This cluster keeps unauthorised people away from information. Layered security perimeters (A.7.1) protect from site boundary to server room; entry controls with audit trails and visitor management permit only authorised access (A.7.2); offices, rooms and facilities are secured against intrusion and shoulder-surfing (A.7.3); premises are continuously monitored (A.7.4, new in 2022); behaviour within secure areas is governed (A.7.6); and clear-desk/clear-screen discipline protects information at the workstation (A.7.7).

Control	Intent & representative metric
A.7.1 Physical security perimeters	Layered, proportionate perimeters — % secure areas with documented perimeter
A.7.2 Physical entry	Authorised-only entry with audit trail and visitor control — tailgating incidents detected
A.7.3 Securing offices, rooms & facilities	Protection against intrusion and shoulder-surfing — physical-security assessment score
A.7.4 Physical security monitoring [NEW]	Continuous monitoring with alert and response — % alerts investigated in SLA
A.7.6 Working in secure areas	Governed behaviour (devices, escorts, photography) — secure-area policy violations
A.7.7 Clear desk & clear screen	Locked screens, secured papers — clear-desk compliance; screen-lock coverage

7.2 Cluster B — Environmental Protection and Utilities (A.7.5, A.7.11–A.7.13)

This cluster keeps the environment from defeating the organisation. Protection against physical and environmental threats addresses fire, flood, earthquake, extreme weather and power failure (A.7.5); supporting utilities are safeguarded with UPS, generators and redundant feeds (A.7.11); cabling carrying power and data is protected from interception and damage (A.7.12); and equipment is correctly maintained to preserve availability and integrity (A.7.13). The AIIMS ransomware case is a reminder that for a hospital or a bank, an environmental or availability failure is a safety event, not an inconvenience.

Control	Intent & representative metric
A.7.5 Protecting against environmental threats	Fire/flood/power/quake protection tied to BC — environmental incidents per period
A.7.11 Supporting utilities	UPS, generators, redundant power, monitoring — UPS availability; generator test pass rate
A.7.12 Cabling security	Power/data cabling protected from interception and damage — cabling-doc completeness
A.7.13 Equipment maintenance	Scheduled, recorded, supervised maintenance — maintenance-schedule compliance

7.3 Cluster C — Equipment and Media Lifecycle (A.7.8–A.7.10, A.7.14)

This cluster protects information through the life of the hardware that holds it. Equipment is sited to reduce environmental and access risk (A.7.8); assets taken off-premises — laptops, phones, media — are protected with full-disk encryption and remote wipe (A.7.9); storage media are managed and securely handled across their lifecycle (A.7.10); and equipment is sanitised at end of life before disposal or re-use (A.7.14), to standards such as NIST SP 800-88. The perimeter and the end-of-life are where physical-control failures most often become data exposures.

Control	Intent & representative metric
A.7.8 Equipment siting & protection	Servers in locked rooms; cabling and positioning secured — % equipment in controlled rooms
A.7.9 Security of assets off premises	Encryption, remote wipe, VPN for mobile assets — % portable devices encrypted; time-to-wipe
A.7.10 Storage media	Lifecycle management and secure handling of media — secure-disposal compliance rate
A.7.14 Secure disposal or re-use [emphasis]	Verified data removal before disposal/ re-use (NIST 800-88) — % disposals with destruction certificate

Case Study: The Casino Aquarium Thermometer (2017) — Where Physical Meets Digital

As reported by the security firm Darktrace, a North American casino was breached in 2017 through an unexpected vector: a smart, internet-connected thermometer in a lobby fish tank, used to monitor the aquarium's temperature and chemistry. The device had been connected to the casino's internal network without adequate physical or logical isolation. Attackers exploited its network connection to gain a foothold inside the corporate network and exfiltrated roughly 10 GB of data — including the casino's high-roller database — back out through the same path.

Physical-control failures

A.7.1 (perimeters): a guest-area IoT device sat on the same network segment as sensitive business systems — no physical or network perimeter divided them.

A.7.8 (equipment siting): no security assessment was made of the device's network connectivity before installation.

A.7.4 (physical monitoring): the path through which the thermometer communicated went unmonitored.

Lessons — The Aquarium Thermometer

- In the IoT era physical and technical controls are inseparable: every installed, connected device is both.
- Attackers seek the path of least resistance — often the device nobody classified as a computer.
- Basic network segmentation between 'things' and 'systems' would have contained the breach.

Regional Lens: The Physical Layer in India and Australia

India — Critical Infrastructure and the Data-Centre Boom

India's rapid build-out of hyperscale data centres has made physical controls a board-level concern: perimeters, biometric entry, continuous monitoring (A.7.4), utilities resilience (A.7.11) and environmental protection (A.7.5) are now competitive and regulatory necessities. The AIIMS Delhi ransomware incident, though logical in origin, is also a physical-resilience lesson — a hospital's utilities, equipment and continuity provisions determine whether a digital outage becomes a patient-safety crisis. For operators of critical infrastructure, A.7 is where availability is ultimately won or lost.

Australia — Sanitisation and Coordinated Security

Australia's ISM is explicit that equipment must be sanitised before disposal or transfer to remove all sensitive data (A.7.14), and that physical and logical security be coordinated rather than siloed — precisely the integration the casino case shows is essential. For Australian government and regulated entities, documented data-destruction certificates and physical-access monitoring of systems holding sensitive data are expected practice, not optional hygiene.

Key Takeaways

- Physical controls (A.7) provide the environmental protection that technical controls depend upon; logical security cannot compensate for uncontrolled physical access.
- Physical security monitoring (A.7.4) is new in 2022 — active monitoring, not mere deterrence, is now the minimum.
- The highest-risk physical controls are at the perimeter (A.7.1–2) and at end-of-life (A.7.14), where exposures most often occur.

- Off-premises assets (A.7.9) and storage media (A.7.10) matter more as workforces become mobile and data volumes grow.
- Physical and technical controls must be managed as one: a physical compromise is frequently the first step of a digital attack.
- The casino aquarium breach shows an unclassified IoT device can be the weakest point on a strong network.

Reflection Questions

1. Could you produce a complete inventory of every networked device on your premises — including IoT sensors, cameras and building-management controllers?
2. Are your 'things' (IoT, facilities systems) segregated from your 'systems' (business data), or do they share a network as the casino's did?
3. When equipment is disposed of, do you hold a written data-destruction certificate to NIST 800-88 or equivalent?
4. Is your physical access actively monitored and the footage actually reviewed, or merely recorded?
5. If a critical facility lost power or cooling today, how long until information availability was affected — and is that within tolerance?

Action Deploy & Checklist

- Conduct a physical asset walk-through within 60 days documenting every networked device, including IoT, printers and access panels.
- Segregate all IoT and facilities-management devices onto a separate VLAN with no direct path to business data (the casino lesson).

- Run quarterly clear-desk and clear-screen inspections and publish the compliance results (A.7.7).
- Require a written data-destruction certificate (NIST 800-88 or equivalent) for every decommissioned device (A.7.14).
- Enable full-disk encryption and remote wipe on all portable devices and verify coverage (A.7.9).
- Commission an annual physical penetration test or independent physical-security walkthrough.

Controls in brief

A.7.1 | Physical Security Perimeters	
Purpose	To prevent unauthorised physical access, damage, and interference to the organisation's information and other associated assets.
Implementation Guidance	Security perimeters shall be defined and used to protect areas that contain information and other associated assets. Perimeter security should be proportionate to the sensitivity of what is protected. Multiple security perimeters are best practice: an outer perimeter (site boundary), an inner perimeter (building access), and a secure zone (data centre, server room, archive). Each perimeter should be clearly defined, physically robust, and independently controlled.
Key Metrics	• Percentage of secure areas with clearly defined and documented perimeters; number of physical security incidents per period; • Results of physical penetration tests.

A.7.1 | Physical Security Perimeters	
ASD ISM 2026	PRO (ISM 2026): Physical access controls must be implemented for all systems containing sensitive information.

A.7.2 | Physical Entry	
Purpose	To ensure that only authorised access to secure areas is permitted.
Implementation Guidance	Secure areas shall be protected by appropriate entry controls to ensure that only authorised personnel are allowed access. Entry controls should include: access cards or biometric systems with audit trail capability; visitor management — all visitors must be signed in, escorted, and recorded; contractor access procedures; challenge procedures for unescorted individuals; and CCTV coverage of all access points.
Key Metrics	• Number of tailgating incidents detected; • Visitor log completeness rate; • Percentage of access card events reviewed within 24 hours (for high-security areas).

A.7.3 | Securing Offices, Rooms and Facilities	
Purpose	To prevent unauthorised physical access, damage, and interference to the organisation's information in offices, rooms, and facilities.

A.7.3 | Securing Offices, Rooms and Facilities	
Implementation Guidance	Physical security for offices, rooms, and facilities shall be designed and applied. This includes: keeping sensitive areas out of publicly accessible directories; ensuring that unauthorised persons cannot overhear or view work in progress (shoulder surfing); securing filing cabinets and desk drawers; installing cable locks on portable equipment; and ensuring that fire-suppression systems, power protection, and air conditioning are appropriate.
Key Metrics	• Physical security assessment score; • Number of physical security incidents in office environments per period.

A.7.4 | Physical Security Monitoring	
Purpose	To detect and deter unauthorised physical access. [NEW in ISO 27002:2022]
Implementation Guidance	Premises shall be continuously monitored for unauthorised physical access. CCTV systems should provide coverage of all entry/exit points, server rooms, and high-security areas. Monitoring must be combined with alert and response procedures — CCTV footage is only useful if it is reviewed and acted upon. Monitoring records should be retained for a defined period consistent with legal requirements.

A.7.4 | Physical Security Monitoring	
Key Metrics	• CCTV system availability rate; • Percentage of physical security alerts investigated within defined timeframes; • CCTV retention period compliance.
ASD ISM 2026	ISM 2026 requires continuous monitoring of physical access to systems containing sensitive data.

A.7.5 | Protecting Against Physical and Environmental Threats	
Purpose	To prevent or reduce the consequences of events originating from physical and environmental threats.
Implementation Guidance	Physical protection against natural disasters, malicious attacks, or accidents shall be designed and applied, taking into account business continuity requirements. Environmental threats include: fire; flooding; earthquake; extreme weather; power failure; chemical contamination; and vandalism. Controls should include: fire detection and suppression; water/leak detection; uninterruptible power supplies (UPS); redundant cooling systems; and climate monitoring.
Key Metrics	• Environmental monitoring system availability; • Number of environmental incidents per period; • BCP test results covering environmental failure scenarios.

A.7.6 | Working in Secure Areas	
Purpose	To protect information and other associated assets in secure areas from damage and interference by personnel.
Implementation Guidance	Security measures for working in secure areas shall be designed and applied. This includes: prohibiting personal electronic devices unless specifically authorised; requiring escorted access for contractors; preventing unsupervised photography; requiring clean-desk practices within secure areas; ensuring that only need-to-know personnel are permitted in high-security areas.
Key Metrics	• Number of secure area policy violations detected per period; • Compliance rate with clean-desk policy in secure areas (from inspection audits).

A.7.7 | Clear Desk and Clear Screen	
Purpose	To reduce the risks of unauthorised access, loss, and damage to information on desks and screens.
Implementation Guidance	Clear desk rules for papers and removable storage media and clear screen rules for information processing facilities shall be defined and appropriately enforced. Workstations should be locked when unattended (automatic screen lock after defined idle period). Sensitive documents should not be left on desks overnight. Whiteboards and flipcharts with sensitive content should be erased after meetings. Printing of sensitive documents should be controlled.

A.7.7 | Clear Desk and Clear Screen	
Key Metrics	• Clear desk compliance rate (from inspection audits); • Percentage of workstations with screen lock configured to lock within defined idle period.

A.7.8 | Equipment Siting and Protection	
Purpose	To reduce the risks from physical and environmental threats and opportunities for unauthorised access.
Implementation Guidance	Equipment shall be sited and protected to reduce the risks from physical and environmental threats and opportunities for unauthorised access. Servers should be located in locked, access-controlled rooms. Cabling infrastructure should be protected against interception or damage. Equipment should be positioned to minimise shoulder surfing. Cooling and power should be adequate for the equipment load.
Key Metrics	• Percentage of server equipment in locked, • Access-controlled rooms; • Equipment siting compliance rate from physical audit.

A.7.9 | Security of Assets Off-Premises	
Purpose	To prevent loss, damage, theft, or compromise of off-premises equipment.
Implementation Guidance	Off-premises assets shall be protected. Assets taken off-premises — laptops, mobile phones, USB drives, paper documents — are at heightened risk of loss or theft. Controls include: full-disk encryption on all portable computing devices; remote wipe capability; VPN requirement when using public networks; prohibition on storing sensitive data on local storage without encryption; physical security of equipment when not in use.
Key Metrics	• Percentage of portable devices with full-disk encryption enabled; • Number of off-premises asset loss/theft incidents per period; • Mean time to remote-wipe after loss report.

A.7.10 | Storage Media	
Purpose	To prevent unauthorised disclosure, modification, removal, or destruction of information stored on storage media.
Implementation Guidance	Storage media shall be managed through their lifecycle of acquisition, use, transportation, and disposal in accordance with the organisation's classification scheme and handling requirements. Requirements include: formal media management procedures; encrypted storage for sensitive data; secure transfer procedures for physical media; and secure erasure or physical destruction at end of life.

A.7.10 | Storage Media	
Key Metrics	• Percentage of storage media inventoried and tracked; • Secure disposal compliance rate; • Number of media loss incidents per period.

A.7.11 | Supporting Utilities	
Purpose	To prevent loss, damage or compromise of information and other associated assets, or interruption to the organisation's operations due to failures in supporting utilities.
Implementation Guidance	Information processing facilities shall be protected from power failures and other disruptions caused by failures in supporting utilities. This includes: UPS systems; generator backup for critical facilities; redundant power feeds; regular testing of backup power systems; temperature and humidity monitoring; and emergency lighting.
Key Metrics	• UPS system availability; generator test frequency and pass rate; • Power event incidents per period.

A.7.12 | Cabling Security	
Purpose	To protect cables carrying power or data or supporting information services from interception, interference, or damage.

A.7.12 | Cabling Security	
Implementation Guidance	Cables carrying power or data or supporting information services shall be protected from interception, interference, or damage. Network cabling should be routed through conduit; data cables should be clearly identified and labelled; cable ducts should be locked where feasible; wireless networks should be the subject of surveys to detect rogue access points.
Key Metrics	• Number of cabling security incidents per period; • Cabling documentation completeness (percentage of network ports documented).

A.7.13 | Equipment Maintenance	
Purpose	To prevent failures of equipment resulting from insufficient maintenance.
Implementation Guidance	Equipment shall be maintained correctly to ensure its continued availability and integrity. All equipment subject to regular maintenance should have a documented maintenance schedule. Maintenance records should be retained. Maintenance performed by external parties should be supervised. Sensitive data should be removed from equipment before external maintenance.
Key Metrics	• Maintenance schedule compliance rate; • Equipment failure rate attributable to missed maintenance; • Percentage of maintenance activities with documented records.

A.7.14 | Secure Disposal or Re-Use of Equipment	
Purpose	To prevent leakage of information from equipment to be disposed of or re-used.
Implementation Guidance	All items of equipment containing storage media shall be verified to ensure that any sensitive data and licensed software has been removed or securely overwritten prior to disposal or re-use. Acceptable disposal methods include: certified data erasure (meeting NIST 800-88 standards); degaussing for magnetic media; physical shredding/ destruction for high-sensitivity media; use of certified WEEE recyclers with data destruction certificates.
Key Metrics	Percentage of disposed equipment with documented secure disposal record; data destruction certificate retention rate; number of data leakage incidents attributable to improper disposal per period.
ASD ISM 2026	ISM 2026: Equipment must be sanitised before disposal or transfer to remove all sensitive data.

Key Takeaways

- Physical controls (A.7) establish the environmental protection that technical controls depend upon — logical security cannot fully compensate for uncontrolled physical access.
- Physical Security Monitoring (A.7.4) is new in ISO 27002:2022, recognising that active monitoring — not just deterrence — is now a minimum expectation.
- The highest-risk physical controls are at the perimeter (A.7.1, A.7.2) and at end-of-life (A.7.14) — these are

where data exposures are most likely to result from physical control failures.

- Off-premises security (A.7.9) and storage media (A.7.10) are increasingly important as workforces become more mobile and organisations hold ever-larger volumes of sensitive data on portable devices.
- Physical and technical controls must be managed as an integrated whole — a breach of physical security is often the first step in a multi-stage attack that ultimately targets digital assets.

CHAPTER

8

TECHNOLOGICAL CONTROLS

ISO/IEC 27002:2022 A.8 — Thirty-Four Controls for the Technical Security Architecture

S.T.E.P.S.™ Engine — Operational Anchor: DO (the Technical Layer)

The last and largest of the four control chapters. The thirty-four technological controls of A.8 are the implementation layer of the ISMS — endpoints, access, data protection, monitoring, networks and secure development. Their value depends entirely on completeness and consistency: one unprotected account or unpatched system can defeat an otherwise sound architecture.

Chapter Overview

The thirty-four technological controls of ISO/IEC 27002:2022 Annex A.8 are where the ISMS becomes operational — the endpoints, access rules, data protections, monitoring, networks and secure-development practices that defend systems day to day.

The 2022 edition added seven controls that reflect a cloud-and-data-centric world: configuration management, information deletion, data masking, data-leakage prevention, monitoring activities, web filtering and secure coding. Yet the chapter's defining lesson is not about the newest control but the most basic: Colonial Pipeline, like WannaCry and Equifax before it, fell to ordinary gaps — a dormant account without MFA, weak network segregation, slow recovery. Logging and monitoring give the DEPLOY & CHECK step something to check; segregation and authentication remove the single points of failure attackers seek; tested backups shorten the worst day.

For India's SaaS sector these controls satisfy SOC 2 and the DPDPA at once, and Australia's Essential Eight proves that a disciplined handful of A.8 controls stops most attacks. Excellence here is the discipline of leaving no gap.

Chapter Objectives

By the end of this chapter, the reader will be able to:

- Explain why technological controls deliver value only when applied completely and consistently.
- Navigate the thirty-four A.8 controls across seven functional clusters.
- Identify the seven new A.8 controls in the 2022 edition and the gaps they close.
- Connect monitoring and detection controls to the DEPLOY & CHECK step of the S.T.E.P.S.™ framework.
- Draw the lessons of the Colonial Pipeline ransomware attack for authentication, segregation and resilience.

The Implementation Layer — and Its Fragility

Technological controls are where strategy finally touches the machine. They are the technical implementation of the information security architecture — the systems, tools, configurations, and technical processes that protect the organization's information assets in cyberspace.

With 34 controls, this is the largest control category in ISO 27002:2022. It covers endpoint security through to secure development, from access control mechanisms through to business continuity of information systems.

They are also where a single omission undoes everything above them: one legacy VPN account without multi-factor authentication, one unpatched server, one misconfigured firewall rule can hand an attacker the keys to an otherwise well-governed enterprise

The thirty-four controls of A.8 — the second-largest category — are therefore governed by a single principle: completeness and consistency matter more than sophistication.

Australia's Essential Eight, almost entirely an A.8 subset, exists precisely because a handful of these controls, applied without exception, prevent the majority of known attacks. This chapter presents the thirty-four in seven functional clusters.

Executive Insight

The most consequential technical-control failures of the era — Colonial Pipeline, WannaCry, Equifax — were not exotic. They were a missing MFA, an unapplied patch, an expired certificate. Excellence in A.8 is not about buying the newest tool; it is about leaving no gap in the controls you already have.

8.1 Cluster A — Endpoints, Access and Privilege (A.8.1–A.8.5, A.8.18, A.8.19)

This cluster governs who and what can act on systems. It secures endpoint devices (A.8.1), tightly manages privileged access rights (A.8.2), restricts information access to need-to-know (A.8.3), controls access to source code (A.8.4), enforces secure authentication including MFA (A.8.5), constrains the use of privileged utility programs (A.8.18), and controls the installation of software on operational systems (A.8.19).

Control	Intent & representative metric
A.8.1 User endpoint devices	Secure, managed endpoints — % endpoints under management/EDR
A.8.2 Privileged access rights	Tightly controlled, reviewed privilege — privileged accounts vs. baseline
A.8.3 Information access restriction	Need-to-know access to information — access-review findings
A.8.4 Access to source code	Controlled read/write to code repositories — unauthorised-access attempts
A.8.5 Secure authentication	Strong auth; MFA for privileged/remote access — MFA coverage rate
A.8.18 Privileged utility programs	Restricted, logged use of powerful utilities — utility-use exceptions
A.8.19 Software installation	Controlled installation on operational systems — unauthorised-software incidents

8.2 Cluster B — Malware, Vulnerability and Configuration (A.8.7–A.8.9)

This cluster keeps systems hardened and current. Protection against malware combines technical defences with awareness (A.8.7); management of technical vulnerabilities provides the patch discipline whose absence enabled WannaCry and Equifax (A.8.8); and configuration management, new in 2022, ensures systems are hardened to a known-good baseline and drift is detected (A.8.9).

Control	Intent & representative metric
A.8.7 Protection against malware	Layered anti-malware plus user awareness — malware-detection/dwell metrics
A.8.8 Management of technical vulnerabilities	Timely, tracked patching against SLAs — critical-patch SLA compliance
A.8.9 Configuration management [NEW]	Hardened baselines; drift detected and corrected — % systems on approved baseline

8.3 Cluster C — Data Protection (A.8.10–A.8.12, A.8.24)

Three of these four controls are new in 2022, reflecting how decisively data protection has moved to the centre. Information deletion ensures data is removed when no longer needed, shrinking the blast radius (A.8.10); data masking limits exposure of sensitive data and PII (A.8.11); data-leakage prevention detects and blocks unauthorised exfiltration (A.8.12); and the use of cryptography protects confidentiality and integrity in transit and at rest (A.8.24). The Latitude breach — enlarged by excessive retention of legacy identity data — is the cautionary tale for this cluster.

Control	Intent & representative metric
A.8.10 Information deletion [NEW]	Delete data when no longer required — retention-policy compliance
A.8.11 Data masking [NEW]	Mask/obfuscate sensitive data and PII — % non-prod data masked

Control	Intent & representative metric
A.8.12 Data leakage prevention [NEW]	Detect and prevent unauthorised exfiltration — DLP events; blocked transfers
A.8.24 Use of cryptography	Encryption and key management in transit/at rest — % regulated data encrypted

8.4 Cluster D — Logging, Monitoring and Time (A.8.15–A.8.17)

You cannot improve what you cannot see, and this cluster is the technical foundation of the DEPLOY & CHECK step. Logging captures events for detection and forensics (A.8.15); monitoring activities, new in 2022, analyses those logs to detect abnormal behaviour and potential incidents (A.8.16); and clock synchronisation ensures timestamps across systems are consistent enough to reconstruct an attack (A.8.17). Detection latency — the months that elapsed at SolarWinds, Marriott and Equifax — is the failure this cluster exists to prevent.

Control	Intent & representative metric
A.8.15 Logging	Capture security-relevant events for detection and forensics — log-coverage of critical systems
A.8.16 Monitoring activities [NEW]	Analyse activity to detect abnormal behaviour — MTTD; alert investigation rate
A.8.17 Clock synchronisation	Consistent time across systems for correlation — % systems time-synchronised

8.5 Cluster E — Capacity, Backup and Resilience (A.8.6, A.8.13, A.8.14)

This cluster keeps information available. Capacity management ensures resources meet demand (A.8.6); information backup provides tested, recoverable copies — ideally immutable or air-gapped against ransomware (A.8.13); and redundancy of information-processing facilities provides failover for critical services (A.8.14). The slow recovery at Colonial Pipeline, where operational systems had to be integrity-checked before restart, shows why tested recovery, not just backup, is the real control.

Control	Intent & representative metric
A.8.6 Capacity management	Resources matched to demand — capacity-related incidents
A.8.13 Information backup	Tested, recoverable, ransomware-resistant backups — restore-test success rate
A.8.14 Redundancy of facilities	Failover for critical processing — redundancy coverage of critical systems

8.6 Cluster F — Network Security (A.8.20–A.8.23)

This cluster defends the connective tissue. Networks security protects the network and its devices (A.8.20); security of network services governs the security mechanisms and service levels of network services (A.8.21); segregation of networks separates environments by trust — the IT/OT division whose absence amplified Colonial Pipeline (A.8.22); and web filtering, new in 2022, blocks access to malicious or unauthorised web resources (A.8.23).

Control	Intent & representative metric
A.8.20 Networks security	Protect networks and networked devices — network-security incidents
A.8.21 Security of network services	Security mechanisms and SLAs for network services — service-security coverage
A.8.22 Segregation of networks	Separate environments by trust (e.g., IT/OT, guest/IoT) — % critical zones segmented
A.8.23 Web filtering [NEW]	Block malicious/unauthorised web resources — blocked-access events

8.7 Cluster G — Secure Development and Change (A.8.25–A.8.34)

The largest cluster, vital for any organisation that builds software. It establishes a secure development lifecycle (A.8.25), defines application security requirements (A.8.26), applies secure architecture and engineering principles (A.8.27), mandates secure coding — new in 2022 (A.8.28), requires security testing in development and acceptance (A.8.29), governs outsourced development (A.8.30), separates development, test and production environments (A.8.31), controls change (A.8.32), protects test information (A.8.33), and protects information systems during audit testing (A.8.34). The governing idea is to 'shift security left': a vulnerability caught in design costs a fraction of one found in production.

Control	Intent & representative metric
A.8.25 Secure development lifecycle	Security built into the SDLC — % releases through secure SDLC
A.8.26 Application security requirements	Security requirements defined per application — requirements coverage

Control	Intent & representative metric
A.8.27 Secure architecture & engineering	Secure-by-design principles applied — architecture-review coverage
A.8.28 Secure coding [NEW]	Secure coding standards reduce vulnerabilities — defect density in code review
A.8.29 Security testing	Testing in development and acceptance — % builds with security tests
A.8.30 Outsourced development	Security governed for outsourced code — supplier-code assurance rate
A.8.31 Separation of environments	Dev/test/prod separated — environment-separation compliance
A.8.32 Change management	Controlled, reviewed change — unauthorised-change incidents
A.8.33 Test information	Protect data used in testing — % test data masked/synthetic
A.8.34 Protection during audit testing	Limit audit-test impact on live systems — audit-related incidents

Case Study: Colonial Pipeline (2021) — Technological Controls Under Fire

On 7 May 2021, the DarkSide ransomware group struck Colonial Pipeline, operator of the largest refined-fuel pipeline in the United States, carrying roughly 45% of the East Coast's fuel. Initial access came through a single compromised password for a legacy VPN account that was no longer in active use and — critically — did not require multi-factor authentication. The attackers exfiltrated around 100 GB of data and encrypted IT systems. Unable to be certain the operational-technology environment was safe, Colonial shut the pipeline down preemptively, triggering fuel shortages and panic buying across the East Coast. The company paid a ransom of 75 Bitcoin (about US$4.4 million); the Department of Justice later recovered 63.7 Bitcoin (about US$2.3 million).

Technological-control failures

A.8.5 (secure authentication): a dormant legacy VPN account, still live and without MFA, was the entire entry point.

A.8.2 (privileged access): the compromised account carried broader access than its purpose required.

A.8.22 (segregation of networks): inadequate IT/OT separation meant a corporate-network compromise threatened the operational pipeline, forcing the shutdown.

A.8.13 (backup & recovery): recovery was slowed by the need to verify operational-system integrity before restart.

Lessons — Colonial Pipeline

Decommission dormant accounts and enforce MFA everywhere: the breach hinged on one forgotten VPN login.

Segregate IT from OT so an office compromise cannot threaten physical operations.

Backups are only as good as tested recovery; a clean restore path shortens the worst day of the year.

Regional Lens: The Technical Layer in India and Australia

India — Cloud-Native Security and the Essential Controls

For India's cloud-native technology and SaaS sector, A.8 is the daily operating reality: secure authentication and MFA (A.8.5), patch and configuration discipline (A.8.8–9), encryption (A.8.24), monitoring (A.8.15–16) and a secure SDLC (A.8.25–29) are precisely the controls that satisfy SOC 2 and the DPDPA's 'reasonable security safeguards' simultaneously. The Cosmos Bank heist examined earlier was, at the technical layer, a failure of monitoring (A.8.15–16) and segregation (A.8.22) — the switch traffic was never watched — underscoring that detection at the right layer is the decisive control in a digital-finance environment.

Australia — The Essential Eight as A.8 in Practice

Australia's ASD Essential Eight is essentially the A.8 core distilled into a prioritised baseline: application control and software restriction (A.8.19), patching applications and operating systems (A.8.8), MFA (A.8.5), restricting admin privileges (A.8.2), application hardening and configuration (A.8.9, A.8.27), malware protection (A.8.7), logging and monitoring (A.8.15–16) and backups (A.8.13). Implemented consistently, these few controls — the same ones whose absence enabled Colonial Pipeline — stop the majority of known intrusions, which is exactly why Australia mandates them as a maturity model.

Key Takeaways

- Technological controls (A.8) are the implementation layer; their value depends on completeness and consistency, not sophistication.
- Seven A.8 controls are new in 2022: configuration management (A.8.9), information deletion (A.8.10), data masking (A.8.11), DLP (A.8.12), monitoring activities (A.8.16), web filtering (A.8.23) and secure coding (A.8.28).
- Logging and monitoring (A.8.15–16) are the technical foundation of the DEPLOY & CHECK step — you cannot improve what you cannot see.
- Secure-development controls (A.8.25–29) make 'shifting security left' concrete and far cheaper than fixing production.
- Network segregation (A.8.22) and secure authentication (A.8.5) are recurring single points of failure in major breaches.
- Colonial Pipeline turned on a dormant VPN account without MFA and weak IT/OT segregation — ordinary controls, extraordinary consequences.

Controls in Brief

The ASD ISM 2026 PRO (Protect) and DET (Detect) principles find their fullest expression in technological controls. The Essential Eight — the ASD's baseline cybersecurity controls — are almost entirely addressed within the A.8 technological control set. This chapter is the practical engineering backbone of the ISMS.

A.8.1 | User End Point Devices	
Purpose	To protect information processed by, stored on, or transmitted over user endpoint devices.
Implementation Guidance	Policies and supporting security measures shall be implemented to protect information accessed from, processed on, or via user endpoint devices. Controls include: mobile device management (MDM) or equivalent for all endpoints; application whitelisting or app store restrictions; remote wipe capability; automatic screen lock and strong authentication; full-disk encryption; endpoint protection software (anti-malware, EDR); and control of removable media.
Key Metrics	Percentage of endpoints enrolled in MDM; endpoint protection deployment rate; mean time to detect and remediate endpoint threats.
ASD ISM 2026	PRO (ISM 2026): Endpoints must be hardened, patched, and monitored. The ASD Essential Eight requires application control, patch management, and MFA for all endpoints.

A.8.2 | Privileged Access Rights	
Purpose	To ensure authorised user access and prevent unauthorised access to systems and services.
Implementation Guidance	The allocation and use of privileged access rights shall be restricted and controlled. Privileged accounts should be used only when necessary and for the minimum time required. Separation of administrator accounts from standard user accounts is essential. Privileged Access Management (PAM) solutions should be used to manage, rotate, and audit the use of privileged credentials. All privileged actions should be logged.

A.8.2 | Privileged Access Rights	
Key Metrics	Number of privileged accounts; ratio of privileged to standard accounts; privileged account activity audit coverage; mean time to revoke privilege after role change.
ASD ISM 2026	PRO-04 (ISM 2026): Privileged access must be restricted and subject to additional authentication and logging requirements.

A.8.3 | Information Access Restriction	
Purpose	To ensure that information and application system functions are restricted in accordance with the access control policy.
Implementation Guidance	Access to information and application system functions shall be restricted in accordance with the access control policy. Role-based access control (RBAC) should be implemented so that access is determined by business role, not individual negotiation. Access to sensitive information should require explicit authorisation from the information owner. Access logs should be reviewed regularly.
Key Metrics	Percentage of systems with RBAC implemented; access review finding rate (inappropriate access found per 100 accounts reviewed).

A.8.4 | Access to Source Code	
Purpose	To prevent the introduction of unauthorised functionality and to avoid unintentional changes to valuable software.

A.8.4 | Access to Source Code	
Implementation Guidance	Read and write access to source code, development tools, and software libraries shall be appropriately managed. Source code should be stored in a version control system with access controls. Separation of duties should prevent the same individual from writing, testing, and deploying code in production. Code review processes should be enforced.
Key Metrics	Percentage of code repositories with enforced access controls; percentage of code changes reviewed before merge; number of unauthorised code changes per period.

A.8.5 | Secure Authentication	
Purpose	To ensure that a user, service, or system has proven its identity.
Implementation Guidance	Secure authentication technologies and procedures shall be implemented based on information access restrictions. Authentication strength should be proportionate to the sensitivity of what is being accessed. Multi-factor authentication (MFA) should be mandatory for: all privileged accounts; all remote access; all cloud service administration; and any access to sensitive or regulated data. Passwordless authentication (FIDO2, passkeys) should be adopted where technically feasible.
Key Metrics	MFA adoption rate by access tier; number of authentication-related incidents per period; percentage of systems supporting MFA.

A.8.5 | Secure Authentication	
ASD ISM 2026	PRO (ISM 2026): Multi-factor authentication is required for all privileged access and all remote access. The ASD Essential Eight mandates MFA for privileged users, remote access, and important data repositories.

A.8.6 | Capacity Management	
Purpose	To ensure that the required capacity of information processing facilities, resources, and systems is provided.
Implementation Guidance	The use of resources shall be monitored and adjusted, and projections shall be made of future capacity requirements to ensure the required system performance. Capacity planning should cover: storage; network bandwidth; compute resources; and cloud service quotas. Alerts should trigger when thresholds are approached. Capacity incidents (performance degradation, outages caused by resource exhaustion) should be tracked.
Key Metrics	Percentage of critical systems with capacity monitoring alerts configured; number of capacity-related incidents per period.

A.8.7 | Protection against Malware	
Purpose	To ensure that information and other associated assets are protected against malware.

A.8.7 | Protection against Malware	
Implementation Guidance	Protection against malware shall be implemented and supported by appropriate user awareness. Controls include: anti-malware software on all endpoints and servers; email gateway filtering; web proxy filtering; application control/whitelisting; regular malware scan schedules; automatic update of malware signatures; and incident response procedures for malware infections.
Key Metrics	Anti-malware deployment coverage; malware detection rate; mean time to contain malware incidents; number of malware incidents per period.
ASD ISM 2026	PRO (ISM 2026): All endpoints and servers must have anti-malware protection. The ASD Essential Eight includes application control and patching as the primary malware defences.

A.8.8 | Management of Technical Vulnerabilities	
Purpose	To prevent exploitation of technical vulnerabilities.
Implementation Guidance	Information about technical vulnerabilities of information systems in use shall be obtained, the organisation's exposure to such vulnerabilities shall be evaluated, and appropriate measures shall be taken. Vulnerability management should include: regular vulnerability scans of all systems; penetration testing on a risk-based schedule; a patch management process with defined SLAs for patching (critical within 48 hours; high within 14 days); and tracking of vulnerability remediation.

A.8.8 | Management of Technical Vulnerabilities	
Key Metrics	Mean time to patch critical vulnerabilities; percentage of systems scanned within the last 30 days; number of known exploited vulnerabilities open for more than 30 days.
ASD ISM 2026	PRO (ISM 2026): Systems must be patched within defined timeframes. The ASD Essential Eight requires patching of operating systems, applications, and firmware within defined timeframes based on criticality.

A.8.9 | Configuration Management	
Purpose	To ensure hardware, software, services, and networks function correctly with required security settings, and settings are not altered by unauthorised or incorrect changes.
Implementation Guidance	Configurations, including security configurations, of hardware, software, services, and networks shall be established, documented, implemented, monitored, and reviewed. Secure baseline configurations (hardening standards) should be defined for all system types. Configuration management should be integrated with change management. Configuration drift should be detected automatically and remediated.
Key Metrics	Percentage of systems compliant with baseline configuration standards; configuration drift detection coverage; number of configuration-related security incidents per period.

A.8.9 | Configuration Management	
ASD ISM 2026	PRO (ISM 2026): Systems must be configured securely prior to deployment. The ASD Essential Eight includes application hardening as a baseline control.

A.8.10 | Information Deletion	
Purpose	To prevent unnecessary exposure of sensitive information and to comply with legal, statutory, regulatory, and contractual requirements for information deletion. [NEW in ISO 27002:2022]
Implementation Guidance	Information stored in information systems, devices, or any other storage media shall be deleted when it is no longer required. Deletion should be secure — meeting NIST 800-88 standards for the sensitivity of the data. Automated data lifecycle management tools should be used where volumes make manual deletion impractical. Deletion should be evidenced for regulated data categories.
Key Metrics	Percentage of data subject to automated lifecycle management; number of confirmed data retention violations per period; deletion certificate retention rate for regulated data.

A.8.11 | Data Masking	
Purpose	To limit the exposure of sensitive data including PII and to comply with legal, statutory, regulatory and contractual requirements. [NEW in ISO 27002:2022]

A.8.11 | Data Masking	
Implementation Guidance	Data masking shall be used in accordance with the organisation's topic-specific policy on access control and other related topic-specific policies, and business requirements, taking applicable legislation into consideration. Data masking should be applied to: test environments (never use real personal data in testing); analytics environments; customer-facing displays of sensitive data (e.g., partial card number display); and development environments.
Key Metrics	Percentage of non-production environments using masked data; number of data masking violations per period.

A.8.12 | Data Leakage Prevention	
Purpose	To detect and prevent the unauthorised disclosure and extraction of information by individuals or systems. [NEW in ISO 27002:2022]
Implementation Guidance	Data leakage prevention (DLP) measures shall be applied to systems, networks, and any other devices that process, store, or transmit sensitive information. DLP should cover: email (outbound); web (HTTP/HTTPS upload); endpoint (USB, local print); and cloud applications. DLP policies should be tuned to minimise false positives while ensuring that intentional exfiltration attempts are detected.
Key Metrics	Number of DLP alerts per period; percentage of DLP alerts investigated within defined SLA; number of confirmed data exfiltration incidents per period.

A.8.12 | Data Leakage Prevention	
ASD ISM 2026	DET (ISM 2026): Organisations must have visibility of data movements, particularly for sensitive and regulated data.

A.8.13 | Information Backup	
Purpose	To enable recovery from loss of data or systems.
Implementation Guidance	Backup copies of information, software, and systems shall be maintained and regularly tested in accordance with the agreed topic-specific policy on backup. Backup requirements should include: frequency (backup schedule aligned with RPO); retention (how long backups are kept); coverage (which systems and data are backed up); storage location (including offsite or cloud backup); encryption (backups should be encrypted); and testing (restoration tests must be performed regularly).
Key Metrics	Backup completion rate; backup restoration test success rate; mean time to restore from backup; RPO/RTO test results.
ASD ISM 2026	REC (ISM 2026): Data backups must be maintained and regularly tested to ensure recovery capability.

A.8.14 | Redundancy of Information Processing Facilities	
Purpose	To ensure continued availability of information processing facilities.

A.8.14 | Redundancy of Information Processing Facilities	
Implementation Guidance	Information processing facilities shall be implemented with redundancy sufficient to meet availability requirements. Redundancy measures include: clustered servers; load-balanced applications; redundant network paths; multi-zone cloud deployments; hot/warm/cold standby configurations; and regular failover tests to verify that redundancy is effective.
Key Metrics	System availability rate against SLA; redundancy test frequency and pass rate; number of availability incidents attributable to single points of failure.

A.8.15 | Logging	
Purpose	To record events and generate evidence of the integrity of the ISMS by detecting anomalous events.
Implementation Guidance	Event logs that record user activities, exceptions, faults, and information security events shall be produced, stored, protected, and analysed. Log management should ensure: comprehensive coverage of critical systems; tamper-proof storage; defined retention periods; centralisation (SIEM); and regular review. Minimum logging events include: authentication attempts (success and failure); privileged account activities; configuration changes; access to sensitive data; and network connection events.

A.8.15 | Logging	
Key Metrics	Percentage of critical systems with logging enabled; log storage retention compliance; SIEM alert review rate within defined SLA.
ASD ISM 2026	DET (ISM 2026): Logging must be enabled for all systems handling sensitive data. Log retention must meet defined minimum periods.

A.8.16 | Monitoring Activities	
Purpose	To detect abnormal behaviour and potential information security incidents. [NEW in ISO 27002:2022]
Implementation Guidance	Networks, systems, and applications shall be monitored for anomalous behaviour and potential information security incidents. A Security Operations Centre (SOC) or equivalent function should provide real-time monitoring capability. Anomaly detection should be based on defined baselines for normal behaviour. Alerts should be tiered by severity and have documented response procedures.
Key Metrics	SOC coverage rate (percentage of critical systems monitored); mean time to detect (MTTD); number of alerts per period and alert-to-incident conversion rate.
ASD ISM 2026	DET (ISM 2026): Continuous monitoring must be in place for all systems containing sensitive data. The ISM emphasises behavioural analytics and anomaly detection as key detection mechanisms.

A.8.17 | Clock Synchronisation	
Purpose	To enable correlation of security events and other recorded data, and to support investigations of information security incidents.
Implementation Guidance	The clocks of all information processing systems within an organisation shall be synchronised to a single reference time source. NTP (Network Time Protocol) should be used with a trusted time source. Clock drift should be monitored and alerted on. Correct timestamps are essential for log correlation, incident investigation, and legal evidence.
Key Metrics	Percentage of systems synchronised to approved NTP sources; number of systems with clock drift exceeding defined threshold.

A.8.18 | Use of Privileged Utility Programs	
Purpose	To ensure that the use of utility programs that might be capable of overriding system and application controls is restricted and tightly controlled.
Implementation Guidance	The use of utility programs that might be capable of overriding system and application controls shall be restricted and tightly controlled. System utilities (e.g., password crackers, network scanners, debugging tools) should be: inventoried; restricted to authorised users; used only for legitimate purposes; subject to enhanced logging; and removed from production systems where not required.

A.8.18 | Use of Privileged Utility Programs	
Key Metrics	Number of unapproved utilities detected on systems per period; privileged utility access review frequency.

A.8.19 | Installation of Software on Operational Systems	
Purpose	To ensure the integrity of operational systems and prevent exploitation of technical vulnerabilities.
Implementation Guidance	Procedures and measures shall be implemented to securely manage software installation on operational systems. Controls include: application whitelisting (only approved software can run); formal software approval process; prohibition on user installation of unauthorised software; software inventory maintained; and SCCM or equivalent for managed deployment.
Key Metrics	Percentage of endpoints with application control enabled; number of unauthorised software installations detected per period.
ASD ISM 2026	PRO (ISM 2026): The ASD Essential Eight requires application control — whitelisting — as a baseline control on all endpoints and servers.

A.8.20 | Networks Security	
Purpose	To protect networks and their supporting infrastructure from threats and to maintain security for systems and applications communicating over networks.

A.8.20 | Networks Security	
Implementation Guidance	Networks shall be managed and controlled to protect information in systems and applications. Network security controls include: network segmentation; firewall policies; IDS/IPS; network access control (NAC); monitoring of network traffic; prohibition on connecting unauthorised devices; and regular review of firewall rule sets.
Key Metrics	Network security assessment score; number of firewall rule review findings; number of unauthorised network connections detected per period.
ASD ISM 2026	PRO/DET (ISM 2026): Networks must be segmented and monitored. Network-based detection capabilities are essential for identifying lateral movement.

A.8.21 | Security of Network Services	
Purpose	To ensure security of network services, whether provided internally or outsourced.
Implementation Guidance	Security mechanisms, service levels, and management requirements of network services shall be identified and included in network services agreements, whether these services are provided in-house or outsourced. Requirements include: encryption of traffic between sites; DDoS mitigation for internet-facing services; network service SLAs including security incident notification.

A.8.21 | Security of Network Services	
Key Metrics	Percentage of network service agreements with security requirements; network service SLA compliance rate; number of network service security incidents per period.

A.8.22 | Segregation of Networks	
Purpose	To limit the impact of a security incident by creating network boundaries between different types of systems and data.
Implementation Guidance	Groups of information services, users, and information systems shall be segregated in networks. Network segregation should reflect data sensitivity and system criticality. Minimum segmentation: separate OT/IT networks; DMZ for internet-facing services; separate VLAN for management traffic; separate guest Wi-Fi network; and zero-trust micro-segmentation for high-sensitivity environments.
Key Metrics	Number of network segments defined and documented; percentage of critical systems in appropriately segregated network zones; number of lateral movement incidents detected per period.
ASD ISM 2026	PRO (ISM 2026): Network segmentation is essential for containing the impact of security incidents.

A.8.23 | Web Filtering	
Purpose	To protect systems from being compromised by malware and to prevent use of unauthorised web resources. [NEW in ISO 27002:2022]

A.8.23 | Web Filtering	
Implementation Guidance	Access to external websites shall be managed to reduce exposure to malicious content. Web filtering should: block known malicious categories (malware, phishing, C2 infrastructure); block non-business categories (adult content, gambling etc.) per policy; provide HTTPS inspection capability; and log all web access for security review. DNS filtering provides a complementary layer of protection.
Key Metrics	Malicious site blocking rate (from threat intelligence testing); number of malware downloads blocked per period; web filtering coverage across all internet egress points.
ASD ISM 2026	PRO (ISM 2026): Web content filtering is a baseline protection mechanism.

A.8.24 | Use of Cryptography	
Purpose	To ensure proper and effective use of cryptography to protect the confidentiality, authenticity, and integrity of information.
Implementation Guidance	Rules for the effective use of cryptography, including cryptographic key management, shall be defined and implemented. Cryptographic controls should include: approved cipher suites and key lengths (aligned with NIST or equivalent guidance); TLS 1.2 minimum for all network communications (TLS 1.3 preferred); full-disk encryption for all endpoints and portable media; database encryption for sensitive data; key management procedures including key rotation, escrow, and revocation; and prohibition of deprecated algorithms (MD5, SHA-1, DES, RC4).

A.8.24 | Use of Cryptography	
Key Metrics	Percentage of data in transit protected by TLS 1.2+; percentage of endpoints with full-disk encryption; cryptographic algorithm compliance rate against approved standards.
ASD ISM 2026	PRO (ISM 2026): Strong cryptography must be used for all sensitive data in transit and at rest. Deprecated algorithms must not be used.

A.8.25 | Secure Development Lifecycle	
Purpose	To ensure that information security is designed and implemented within the secure development lifecycle.
Implementation Guidance	Rules for the secure development of software and systems shall be established and applied. The Secure Development Lifecycle (SDLC) should incorporate: security requirements definition at project initiation; threat modelling; secure design review; secure coding standards; peer code review; SAST (static application security testing); DAST (dynamic application security testing); penetration testing before go-live; and security acceptance testing criteria.
Key Metrics	Percentage of development projects with security reviews at defined SDLC gates; number of security vulnerabilities identified in code review versus production; SAST/DAST scan coverage.

A.8.26 | Application Security Requirements	
Purpose	To ensure information security is identified and addressed when developing or acquiring applications.
Implementation Guidance	Information security requirements shall be identified, specified, and approved when developing or acquiring applications. Security requirements should address: authentication and authorisation; input validation and output encoding; error handling and logging; session management; cryptographic requirements; and third-party component security.
Key Metrics	Percentage of new applications with documented security requirements; number of security requirements fulfilled vs. deferred at go-live.

A.8.27 | Secure System Architecture and Engineering Principles	
Purpose	To ensure systems and architectures are designed securely.
Implementation Guidance	Principles for engineering secure systems shall be established, documented, maintained, and applied to any information system implementation efforts. Security architecture principles include: defence in depth; least privilege; fail-safe defaults; zero trust architecture; security by design; minimise attack surface; and separation of privilege. Architecture decisions should be documented and subject to security review.

A.8.27 | Secure System Architecture and Engineering Principles	
Key Metrics	Security architecture review coverage (percentage of significant architectural changes reviewed); number of architecture-level security defects found in production per period.

A.8.28 | Secure Coding	
Purpose	To ensure software is written securely in order to reduce the number of possible information security vulnerabilities in software. [NEW in ISO 27002:2022]
Implementation Guidance	Secure coding principles shall be applied to software development. The OWASP Secure Coding Practices and OWASP Top 10 provide the industry-standard baseline. Secure coding should be taught to all developers; enforced through code review; validated through SAST tools; and verified through penetration testing. Common vulnerabilities to prevent include: SQL injection; XSS; CSRF; insecure deserialisation; and use of components with known vulnerabilities.
Key Metrics	Secure coding training completion rate for developers; OWASP Top 10 vulnerability prevalence in codebase (tracked over time); mean time to remediate code-level security findings.

A.8.29 | Security Testing in Development and Acceptance	
Purpose	To verify conformance to information security requirements when systems are developed or acquired.

A.8.29 | Security Testing in Development and Acceptance	
Implementation Guidance	Security testing processes and criteria shall be defined and implemented in the development lifecycle. Security testing should be: integrated into CI/CD pipelines (automated SAST, dependency scanning); performed by security specialists (DAST, penetration testing); conducted in a dedicated test environment; and documented with formal acceptance criteria. Security test results must be reviewed and tracked to remediation before go-live.
Key Metrics	Percentage of releases with completed security testing; security defect escape rate (vulnerabilities found in production versus development); mean time to remediate security test findings.

A.8.30 | Outsourced Development	
Purpose	To ensure the information security of outsourced software development.
Implementation Guidance	The organisation shall direct, monitor, and review the activities related to outsourced system development. Requirements for outsourced development include: security requirements in development contracts; right to review code and conduct security audits; background checks on developers with access to sensitive systems; secure handover procedures; and retention of source code in escrow.
Key Metrics	Percentage of outsourced development contracts with security requirements; security audit completion rate for outsourced development projects.

A.8.31 | Separation of Development, Test and Production Environments	
Purpose	To protect the production environment and data by separating development, test, and production environments.
Implementation Guidance	Development, testing, and production environments shall be separated and secured. Production data must not be used in development or test environments. Developers should not have access to production systems except through a formal change management process. System migrations between environments should follow documented procedures.
Key Metrics	Percentage of organisations with documented separation policy; number of incidents caused by inadequate environment separation per period; production data in non-production environment detection rate.

A.8.32 | Change Management	
Purpose	To preserve information security when executing changes.
Implementation Guidance	Changes to information processing facilities and information systems shall be subject to change management procedures. Change management should include: formal change request and approval process; risk assessment for all significant changes; testing in non-production environments; rollback plan; communication to affected parties; and post-implementation review. Emergency changes should have a rapid approval path but must still be documented.

A.8.32 | Change Management	
Key Metrics	Percentage of changes implemented through formal change management process; number of incidents caused by unauthorized or inadequately tested changes per period; emergency change rate.

A.8.33 | Test Information	
Purpose	To ensure the relevance of testing and protection of operational information used for testing.
Implementation Guidance	Test information shall be appropriately selected, protected, and controlled. Production data — particularly personal data — must not be used in testing without appropriate anonymisation or masking. Test data should be created or generated to reflect realistic conditions without exposing real personal information. Test data should be disposed of securely after use.
Key Metrics	Percentage of test environments using anonymised/masked data; number of incidents involving real personal data in test environments per period.

A.8.34 | Protection of Information Systems during Audit Testing	
Purpose	To minimise the impact of audit activities on operational systems.
Implementation Guidance	Audit tests and other assurance activities involving assessment of operational systems shall be planned and agreed between the auditor, system owner, and authorising officer. Audit activities should be: scheduled to minimise operational impact; conducted using read-only access where possible; agreed with system owners in advance; monitored to prevent degradation; and documented with access logs retained.
Key Metrics	Number of operational incidents caused by audit activities per period; audit planning completeness rate.

Key Takeaways

- Technological controls (A.8) are the technical implementation backbone of the ISMS — 34 controls covering endpoint security, access management, network security, cryptography, monitoring, and secure development.
- The ASD Essential Eight — application control, patch applications, patch operating systems, MFA, restrict administrative privileges, back up data, disable macOS macros, and application control — are almost entirely addressed within the A.8 control set.
- New 2022 controls — Information Deletion (A.8.10), Data Masking (A.8.11), Data Leakage Prevention (A.8.12), Monitoring Activities (A.8.16), Web Filtering (A.8.23), and Secure Coding (A.8.28) — reflect the contemporary threat and technology landscape.

- Monitoring (A.8.15, A.8.16) and detection capability is the technical foundation for the Deploy & Check step of the 7-Step Framework — you cannot improve what you cannot see.
- The secure development lifecycle controls (A.8.25-A.8.29) are critical for organizations that develop software — shifting security left into design and development is dramatically more cost-effective than finding vulnerabilities in production.

Reflection Questions

1. Do you have any dormant or legacy accounts — like Colonial's VPN profile — still live and without MFA?
2. Are your most sensitive networks (and any OT or IoT) segregated from your corporate IT, or flat enough that one compromise reaches everything?
3. When did you last successfully restore from backup in a test — not merely confirm a backup ran?
4. Which of the seven new 2022 controls (deletion, masking, DLP, monitoring, config, web filtering, secure coding) are not yet implemented?
5. Could your monitoring detect an intruder moving laterally today, or would detection take the months it took the largest victims?

Action Deploy & Checklist

- Inventory and disable dormant/legacy accounts and enforce MFA on all remote and privileged access within 30 days (A.8.5, A.8.2).
- Implement the Essential Eight as a prioritised A.8 baseline and measure maturity against it.

- Establish patch SLAs for critical vulnerabilities and track compliance (A.8.8); define hardened configuration baselines (A.8.9).
- Run a backup-restore test for your most critical systems and record recovery time and integrity (A.8.13).
- Segregate IT from OT/IoT and confirm critical zones are isolated (A.8.22).
- Stand up centralised logging and monitoring with a measured mean-time-to-detect (A.8.15–16).

CHAPTER

9

ENSURING SUCCESS FOR YOUR ORGANISATION WITH ISO/IEC 27002:2022

From control implementation to sustainable ISMS excellence

Chapter Overview

S.T.E.P.S.™ Engine — Operational Anchor: DO & DEPLOY & CHECK and DRIVE

Implementing the 93 controls is the beginning, not the destination. This chapter is the engine room of the DEPLOY & CHECK and DRIVE steps: the measurement, maturity and integration disciplines that turn a control architecture into a system that demonstrably reduces risk and keeps improving.

Implementing controls builds the architecture of security; measuring, maturing and integrating that architecture is what makes it deliver. This chapter supplies the disciplines of the DEPLOY & CHECK and DRIVE steps: a three-tier measurement model that serves board, programme and operations; the ROSI and ALE models that express value and exposure in financial terms; the Balanced Scorecard and CISO dashboard that report performance across the dimensions stakeholders care about; and the five-level maturity model that turns 'are we certified?'

into the better question, 'are we improving, and can we prove it?' The recurring causes of failure — documentation theatre, weak management commitment, narrow scope, compliance-only risk assessment, neglect of the human element, and above all inadequate measurement — are all avoidable once named. Integration with privacy, continuity and quality management multiplies the return on the investment. As maturity-led programmes show, security measured and matured becomes a competitive advantage; for India it is the climb to Level 4 that wins global trust, and in Australia it is board-level reporting enforced as regulation.

Chapter Objectives

By the end of this chapter, the reader will be able to:

- Explain why measurement is the precondition for evidence-based security governance.
- Apply a three-tier metrics model and quantify value using ROSI and ALE.
- Assess ISMS maturity against the five-level Capability Maturity Model and target the next level.
- Recognise and avoid the most common causes of ISMS implementation failure.
- Integrate the ISMS with privacy, continuity and quality management systems for efficiency and value.

The Certificate Is Not the Destination

Implementing the 93 controls of ISO/IEC 27002:2022 provides the architecture of information security. It does not, by itself, deliver the outcome — reduced risk, greater resilience, enabled business. That outcome requires sustained management attention, disciplined measurement, and a culture that treats security as a shared responsibility rather than the security team's problem. A certificate on the wall proves a system existed on audit day; a measured, maturing programme proves the system is working every day. This chapter is about the difference between the two.

> **Executive Insight**
>
> Certification proves conformance at a moment in time; maturity proves capability over time. The boards that ask "are we certified?" get a yes-or-no answer. The boards that ask "are we maturing, and can you show me the trend?" get a security programme.

9.1 The Measurement Imperative

As W. Krag Brotby observed, security is one of the few areas of management without a well-understood canon of measurement — and without measurement, governance is intuition, not evidence. Senior management cannot make sound decisions about investment, prioritisation or risk acceptance without reliable data. Effective measurement operates at three levels, each serving a different audience, so that the right information reaches the right decision-maker at the right altitude.

Metric level	Audience	Example measures
Strategic / governance	Board, C-suite	Residual-risk posture; risks above appetite; alignment with strategy
Security programme	CISO, security management	Control-maturity scores; incident trends; remediation rates

Metric level	Audience	Example measures
Technical / operational	Security operations, IT	Patch rates; MTTD/MTTR; vulnerability counts; alert volumes

9.2 Quantifying Value: ROSI and ALE

Two models let security speak the language of capital. Return on Security Investment expresses the business value of a control; Annual Loss Expectancy expresses the financial exposure a risk represents. Neither requires false precision — even order-of-magnitude estimates are vastly superior to purely qualitative judgement when justifying spend to a board.

Return on Security Investment (ROSI)

ROSI = (Asset Value × Threat Probability × Vulnerability Factor × Control Effectiveness) – Cost of Control

Equivalently: ROSI = Risk Reduction × Asset Value – Cost of Control. The model forces every proposed control to justify its cost against the loss it actually prevents.

Annual Loss Expectancy (ALE)

ALE = Single Loss Expectancy (SLE) × Annual Rate of Occurrence (ARO)

ALE gives the expected yearly cost of a risk left untreated — the number against which a control's cost is weighed, and the natural complement to the FAIR-based quantification of the risk-leadership discipline.

9.3 The Balanced Scorecard for Security

Introduced in Chapter 2 as a governance lens, the Balanced Scorecard becomes, at this stage, the reporting structure that presents security performance across the four dimensions stakeholders care about — so that no single number masks a weakness in another quadrant.

Perspective	Representative security measures
Financial	ROSI; cost per incident; budget variance; insurance-premium trend; losses avoided
Customer / stakeholder	Security-SLA compliance; breach-notification compliance; customer-audit findings
Internal process	Control-maturity scores; finding-closure rates; patch and access-review performance
Learning & growth	Awareness scores; training completion; competence development; intel-programme maturity

9.4 ISMS Maturity: The Five-Level Model

The Capability Maturity Model, adapted from software-process improvement, is the most useful lens for assessing and steering an ISMS. Certification to ISO/IEC 27001 broadly corresponds to Level 3 (Defined); the strategic goal is to progress toward Level 4 (Quantitatively Managed) and Level 5 (Optimizing), where decisions are driven by data and improvement is continuous and increasingly automated.

Level	Name	What it looks like
1	Initial	Informal, inconsistent, dependent on individuals; incidents handled ad hoc

Level	Name	What it looks like
2	Managed	Basic processes documented and followed, but practice varies across units
3	Defined	Standardised, organisation-wide, formally approved processes (typical ISO 27001 certification)
4	Quantitatively Managed	Processes measured and controlled with metrics (e.g., MTTD/MTTR) for predictable outcomes
5	Optimizing	Continuous improvement via analytics, automation and lessons learned (e.g., AI-driven detection tuning)

9.5 The CISO's Board Dashboard

Australia's ASD ISM (GOV-02) requires the CISO to provide regular, risk-based reporting to the board on posture, control effectiveness, current risks and emerging threats. The dashboard below gives that reporting a repeatable structure — the practical answer to the question of what security should actually put in front of a board.

Dimension	Metrics to include
Risk posture	Top risks by residual level; risks above appetite; new risks since last report
Control effectiveness	Maturity scores by category; findings open >90 days; critical control failures
Incident performance	Incidents by severity; MTTD/MTTR; breach notifications; period-on-period trend
Compliance status	Regulatory compliance rate; audit findings open/ closed; certification status

Dimension	Metrics to include
Investment & resource	Budget spent vs. planned; headcount vs. establishment; capability gaps
Emerging threats	Threat-intelligence highlights; sector incidents; new regulatory developments

9.6 Common ISMS Implementation Pitfalls

Decades of advisory experience surface the same recurring causes of failure. Naming them is the cheapest way to avoid them.

- **ISO 27001 as a documentation exercise:** policies that bear no relationship to practice — the first audit exposes the gap.
- **Insufficient top-management commitment:** a CISO without board support cannot drive the decisions, resources and culture change required.
- **Scope defined too narrowly:** excluding the hardest parts eases certification but leaves actual risk untouched.
- **Risk assessment as compliance theatre:** if the register never changes the security posture, it was not a genuine assessment.
- **Controls without business alignment:** sophisticated controls the organisation cannot sustain are worse than simple controls operated well.
- **Neglecting the human element:** controls fail when staff are untrained or when controls are so cumbersome they are circumvented.
- **Inadequate measurement:** an ISMS without metrics cannot prove value, detect failure, or improve.

9.7 Integrating the ISMS With Other Management Systems

The shared Annex SL structure makes integration across standards efficient. An Integrated Management System eliminates duplication in policy, documented information, internal audit, management review and competence programmes — turning several separate compliance burdens into one.

The highest-value integrations:

1. ISO/IEC 27701 extends the ISMS into a privacy-information management system directly relevant to GDPR and the DPDPA;
2. ISO 22301 aligns with the continuity controls (A.5.29–30, A.8.13–14); ISO 9001 shares the documentation, audit and review machinery; and
3. The NIST Cybersecurity Framework (Identify–Protect–Detect–Respond–Recover) offers a complementary communication structure for US-market stakeholders.

Case Study: Maturity as Competitive Advantage

Cloudflare, a global internet-security and performance company, is widely cited as an example of security maturity treated as a business asset rather than a compliance cost. Its programme illustrates the principles of this chapter: measurement at all three tiers — technical (mean time to detect and respond, vulnerability-remediation rates), programme (training completion, incident-trend analysis, third-party audit findings) and strategic (risk posture reported to the board, investment analysis, external benchmarking via penetration testing). The company is also known for radical transparency — public post-incident write-ups and a public bug-bounty programme that turns external researchers into a continuous quality-assurance function.

Read through the maturity model, such a programme illustrates the journey this chapter describes: from ad hoc response (Level 1), through documented, audited processes (Level 3, the ISO 27001 baseline), toward statistically managed metrics (Level 4) where security performance is tracked with the rigour of any other operational discipline. The lesson is that maturity, made visible through measurement, becomes a trust signal to enterprise customers — security as differentiator, not overhead.

Lessons — Maturity As Advantage

Measurement is the engine of the maturity journey; without it, an organisation cannot know which level it occupies.

Transparency — public post-mortems, bug bounties — converts external scrutiny into continuous improvement.

Demonstrable maturity is a commercial asset: enterprise buyers increasingly select on evidence of it.

Regional Lens: Maturity and Assurance in India and Australia

India — The Climb to Level 4 for Global Trust

For Indian SaaS and services firms selling globally, the maturity journey is a commercial strategy. ISO 27001 certification (Level 3) opens doors; demonstrable Level 4 measurement — MTTD/ MTTR trends, control-maturity scores, audited metrics — is what closes enterprise and regulated-sector deals, and the same evidence simultaneously satisfies SOC 2 and the DPDPA's expectation of reasonable, demonstrable safeguards. CERT-In's reporting and log-retention directions effectively mandate the operational metrics on which higher maturity is built.

Australia — Board Reporting as Regulation

Australia turns the CISO dashboard into a regulatory expectation. APRA's CPS 234 and ASIC's cyber-resilience good practices require board-visible reporting on posture, control effectiveness and incident performance — exactly the dimensions of the dashboard above — and the ASD ISM's GOV-02 makes that reporting a named principle. In the Australian context, the measurement disciplines of this chapter are not optional maturity; they are supervised practice.

Key Takeaways

- ISMS success is determined by consistent operation, measurement and improvement — not by the existence of policies and controls.
- The three-tier metrics model delivers the right information to the right stakeholder at the right altitude.
- ROSI and ALE communicate security value and exposure in the financial language boards act on.
- ISMS maturity is a journey: certification is roughly Level 3; the goal is to progress toward Levels 4 and 5.

- Most ISMS failures stem from a short list of avoidable pitfalls — chief among them weak management commitment and inadequate measurement.
- Integration with ISO 27701, 22301, 9001 and the NIST CSF multiplies value and cuts compliance overhead.

Key Takeaways

1. ISMS success is determined not by the existence of policies and controls, but by their consistent operation, measurement, and improvement.
2. The three-tier measurement model — strategic/governance, programme, and technical/operational — ensures that the right information reaches the right stakeholder at the right time.
3. ROSI and the Balanced Scorecard provide the frameworks for communicating security value in business terms that boards and executive committees can act on.
4. ISMS maturity is a journey: ISO 27001 certification represents Level 3 (Defined); the goal is to progress toward Level 4 (Quantitatively Managed) and Level 5 (Optimizing).
5. Integration with ISO 27701, ISO 22301, ISO 9001, and the NIST CSF maximises the business value of the ISMS investment and reduces compliance overhead.

Reflection Questions

1. If your board asked "are we improving, and can you show the trend?", could your metrics answer — or only confirm a certificate?
2. At which maturity level does your ISMS honestly sit, and what single change would move it up one?

3. Can you express your top control investment as an ROSI or your top risk as an ALE in rupees?
4. Which of the seven common pitfalls is most alive in your organisation right now?
5. What duplication exists across your security, privacy, continuity and quality systems that integration could remove?

Action Deploy & Checklist

- Stand up a three-tier metrics set — board, programme, operational — and assign an owner to each tier within 30 days.
- Run a five-level maturity self-assessment of your ISMS and document the target level and the gap to reach it.
- Express your three largest security investments as ROSI estimates and your three top risks as ALE figures for the next board pack.
- Build the six-dimension CISO dashboard and present it to the board at the next meeting (GOV-02).
- Audit your programme against the seven common pitfalls and remediate the most material one this quarter.
- Map overlaps with ISO 27701, 22301 and 9001 and consolidate shared policy, audit and review processes into an Integrated Management System.

CHAPTER

10

THE FUTURE OF INFORMATION SECURITY, CYBERSECURITY AND PRIVACY PROTECTION

Navigating the horizon in a world of relentless digital transformation

The only certainty about the future of cybersecurity is uncertainty. The threat landscape will evolve faster than our defences. The organisations that will prevail are those that build adaptive governance systems, not static compliance architectures.

— Ajai Srivastava, Founder Director, Seven Step Consulting Private Limited.

S.T.E.P.S.™ Engine — Operational Anchor: DRIVE, Extended Into the Future

The closing chapter looks forward. Its argument is that the DRIVE step — continual improvement — must become continuous adaptation: an intelligence-led, ever-adjusting governance system rather than a static, annual compliance architecture. The future belongs to organisations that build adaptive systems, not fixed ones.

Chapter Overview

The closing argument of this book is that security must be built to adapt, because the threat landscape will not hold still. Five forces — dual-use artificial intelligence, the quantum cryptographic horizon, persistent nation-state and supply-chain threats, accelerating regulation, and the convergence of IT with operational technology — will render today's best controls obsolete, and a new generation of frameworks (ISO/IEC 42001, the NIST AI RMF, NIS2 and DORA) is rising to govern what comes next. The response is not a better static fortress but an adaptive, intelligence-led ISMS: continuously monitored, zero-trust by design, resilient over merely defended, and private by default. The MOVEit breach already demonstrates every one of these forces at once, rewarding the organisations that built for detection and response over those that trusted the perimeter. Across three plausible scenarios for 2030 — a trust dividend, a widening gap, or a cryptographic shock — the same preparation serves: adaptive governance and cryptographic agility. Infosec Nirvana is a direction, not a destination, and the S.T.E.P.S.™ journey is how an organisation keeps moving toward it.

Chapter Objectives

By the end of this chapter, the reader will be able to:

- Describe the five forces reshaping information security over the coming decade.
- Explain the 'harvest now, decrypt later' threat and why post-quantum planning must begin today.
- Identify the emerging frameworks — ISO/IEC 42001, NIST AI RMF, NIS2, DORA — that will govern the next phase.
- Describe the characteristics of an adaptive, intelligence-led, future-ready ISMS.

- Weigh three plausible scenarios for 2030 and what each demands of leadership now.

Building for a Future That Will Not Hold Still

Every preceding chapter has described how to build a security management system that works today. This one asks the harder question: how to build one that will still work when today's controls are obsolete. The McKinsey observation is sobering — even the most sophisticated current controls will soon be outdated — and the implication is not despair but design. A governance system built to adapt will outlast one built to comply. The five forces below are the reasons why, and the adaptive ISMS is the response.

10.1 Five Forces Reshaping the Landscape

1. Artificial Intelligence — Dual-Use at Scale

AI is at once the defender's most powerful tool and the attacker's most dangerous capability enhancement. Attackers wield it for hyper-personalised phishing that defeats traditional awareness training, deepfakes that undermine authentication, and automated vulnerability discovery that compresses the gap between disclosure and exploit to hours. Defenders wield it for behavioural analytics that sharpen detection, AI-assisted threat hunting that accelerates investigation, and automated secure-code review. Australia's ASD ISM responds with a new board-level accountability (GOV-08): ensuring AI is secure, controllable, human-supervised and used ethically — the first major framework to make AI governance an explicit board obligation.

2. Quantum Computing — The Cryptographic Horizon

A sufficiently powerful quantum computer will break the asymmetric algorithms (RSA, ECC) that secure the internet.

Such machines are not yet operational, but the 'harvest now, decrypt later' threat — adversaries collecting encrypted data today to decrypt when quantum matures — means organisations holding data with long-term sensitivity must begin their post-quantum transition now. NIST published its first post-quantum standards in 2024 (including ML-KEM, derived from CRYSTALS-Kyber, and ML-DSA, from CRYSTALS-Dilithium). The practical steps: inventory cryptographic assets, assess data longevity, design for cryptographic agility, and press cloud and software vendors on their PQC roadmaps.

3. Nation-State and Advanced Persistent Threats

The line between criminal and state-sponsored operations has blurred. Nation-state actors pursue espionage, destructive attacks on critical infrastructure and economic theft, often as persistent, long-dwell presences — and the supply-chain attack, compromising a target through a trusted supplier or update, has become a primary vector. The governance implications: supply-chain security (A.5.19–22) needs board attention, not just procurement scrutiny; threat intelligence (A.5.7) must include nation-state tradecraft; and incident response must plan for stealthy persistence, not only smash-and-grab ransomware.

4. Regulatory Acceleration

The regulatory environment is intensifying worldwide: India's DPDPA 2023 and its Rules; the EU's NIS2 Directive (with 24-hour-class incident reporting and personal liability for senior management); the EU's DORA for financial entities; the US SEC's cyber-disclosure rules for listed companies; and Australia's expanded critical-infrastructure obligations. The lesson is that compliance is neither a one-time exercise nor the ceiling of ambition — it is a continuous process, and the legal register (A.5.31) must be a living document.

5. IoT and OT Convergence

The explosion of IoT devices — sensors, controllers, medical and industrial equipment — has vastly enlarged the attack surface with devices that often cannot run security agents, cannot be patched easily, and speak protocols built for availability over security. As IT and operational technology converge in manufacturing, healthcare, utilities and transport, a cyberattack can now cause physical harm. ISMS scope must routinely include OT, and risk assessment must respect its distinct character: safety implications, an availability-first priority, and long-lived legacy systems.

10.2 Emerging Frameworks and Standards

The standards landscape is moving to meet these forces. ISO/IEC 42001:2023 is the first AI management-system standard — the certifiable governance complement to ISO 27001 for organisations building or deploying AI, and the natural next step for an ISMS-mature organisation. The NIST AI Risk Management Framework provides a structured approach (Govern, Map, Measure, Manage) to AI-specific risk. The EU's NIS2 broadens scope and adds supply-chain obligations, rapid incident reporting and management liability. DORA imposes ICT risk-management and resilience-testing requirements on financial entities, closely aligned with ISO 27001 but going further on third-party ICT risk. Together they signal that AI governance and operational resilience are the next certification frontiers.

10.3 The Future ISMS: Adaptive, Integrated, Intelligence-Led

The ISMS of the future is not a static compliance framework but an adaptive governance system that continuously ingests threat intelligence, adjusts controls in near real time, and delivers actionable evidence to decision-makers at every level. Six characteristics define it.

- **Continuous control monitoring:** automated, real-time testing of control effectiveness — not just annual audits.
- **Intelligence-led security:** threat intelligence (A.5.7) as a continuous input to risk, prioritisation and response.
- **Zero-trust architecture:** assume breach, verify continuously, grant least privilege — the direction of A.8.22 and the ISM Protect principles.
- **Security as code:** policies, configurations and controls defined as version-controlled, tested, automatically deployed code.
- **Resilience over perimeter:** invest in detection, containment and recovery as heavily as prevention, accepting that breaches will occur.
- **Privacy by design:** privacy embedded at the design stage, consistent with the DPDPA, GDPR and ISO 27701.

10.4 Three Scenarios for 2030

No one can predict the future, but leaders can prepare for a range of them. The three scenarios below — optimistic, realistic and disruptive — are not forecasts but planning aids: each implies actions worth taking now, and the adaptive ISMS is the common preparation that serves all three.

Scenario 1 — Optimistic: The Trust Dividend Post-quantum cryptography is adopted ahead of any cryptographically relevant quantum computer. AI defenders consistently outpace AI attackers. Certifiable AI governance (ISO 42001) and integrated privacy-security management become mainstream, and the world's privacy regimes move toward interoperability. Trust becomes a measurable market advantage, and organisations that invested early in adaptive governance capture it.
Scenario 2 — Realistic: The Widening Gap Adoption is uneven. The AI arms race stays roughly balanced, breaches continue, and a thickening patchwork of regulation raises compliance cost. Post-quantum migration proceeds in fits and starts. The decisive divide is between organisations with adaptive, measured governance — which absorb shocks and pull ahead — and those running static compliance, which fall progressively behind. Maturity, not luck, determines which side an organisation lands on.
Scenario 3 — Disruptive: The Cryptographic Shock A cryptographically relevant quantum computer arrives sooner than expected, and the 'harvest now, decrypt later' bet pays off for adversaries holding years of stolen ciphertext. A major AI-driven supply-chain cascade compromises thousands of organisations at once, and geopolitical fracture splinters the internet into less-trusting zones. Organisations without cryptographic agility and adaptive governance suffer existential damage; those that prepared survive because they designed for breach, not for calm.

Case Study: MOVEit (2023) — The Future Is Already Here

In May 2023, the Cl0p ransomware group exploited a zero-day SQL-injection vulnerability (CVE-2023-34362) in MOVEit Transfer, a widely used managed file-transfer product from Progress Software. Exploitation began around 27 May, before any public knowledge; Progress disclosed and patched the flaw on 31 May, but mass data theft was already underway via a custom web shell. Rather than encrypt, Cl0p simply exfiltrated data and extorted victims. Over the following months the victim count grew to more than 2,600 organisations and over 77 million individuals worldwide — including the BBC, British Airways, Boots (through the Zellis payroll provider) and the US Department of Energy. Evidence suggests the attackers had pre-positioned the exploit, ready to launch a mass campaign the moment they chose.

Every future trend, at once

Supply-chain amplification: a single zero-day in a product embedded across thousands of supply chains cascaded instantly and globally.

Regulatory complexity: one incident triggered simultaneous obligations under GDPR, UK GDPR, US SEC rules and numerous state breach laws.

Detection over prevention: organisations with threat intelligence (A.5.7) and monitoring (A.8.16) blocked MOVEit within hours; most discovered their exposure weeks later.

Lessons — MOVEit

The future of security is already the present for organisations without adaptive, intelligence-led governance.

A trusted, widely embedded product is the ideal supply-chain target; trust must be verified, not assumed (A.5.21).

When a zero-day arrives with no patch, the premium shifts decisively to detection, containment and tested response.

A Word to the Senior Leader

If you have read this far, you understand that information security, cybersecurity and privacy are not technical problems to be delegated and forgotten. They are board-level governance responsibilities requiring sustained attention, adequate resources and personal accountability. The S.T.E.P.S.™ Framework gives your organisation its roadmap; ISO/IEC 27001:2022 gives the internationally recognised structure; the 93 controls of ISO/IEC 27002:2022 give the architecture; and the measurement disciplines — from ROSI to the board dashboard — give the evidence base for the decisions only you can make.

Infosec Nirvana is not a destination; it is a direction. The organisation that commits to the journey — systematically, continuously, and with genuine management commitment — will be more resilient, more trustworthy and better positioned to pursue its objectives than the one that treats security as a compliance exercise to be discharged and forgotten. The journey begins with a single step, and the framework tells you which step to take first.

Key Takeaways

- Five forces will define the next decade: AI (dual-use), quantum computing, nation-state/APT and supply-chain threats, regulatory acceleration, and IoT/OT convergence.
- Australia's ASD ISM introduces AI-governance accountability (GOV-08) as a board obligation — a sign of where governance is heading.
- Post-quantum transition must begin now because of 'harvest now, decrypt later'; NIST published its first PQC standards in 2024.

- Emerging frameworks — ISO/IEC 42001, NIST AI RMF, NIS2, DORA — mark AI governance and operational resilience as the next frontiers.
- The future ISMS is adaptive, intelligence-led and continuous, not static and annual.
- MOVEit shows the future is already here: supply-chain amplification, regulatory complexity, and a premium on detection over prevention.

Reflection Questions

1. Have you begun a cryptographic inventory and a post-quantum transition plan for your longest-lived sensitive data?
2. Who on your board is accountable for AI governance — and is your ISMS extending toward ISO/IEC 42001?
3. Does your ISMS scope include your OT and IoT estate, with risk assessed for safety and availability, not just confidentiality?
4. If a MOVEit-style zero-day hit a product embedded in your supply chain tomorrow, how fast would you detect and contain it?
5. Of the three 2030 scenarios, which would expose your organisation most — and what would you wish you had started today?

Action Deploy & Checklist

- Start a cryptographic-asset inventory and a post-quantum migration plan prioritised by data longevity (begin within 90 days).
- Assign board-level accountability for AI governance and evaluate ISO/IEC 42001 alongside your existing ISMS.

- Extend ISMS scope to OT and IoT, assessing safety and availability impacts explicitly.
- Make threat intelligence (A.5.7) a continuous input to risk and response, including nation-state tradecraft.
- Stand up continuous control monitoring for your highest-value controls, moving beyond annual audit.
- Shift investment toward detection, containment and tested recovery in line with a 'resilience over perimeter' posture.

ANNEXURE

A. S.T.E.P.S.™: FROM COMPLIANCE TO TRUST – ONE STEP AT A TIME

A Governance Framework for the 21st Century

Introduction: Why Trust is the New Currency of Business

The 21st century has fundamentally changed the relationship between organizations and their stakeholders. Customers, employees, regulators, investors, partners, and society no longer judge organizations solely by their products, profits, or compliance status. They increasingly evaluate organizations based on trust.

Trust has become the most valuable intangible asset an organization can possess and the most fragile asset it can lose. In an era characterized by digital transformation, artificial intelligence, cybersecurity threats, privacy concerns, misinformation, regulatory complexity, and heightened stakeholder expectations, trust is no longer a by-product of good business—it is a strategic imperative for survival and growth.

Traditional governance models were designed primarily to ensure compliance. While compliance remains essential, compliance alone does not create trust. Organizations can comply with regulations and still lose the confidence of customers, employees, and society. The future belongs to organizations that move beyond compliance and intentionally build, demonstrate, and sustain trust.

The S.T.E.P.S.™ Governance Framework provides a practical roadmap for achieving this objective.

S.T.E.P.S.™ consists of five interconnected elements:

1. **S – See Reality Clearly**
2. **T – Think Deliberately**
3. **E – Enact Governance**
4. **P – Prove Trust**
5. **S – Sustain Trust**

Together, these elements create a continuous cycle of governance excellence that transforms compliance obligations into sustainable stakeholder trust.

S – See Reality Clearly

Understanding the Truth Before Managing It

The first responsibility of governance is not control—it is awareness.

Many governance failures occur because organizations operate on assumptions rather than realities. Leaders often receive filtered information, incomplete risk assessments, or outdated data that create a false sense of security.

Seeing reality clearly requires organizations to develop a culture of transparency, visibility, and situational awareness.

Organizations must continuously assess:

- Strategic risks
- Operational vulnerabilities
- Cybersecurity threats
- Regulatory obligations
- Stakeholder expectations
- Emerging technologies
- Market disruptions
- Ethical implications

The objective is to establish a single source of truth that enables informed decision-making.

Key Governance Questions

- What risks are we facing today?
- What risks are emerging tomorrow?
- Where are our blind spots?
- What are stakeholders telling us?
- What evidence supports our assumptions?

Leadership Imperative

Leaders must encourage uncomfortable truths, challenge assumptions, and reward transparency rather than concealment.

Organizations that fail to see reality clearly eventually become victims of reality.

T – Think Deliberately

Governance Begins with Intentional Decision-Making

Information alone does not create trust. Trust emerges when leaders use information responsibly.

Thinking deliberately means ensuring that decisions are guided by purpose, ethics, values, and long-term impact rather than short-term gains.

In today's environment, organizations must evaluate decisions through multiple lenses:

- Business impact
- Regulatory compliance
- Ethical considerations
- Security implications
- Privacy requirements
- Social responsibility
- Sustainability outcomes
- Stakeholder expectations

The age of siloed decision-making is over.

Every significant decision should answer a simple question:

"Will this decision strengthen or weaken stakeholder trust?"

Key Governance Questions

- Why are we making this decision?
- Who benefits?
- Who may be harmed?

- Are we balancing innovation with responsibility?
- Does this align with our organizational values?

Leadership Imperative

Trustworthy organizations are built by leaders who demonstrate judgment, accountability, and ethical courage.

Thinking deliberately transforms governance from a compliance exercise into a strategic capability.

E – Enact Governance

Turning Intent into Action

Good intentions without execution create disappointment.

Governance becomes meaningful only when policies, principles, and decisions are consistently translated into operational reality.

Enacting governance means embedding trust into everyday business processes.

This includes:

- Clear accountability structures
- Defined roles and responsibilities
- Risk management frameworks
- Security controls
- Privacy safeguards
- Ethical AI practices
- Performance monitoring
- Compliance management systems

Governance should not exist only in boardrooms or policy documents. It must be visible in daily operations.

Characteristics of Effective Governance Execution

- Consistency
- Accountability
- Transparency
- Repeatability
- Measurability
- Continuous oversight

Key Governance Questions

- Are our policies being followed?
- Who owns each governance responsibility?
- How do we monitor effectiveness?
- Are controls working as intended?

Leadership Imperative

Trust is built when promises become practices.

Execution is where governance becomes visible to stakeholders.

P – Prove Trust

Evidence Matters More Than Claims

In the trust economy, stakeholders no longer accept declarations without validation.

Organizations must demonstrate—not merely claim—that they are trustworthy.

This requires credible evidence.

Trust must be measurable, observable, and verifiable.

Examples include:

- Independent audits
- Certifications
- Compliance reports
- Risk assessments
- Security testing
- Privacy impact assessments
- ESG disclosures
- Transparency reports
- Customer assurance programs

The principle is simple:

Trust grows when evidence exceeds expectation.

Modern Trust Indicators

- ISO Certifications
- SOC Reports
- Privacy Compliance Demonstrations
- Cybersecurity Maturity Assessments
- Ethical AI Assurance Reports
- Sustainability Metrics
- Governance Performance Dashboards

Key Governance Questions

- Can we prove what we claim?
- What evidence supports stakeholder confidence?
- How transparent are we?
- Are our assurances independently validated?

Leadership Imperative

Trust is earned through evidence, not marketing.

Organizations that consistently provide credible assurance become preferred partners, employers, and service providers.

S – Sustain Trust

Trust is a Journey, Not a Destination

The final and most critical element of governance is sustaining trust over time.

Trust can take years to build and moments to destroy.

Organizations must therefore develop resilience, adaptability, and continuous improvement capabilities.

Sustaining trust requires:

- Continuous learning
- Governance reviews
- Lessons learned programs
- Incident analysis
- Stakeholder feedback
- Innovation oversight
- Culture development
- Leadership accountability

Organizations must recognize that risks, technologies, regulations, and societal expectations evolve continuously.

Governance frameworks must evolve with them.

Key Governance Questions

- What have we learned?
- What needs improvement?
- Are stakeholder expectations changing?
- How do we remain relevant and trustworthy?

Leadership Imperative

The most trusted organizations are not those that never fail; they are those that learn, adapt, and improve faster than others.

Sustained trust becomes a competitive advantage that compounds over time.

The S.T.E.P.S.™ Trust Cycle

The true strength of the framework lies in its continuous nature.

Organizations:

- **See** emerging realities.
- **Think** carefully about implications.
- **Enact** effective governance measures.
- **Prove** trust through evidence.
- **Sustain** trust through learning and improvement.

The cycle then begins again.

This creates a self-reinforcing system where governance becomes proactive rather than reactive and trust becomes institutionalized rather than incidental.

Why S.T.E.P.S.™ Matters for the Future

The next decade will be defined by artificial intelligence, digital ecosystems, data-driven economies, geopolitical uncertainty, climate challenges, and increasing stakeholder scrutiny.

Organizations that focus solely on compliance will struggle to keep pace.

Organizations that focus on trust will thrive.

S.T.E.P.S.™ provides a practical governance framework that bridges the gap between compliance obligations and stakeholder confidence.

It enables organizations to:

- Strengthen resilience
- Accelerate innovation responsibly
- Improve regulatory readiness
- Enhance customer confidence
- Attract investors
- Retain talent
- Improve reputation
- Build sustainable growth

Conclusion

The future of governance is not about managing rules—it is about cultivating trust.

Compliance may protect an organization from penalties, but trust protects its future.

The S.T.E.P.S.™ Governance Framework offers a modern approach to leadership and governance by helping organizations move beyond compliance toward enduring trust.

By learning to **See Reality Clearly, Think Deliberately, Enact Governance, Prove Trust, and Sustain Trust**, organizations create a culture where trust becomes measurable, repeatable, and sustainable.

In the 21st century, trust is no longer optional.

It is the foundation of survival.

It is the engine of growth.

And it is built—one S.T.E.P.S.™ at a time.

For More details read the book

Mind Your S.T.E.P.S -From Compliance to Trust – One Step at a Time

https://notionpress.com/in/read/mind-your-s-t-e-p-s

https://www.amazon.in/dp/B0H2VPFQC8?&tag=notionpcom-21

https://www.amazon.com/dp/B0H2VPFQC8

https://www.amazon.co.uk/dp/B0H2VPFQC8

B. AADHAAR CASE STUDY

Case Study: The Aadhaar Ecosystem — Data Governance at Population Scale

Incident / Context: Multiple documented data exposure incidents, 2018–2023, involving Aadhaar-linked systems and third-party integrations

Jurisdiction: India (Government of India / UIDAI)

Regulatory Framework: Aadhaar Act 2016; Information Technology Act 2000; DPDP Act 2023 (prospective); Supreme Court judgment in Puttaswamy v. Union of India (2018)

Relevant to Chapter: Chapter 1 (Privacy vs. Security); Chapter 5 (Organisational Controls); Annexure D (DPDP Act)

Background

Aadhaar is the world's largest biometric identity system, administered by the Unique Identification Authority of India (UIDAI). As of 2024, over 1.3 billion Aadhaar numbers have been issued, each linked to an individual's biometric data (fingerprints and iris scans) and demographic information. The system underpins delivery of government subsidies, financial inclusion through Jan Dhan accounts, digital payments infrastructure (via Aadhaar-enabled Payment Systems), KYC processes across banking, telecom, and insurance, and healthcare identity under the Ayushman Bharat Digital Mission.

The concentration of identity data at this scale — for virtually the entire Indian population — creates a governance challenge without precedent: any failure of access control, purpose limitation, or security safeguard carries population-scale consequences.

Key Documented Incidents

Date	Incident	Data Exposed	Source
January 2018	Tribune newspaper reported purchasing Aadhaar data via a WhatsApp-based network; 500 rupees reportedly bought access to UIDAI's internal demographic search system via an unofficial access point.	Name, address, photo, phone, email for ~1 billion Aadhaar holders	The Tribune investigation; UIDAI response
March 2018	UIDAI acknowledged an internal check on misuse of its API revealed 210 government websites had published Aadhaar-linked data in clear text on publicly accessible pages.	Partial demographic data across multiple welfare schemes	UIDAI advisory; RTI disclosures

Date	Incident	Data Exposed	Source
2019	French security researcher Baptiste Robert (Elliot Alderson) identified multiple API endpoints and system misconfigurations in Aadhaar-linked systems exposing demographic data to unauthenticated queries.	Demographic data; authentication session tokens	Published security research
September 2023	Reports emerged of Aadhaar-linked data sets being offered for sale on dark web forums, including names, Aadhaar numbers, and biographic data attributed to a leak from a government utility database.	Unconfirmed volume; UIDAI denied systemic compromise of core UIDAI infrastructure	Cybersecurity researcher reports; CERT-In investigation

Root Cause Analysis

The pattern across these incidents points to three systemic failure categories rather than isolated technical errors:

- **Access Control Architecture**: The Aadhaar ecosystem's breadth — spanning central government, state governments, banking correspondents, telecom operators, and private eKYC providers — created thousands of API integration points, each a potential access control failure. Granting access to the authentication API without rigorous monitoring of query patterns enabled misuse to go undetected.

- **Purpose Creep and Function Expansion**: Aadhaar was originally designed for welfare delivery. Its mandatory linkage to bank accounts, mobile SIMs, tax returns, and health records — subsequently struck down in part by the Supreme Court — represented processing beyond the original purpose, inconsistent with the purpose limitation principle central to both the Aadhaar Act and the DPDP Act 2023.
- **Third-Party Risk**: The most significant exposure vectors were not UIDAI's core biometric database — which remained uncompromised — but downstream systems operated by state governments, Public Sector Undertakings, and private sector eKYC providers that stored Aadhaar-linked data with inadequate controls.

Supreme Court Judgment — Puttaswamy (2018)

In September 2018, a five-judge Constitution Bench of the Supreme Court upheld the constitutional validity of the Aadhaar Act subject to significant restrictions. The Court struck down mandatory private sector Aadhaar linkages (bank accounts, mobile SIMs), holding that the State could not compel citizens to provide biometric data for private commercial purposes. The judgment reinforced purpose limitation and data minimisation as constitutional requirements flowing from the right to privacy — the precise principles subsequently codified in the DPDP Act 2023.

Regulatory and Governance Response

- UIDAI revoked approximately 50,000 operator licences following the 2018 Tribune investigation and introduced biometric authentication for Aadhaar operators.
- UIDAI mandated a "Virtual ID" (VID) system — a 16-digit revocable identifier — to enable Aadhaar-based authentication without disclosing the actual Aadhaar number, implementing a tokenisation control.
- UIDAI introduced a "lock/unlock" facility allowing Data Principals to lock their biometrics against unauthorised authentication attempts.
- CERT-In issued guidelines for entities processing Aadhaar data, including mandatory audit and incident reporting requirements.

ISO 27001:2022 Control Mapping

Failure	ISO 27001:2022 Control	Control Description
Unauthorised API access	A.8.3	Information access restriction
Unmonitored query patterns	A.8.16	Monitoring activities
Third-party eKYC provider exposure	A.5.19	Information security in supplier relationships
Government website data publication	A.5.14	Information transfer

Failure	ISO 27001:2022 Control	Control Description
Purpose creep beyond original mandate	A.5.12	Classification of information
Absence of Data Principal controls (pre-VID)	A.5.34	Privacy and protection of PII
Delayed detection and disclosure	A.5.24–A.5.26	Information security incident management

C. ISMS MATURITY SELF-ASSESSMENT TOOL

This tool enables organisations to assess the maturity of their Information Security Management System (ISMS) across ten control domains, aligned with the five-level maturity model introduced in Chapter 9 and the 93 controls of ISO/ IEC 27002:2022. It is designed to be completed by the CISO or Information Security Manager, ideally in a facilitated workshop with key stakeholders.

How to Use This Tool

- For each control domain, read the maturity level descriptors and select the level (1–5) that most accurately describes your organisation's current state. Partial credit is not applicable — select the highest level at which your organisation fully meets the criteria.
- Use the "Evidence / Notes" column to record the specific evidence that supports your maturity rating. Without evidence, the assessment cannot be used to support an audit or management review.
- Calculate your domain scores and overall maturity score using the scoring guide at the end of this tool.

- Use the Improvement Actions column to document the priority actions required to advance to the next maturity level.
- This assessment should be conducted at least annually and following any material change to the organisation's threat landscape, regulatory environment, or business operations.

Maturity Level Definitions

Level	Label	Definition
1	**Initial**	Security activities are ad hoc, reactive, and largely undocumented. There is no formal ISMS. Responses to incidents are inconsistent. The organisation is unaware of its compliance obligations or risk exposure.
2	**Developing**	Some security policies and controls exist but are inconsistently applied. Risk assessment has been performed but is not systematic or repeatable. The ISMS, if present, is partially implemented and not formally maintained.
3	**Defined**	A documented ISMS exists and is formally implemented across the organisation's scope. Policies, procedures, and controls are consistently applied. Risk assessment is systematic and repeatable. ISO/IEC 27001:2022 certification is either achieved or achievable.
4	**Managed**	The ISMS is measured and monitored through defined metrics and KPIs. Security performance is reported to senior management. Control effectiveness is tested. The organisation manages its security posture proactively rather than reactively.

Level	Label	Definition
5	**Optimising**	The ISMS is continuously improved based on metrics, threat intelligence, and external benchmarking. Security is embedded in business strategy, product development, and supplier governance. The organisation anticipates emerging threats and adapts its controls proactively.

Domain Assessments

Domain 1: Governance and Leadership (Clause 5; A.5.1–A.5.4)

Level	Criteria — Your organisation...
1 — Initial	Has no formal information security policy. Security responsibilities are undefined. Senior management has not committed to or mandated the ISMS.
2 — Developing	Has an information security policy that has been approved but is not consistently communicated or enforced. Security responsibilities are partially defined.
3 — Defined	Has a formally approved and communicated information security policy. CISO or equivalent role exists with defined authority. Management has documented its commitment to the ISMS.
4 — Managed	Senior management receives regular (at least quarterly) security performance reports. Security objectives are set at the executive level and tracked. The security function has appropriate budget and headcount.
5 — Optimising	The Board has cybersecurity literacy sufficient to govern the security function. Security is a standing agenda item at Board level. The CISO has direct access to the Board. External threat intelligence informs leadership decision-making.

Your Maturity Level (1–5)	Evidence / Notes	Priority Improvement Actions

Domain 2: Risk Management (Clause 6.1; A.5.7–A.5.8)

Level	Criteria — Your organisation...
1 — Initial	Has no formal risk assessment process. Risks are identified and addressed reactively, typically after an incident.
2 — Developing	Has conducted a risk assessment but it is not based on a documented methodology and is not repeated on a defined schedule.
3 — Defined	Has a documented, repeatable risk assessment methodology. A complete risk register exists. Risk treatment decisions are documented in a Risk Treatment Plan and Statement of Applicability.
4 — Managed	Risk assessments are conducted on a defined schedule and triggered by material changes. Risk owners are assigned. Residual risk is tracked and reviewed by senior management.
5 — Optimising	Threat intelligence is integrated into the risk assessment process. Risk appetite is formally defined and approved by the Board. Emerging risks (AI, quantum, supply chain) are proactively assessed and treated.

Your Maturity Level (1–5)	Evidence / Notes	Priority Improvement Actions

Domain 3: Asset Management (A.5.9–A.5.12)

Level	Criteria — Your organisation...
1 — Initial	Has no formal asset inventory. Information classification has not been defined or applied.
2 — Developing	Has a partial asset inventory that is not maintained. Some data classification labels exist but are inconsistently applied.
3 — Defined	Maintains a complete, accurate asset inventory with assigned owners. A formal information classification scheme is defined and applied to all information assets.
4 — Managed	The asset inventory is maintained in near-real-time and integrated with change management. Asset lifecycle events (disposal, transfer) trigger security control reviews.
5 — Optimising	Asset discovery is automated. Data flows are mapped and monitored continuously. Sensitive data is identified and protected automatically through DLP and tagging tools.

Your Maturity Level (1–5)	Evidence / Notes	Priority Improvement Actions

Domain 4: People Security (A.6.1–A.6.8)

Level	Criteria — Your organisation...
1 — Initial	Has no security awareness programme. Background checks are not conducted. Security responsibilities are not included in employment contracts.

Level	Criteria — Your organisation...
2 — Developing	Conducts basic annual security awareness training. Some background checks are performed. Security policy acknowledgement is required at onboarding.
3 — Defined	Runs a structured security awareness programme with role-based training. Pre-employment screening is systematically applied. Clear policies govern acceptable use, confidentiality, and incident reporting.
4 — Managed	Security awareness effectiveness is measured (phishing simulation rates, quiz scores). Training completion is tracked and reported. Privileged user training is differentiated and more rigorous.
5 — Optimising	Security culture is measured through surveys and behavioural indicators. Insider threat monitoring is in place. Security champions are embedded in business units. Learning is continuous and adaptive.

Your Maturity Level (1–5)	Evidence / Notes	Priority Improvement Actions

Domain 5: Physical and Environmental Security (A.7.1–A.7.14)

Level	Criteria — Your organisation...
1 — Initial	Physical access to sensitive areas is not controlled. There are no defined security perimeters.
2 — Developing	Physical access controls exist in some areas. A clear desk policy is defined but inconsistently enforced.

Level	Criteria — Your organisation...
3 — Defined	Physical security perimeters are defined and enforced. Access to sensitive areas (data centres, server rooms) is restricted to authorised personnel. Physical access is logged.
4 — Managed	Physical access logs are regularly reviewed. Environmental controls (temperature, power, humidity) are monitored. Visitor management is formally controlled. CCTV covers all sensitive areas.
5 — Optimising	Physical and logical access controls are integrated. Physical security alerts are fed into the SIEM. Physical security assessments are conducted periodically by an independent party.

Your Maturity Level (1–5)	Evidence / Notes	Priority Improvement Actions

Domain 6: Identity and Access Management (A.5.15–A.5.18; A.8.2–A.8.5)

Level	Criteria — Your organisation...
1 — Initial	User access is not formally controlled. Shared credentials are used. Joiners/movers/leavers processes do not include access reviews.
2 — Developing	A formal access provisioning process exists. Some access reviews are conducted. Password policies are defined but not technically enforced.

Level	Criteria — Your organisation...
3 — Defined	Role-based access control (RBAC) is implemented. Access rights are reviewed at least annually. MFA is deployed for remote access and privileged accounts. A joiners/movers/leavers process is formally managed.
4 — Managed	Privileged access is managed through a PAM solution. Access reviews are risk-based and conducted more frequently for privileged accounts. MFA is deployed across all systems. Access anomalies are monitored.
5 — Optimising	Zero Trust principles are applied. Just-in-time privileged access is implemented. Identity governance and administration (IGA) tools automate provisioning and de-provisioning. Access risk is continuously scored.

Your Maturity Level (1–5)	Evidence / Notes	Priority Improvement Actions

Domain 7: Threat and Vulnerability Management (A.8.7–A.8.8; A.5.7)

Level	Criteria — Your organisation...
1 — Initial	Patches are applied reactively, typically after a breach or known exploitation. No vulnerability scanning programme exists.
2 — Developing	Critical patches are applied within a defined window. Vulnerability scanning is conducted but not on a scheduled basis. Results are not tracked to closure.

Level	Criteria — Your organisation...
3 — Defined	A formal vulnerability management programme exists with defined scan frequency, risk-based remediation timelines, and tracked closure. Penetration testing is conducted at least annually.
4 — Managed	Vulnerability remediation SLAs are measured and reported. Threat intelligence is used to prioritise patching. Penetration test findings are tracked through to verified remediation.
5 — Optimising	Continuous vulnerability management is implemented. Exploit probability is integrated into prioritisation. Red team exercises are conducted regularly. Bug bounty programmes may supplement internal testing.

Your Maturity Level (1–5)	Evidence / Notes	Priority Improvement Actions

Domain 8: Incident Detection and Response (A.5.24–A.5.28; A.8.15–A.8.16)

Level	Criteria — Your organisation...
1 — Initial	Incidents are managed on an ad hoc basis. There is no formal incident response plan. Detection depends on user reports.
2 — Developing	An incident response plan exists but has not been tested. Logging is enabled on some systems. Incident classification criteria are defined.

Level	Criteria — Your organisation...
3 — Defined	A formal incident response plan is documented, communicated, and tested annually (tabletop or live exercise). Log collection covers all critical systems. A SIEM or equivalent tool is operational.
4 — Managed	MTTD (Mean Time to Detect) and MTTR (Mean Time to Respond) are measured and tracked. Post-incident reviews are conducted for all significant incidents. Regulatory notification timelines are defined and tested.
5 — Optimising	A 24/7 SOC (internal or managed) provides continuous monitoring. SOAR automation reduces manual response effort. Threat hunting is conducted proactively. Lessons learned are systematically fed back into risk assessment and controls.

Your Maturity Level (1–5)	Evidence / Notes	Priority Improvement Actions

Domain 9: Supplier and Third-Party Risk (A.5.19–A.5.23)

Level	Criteria — Your organisation...
1 — Initial	No formal process exists for assessing supplier security. No security requirements are included in supplier contracts.
2 — Developing	Security questionnaires are sent to some suppliers. Some contracts include basic security clauses. Supplier access is not formally managed.

Level	Criteria — Your organisation...
3 — Defined	A formal TPRM programme exists. All suppliers handling sensitive data are assessed prior to engagement. Security requirements are included in all relevant contracts. Supplier access is controlled and logged.
4 — Managed	Suppliers are classified by risk tier and monitored proportionately. Annual reassessments are conducted for high-risk suppliers. Supplier security performance is reported to management. Right-to-audit clauses are exercised.
5 — Optimising	Continuous supplier monitoring is implemented (via security ratings services or automated questionnaire platforms). Fourth-party risk (suppliers' suppliers) is assessed. Supply chain attacks are modelled in the risk assessment.

Your Maturity Level (1–5)	Evidence / Notes	Priority Improvement Actions

Domain 10: Business Continuity and Compliance (A.5.29–A.5.30; A.5.31–A.5.36)

Level	Criteria — Your organisation...
1 — Initial	No business continuity plan exists. Legal and regulatory compliance obligations are not formally tracked.
2 — Developing	A BCP exists but has not been tested. A legal register exists but is not maintained. Compliance obligations are partially understood.

Level	Criteria — Your organisation...
3 — Defined	A tested BCP and Disaster Recovery Plan exist with defined RTO/RPO targets. A complete legal, regulatory, and contractual obligations register is maintained and reviewed annually.
4 — Managed	BCP tests are conducted at least annually (full simulation). Recovery capability is validated. Regulatory changes are tracked and compliance impact assessed. ISMS integrates with BCM.
5 — Optimising	Resilience is designed into all critical systems and processes (not added on). Compliance management is automated where possible. The organisation proactively engages regulators. Privacy-by-design and security-by-design are standard.

Your Maturity Level (1–5)	Evidence / Notes	Priority Improvement Actions

Scoring and Interpretation

Domain	Your Score (1–5)	Weight	Weighted Score
1. Governance and Leadership		10%	
2. Risk Management		15%	
3. Asset Management		10%	
4. People Security		10%	

Domain	Your Score (1–5)	Weight	Weighted Score
5. Physical and Environmental Security		5%	
6. Identity and Access Management		15%	
7. Threat and Vulnerability Management		15%	
8. Incident Detection and Response		10%	
9. Supplier and Third-Party Risk		5%	
10. Business Continuity and Compliance		5%	
OVERALL WEIGHTED SCORE		100%	

Calculate Weighted Score: multiply each domain score by its weight (as a decimal), sum all weighted scores. Example: Domain 1 score of 3 × 0.10 = 0.30. Repeat for all domains and sum.

Overall Score Range	Maturity Level	Indicative Status	Recommended Action
1.0 – 1.9	Initial	Significant risk exposure; ISMS does not exist or is non-functional.	Immediate foundational investment required. Engage a qualified ISMS implementation partner.

Overall Score Range	Maturity Level	Indicative Status	Recommended Action
2.0 – 2.9	Developing	Basic controls exist but gaps are material. Not audit-ready.	Define implementation roadmap targeting Level 3 within 12 months. Prioritise risk assessment and policy documentation.
3.0 – 3.9	Defined	Functionally compliant ISMS. ISO 27001 certification is achievable.	Pursue certification. Focus measurement and monitoring improvements to close gap to Level 4.
4.0 – 4.9	Managed	Mature ISMS with strong measurement and management. Competitive governance posture.	Focus on automation, threat intelligence integration, and supply chain security to achieve Level 5.
5.0	Optimising	Industry-leading security governance. Genuine security as competitive advantage.	Maintain through continuous improvement, external benchmarking, and contribution to industry standards.

Assessment Record

Field	Details
Organisation Name	
Assessment Date	
Assessment Conducted By	
Next Assessment Due	
Overall Weighted Score	
Overall Maturity Level	
Key Priority Actions (Top 3)	1. 2. 3.
Board / Management Review Date	
Reviewer / Approver	

D. TOOLS AND TEMPLATES

Essential ISMS Documentation Templates

Document	Description
ISMS Scope Statement	Defines the boundary, assets, and locations covered by the ISMS
Information Security Policy	Top-level management statement of security intent and commitment
Risk Assessment Methodology	Documents the risk assessment approach, criteria, and scales
Risk Assessment Register	Records all identified assets, threats, vulnerabilities, likelihood, impact, and risk levels
Risk Treatment Plan	Maps each risk to treatment decision, selected controls, implementation status, and residual risk
Statement of Applicability (SoA)	Maps all 93 Annex A controls to applicability decisions with justification and implementation status
Information Security Objectives Register	Documents measurable security objectives, owners, and progress
Legal and Regulatory Register	Records all applicable legal, regulatory, and contractual requirements
Asset Inventory	Complete register of information assets with classification and ownership

Document	Description
Supplier Security Register	Records security assessments, contract clauses, and monitoring status for all relevant suppliers
Incident Register	Logs all security events and incidents with classification, timeline, actions, and root cause
Internal Audit Schedule and Reports	Annual audit programme and individual audit reports with findings and corrective actions
Management Review Minutes	Records of management review meetings with inputs, outputs, and decisions
Nonconformity and Corrective Action Register	Tracks all nonconformities, root causes, corrective actions, and verification

E. RECOMMENDED TOOLS

- **GRC Platforms:** Seven Step Consulting's Compl AI Platform https://complaiplatform.com; ServiceNow GRC; RSA Archer; MetricStream — for integrated risk, compliance, and control management.
- **Vulnerability Management**: Tenable Nessus; Qualys VMDR; Rapid7 InsightVM — for continuous vulnerability scanning and patch management tracking.
- **SIEM / SOAR**: Microsoft Sentinel; Splunk Enterprise Security; IBM QRadar; Google Chronicle — for security event management, monitoring, and incident response automation.
- **Identity and Access Management**: Microsoft Entra ID; Okta; CyberArk PAM — for identity governance, MFA, and privileged access management.
- **DLP:** Microsoft Purview; Symantec DLP; Digital Guardian — for data leakage prevention and data classification enforcement.
- **Endpoint Protection**: Microsoft Defender; CrowdStrike Falcon; SentinelOne — for EDR and endpoint protection platform.
- **Secure Development:** SonarQube (SAST); OWASP ZAP (DAST); Snyk (dependency scanning); Deploy & Checkmarx — for secure development lifecycle tooling.

F. IMPLEMENTATION CHECKLIST

ISMS Implementation Readiness Checklist

Item	Status
1. Top management commitment documented	
2. CISO/ISO role defined and resourced	
3. ISMS scope defined and documented	
4. Internal and external context analysis completed (PESTLE/SWOT)	
5. Interested party requirements documented	
6. Information Security Policy approved and communicated	
7. Risk assessment methodology documented and approved	
8. Asset inventory completed and owners assigned	
9. Risk assessment completed (all assets in scope)	
10. Risk treatment plan approved by risk owners	
11. Statement of Applicability (SoA) completed and approved	
12. Information security objectives defined and measurable	
13. Policy suite developed (all applicable controls)	
14. Procedure documentation completed	

Item	Status
15. Staff awareness training programme launched	
16. Technical controls implemented (per SoA)	
17. Internal audit programme established	
18. First internal audit completed	
19. Management review conducted	
20. Corrective actions from audit and review tracked	

EPILOGUE

We began this book with Aesop's fable of the Horse and the Hunter — a cautionary tale about the price of seeking protection without understanding the cost. The parallel with information security is precise: the technologies and systems we adopt to manage and protect our information assets can themselves become instruments of constraint and vulnerability if we do not approach them with clear eyes, sound governance, and structured discipline.

The 7-D Framework is our attempt to provide that structure — to give senior leaders and their security teams a compass that is both principled and practical. It draws on the best of what the global information security community has produced: the ISO/IEC 27000 family of standards; the metrics and governance insights of the security measurement movement; and the operational wisdom codified in authoritative guidance such as the Australian Signals Directorate's Information Security Manual.

Information security is ultimately a people discipline. Technology is a tool, standards are a guide, and frameworks are a map. But it is people — leaders who take accountability, practitioners who implement with rigour, and employees who develop awareness and vigilance — who make the ISMS real.

We invite you to take the seven steps. Define your context. Discover your risks. Design your controls. Document your framework. Do and deploy. Deploy & check your performance. And drive toward the continuous improvement that is the only honest definition of Infosec Nirvana.

The journey is worth every step.

Ajai Kumar Srivastava | Susheela Gupta

ABBREVIATIONS

Abbreviation	Full Form
AES	Advanced Encryption Standard
ALE	Annual Loss Expectancy
APT	Advanced Persistent Threat
ASD	Australian Signals Directorate
BCM	Business Continuity Management
BCP	Business Continuity Plan
BYOD	Bring Your Own Device
CCPA	California Consumer Privacy Act
CIA	Confidentiality, Integrity, Availability
CISA	Cybersecurity and Infrastructure Security Agency (US)
CISO	Chief Information Security Officer
CMM	Capability Maturity Model
DAST	Dynamic Application Security Testing
DLP	Data Leakage / Loss Prevention
DPO	Data Protection Officer
DPDP	Digital Personal Data Protection (Act 2023, India)
DORA	Digital Operational Resilience Act (EU)
EDR	Endpoint Detection and Response
GDPR	General Data Protection Regulation (EU)

Abbreviation	Full Form
GRC	Governance, Risk, and Compliance
HIPAA	Health Insurance Portability and Accountability Act (US)
IAM	Identity and Access Management
IDS	Intrusion Detection System
IMS	Integrated Management System
IPS	Intrusion Prevention System
ISM	Information Security Manual (ASD, Australia)
ISMS	Information Security Management System
ISO	International Organization for Standardization
IEC	International Electrotechnical Commission
MFA	Multi-Factor Authentication
MTTD	Mean Time to Detect
MTTR	Mean Time to Respond / Remediate
NIST	National Institute of Standards and Technology
OT	Operational Technology
PAM	Privileged Access Management
PDCA	Plan-Do-Deploy & Check-Act
PCI DSS	Payment Card Industry Data Security Standard
PIMS	Privacy Information Management System
PII	Personally Identifiable Information
PQC	Post-Quantum Cryptography
RBAC	Role-Based Access Control
ROSI	Return on Security Investment
RPO	Recovery Point Objective
RTO	Recovery Time Objective

Abbreviation	Full Form
SABSA	Sherwood Applied Business Security Architecture
SAST	Static Application Security Testing
SDLC	Secure Development Lifecycle
SIEM	Security Information and Event Management
SLE	Single Loss Expectancy
SOC	Security Operations Centre
SoA	Statement of Applicability
SOC 2	Service Organization Control 2
TLS	Transport Layer Security
TPRM	Third-Party Risk Management
UPS	Uninterruptible Power Supply
VPN	Virtual Private Network
WEEE	Waste Electrical and Electronic Equipment

BIBLIOGRAPHY

Standards and Official Publications

- Australian Signals Directorate. Information Security Manual, March 2026. Commonwealth of Australia.
- International Organization for Standardization. ISO/IEC 27000:2018 Information technology — Security techniques — Information security management systems — Overview and vocabulary.
- International Organization for Standardization. ISO/IEC 27001:2022 Information security, cybersecurity and privacy protection — Information security management systems — Requirements.
- International Organization for Standardization. ISO/IEC 27002:2022 Information security, cybersecurity and privacy protection — Information security controls.
- International Organization for Standardization. ISO/IEC 27005:2022 Information security, cybersecurity and privacy protection — Guidance on managing information security risks.
- International Organization for Standardization. ISO/IEC 27701:2019 Security techniques — Extension to ISO/IEC 27001 and ISO/IEC 27002 for privacy information management.

- National Institute of Standards and Technology. NIST Cybersecurity Framework 2.0, 2024.
- National Institute of Standards and Technology. NIST SP 800-12 Rev. 1: An Introduction to Information Security, 2017.
- National Institute of Standards and Technology. NIST SP 800-37 Rev. 2: Risk Management Framework for Information Systems and Organizations, 2018.

Books and Academic Works

- Brotby, W. Krag. Information Security Management Metrics: A Definitive Guide to Effective Security Monitoring and Measurement. Boca Raton: Auerbach Publications / Taylor & Francis Group, 2009.
- Calder, Alan. Implementing the ISO/IEC 27001 ISMS Standard, Second Edition. Ely: IT Governance Publishing.
- Gates, Bill. Business @ the Speed of Thought. New York: Warner Books, 1999.
- Licklider, J.C.R. and Robert W. Taylor. "The Computer as a Communication Device." Science and Technology, April 1968.
- Miller, George A. "The Magical Number Seven, Plus or Minus Two: Some Limits on Our Capacity for Processing Information." Psychological Review, 63(2), 81-97, 1956.
- Warren, Samuel D. and Louis Brandeis. "The Right to Privacy." Harvard Law Review, 4(5), 193-220, December 1890.

Reports and Articles

- Boehm, Jim et al. "Cybersecurity Trends: Looking over the Horizon." McKinsey & Company, March 2022.
- CrowdStrike. CrowdStrike 2022 Global Threat Report. CrowdStrike, 2022.
- Djuraskovic, Ogi. "Big Data Statistics 2022: How Much Data is in The World?" FirstSiteGuide.com, 2022.
- Gartner. Top Cybersecurity Trends and Predictions 2022. Gartner Research, 2022.
- Hemp, Paul. "Death by Information Overload." Harvard Business Review, September 2009.
- ISC2. Cybersecurity Workforce Study 2022. International Information System Security Certification Consortium.

ABOUT THE AUTHORS

Ajai Kumar Srivastava

https://www.linkedin.com/in/ajaisrivastava/

Ajai Kumar Srivastava is a globally recognized cybersecurity strategist, governance and risk advisor, entrepreneur, and author with over 35 years of experience helping organizations strengthen digital trust, cybersecurity, privacy, and organizational resilience.

As the Founder and Managing Director of Seven Step Consulting Pvt. Ltd., based in Gurugram, India, he has advised organizations across the BFSI, healthcare, SaaS, manufacturing, telecommunications, and public sectors on information security, enterprise risk management, business continuity, AI governance, and regulatory compliance.

His expertise spans ISO/IEC 27001, ISO/IEC 27701, ISO 22301, SOC 2, PCI DSS, HIPAA, GDPR, India's Digital Personal Data Protection (DPDP) Act, and other global governance, risk, and compliance frameworks. Renowned for his practical, business-focused approach, Ajai helps organizations move beyond compliance to build sustainable cyber resilience and governance excellence.

Ajai is the creator of the S.T.E.P.S.™ Governance Trust Cycle and the 7-Step Framework for Information Security Management, methodologies that integrate governance, risk, security, and continuous improvement into everyday business operations. He is also the architect of Compl AI, an AI-powered Governance, Risk, and Compliance (GRC) platform, and the TCF (The Compliance First) SaaS suite.

An accomplished author and thought leader, Ajai has written or co-authored several books, including Digital Dragons and Defenders, MIND Your S.T.E.P.S., Beyond Firewalls: Cybersecurity and Privacy in the Digital Age, The Endless Becoming, and Code vs Constitution. He also leads the Wisdom Code Series, an initiative dedicated to making complex governance, cybersecurity, and compliance concepts practical and accessible for leaders and professionals.

A graduate of St. Stephen's College, University of Delhi, where he earned both his bachelor's and master's degrees, Ajai combines academic insight with decades of consulting and executive leadership experience.

In Seven Steps to Infosec Nirvana, he presents a practical roadmap for executives, security leaders, and technology professionals to build resilient organizations where cybersecurity becomes a strategic business enabler rather than merely a compliance requirement.

Susheela (Sush) Gupta

CISA | CISM | CDPSE | ISO/IEC 27001 Lead Auditor | Certified Scrum Master | B.Tech (Computer Science) | PGDIT (Information Technology)

https://www.linkedin.com/in/susheelagupta

What does it take to build trust in an increasingly digital world? How can organisations stay resilient in the face of evolving cyber threats, changing regulations, and growing privacy expectations? These are the questions that have shaped Susheela Gupta's 16-year career in information security, governance, risk, compliance (GRC), and assurance.

A highly respected cybersecurity and GRC professional based in Melbourne, Australia, Susheela has helped organisations across telecommunications, government, banking, financial services, healthcare, and technology strengthen their security posture, manage enterprise risk, and build resilient governance frameworks. Her experience spans both large enterprises and mid-sized organisations, where she has successfully led information security, risk, privacy, compliance, and assurance initiatives that align security with business strategy.

Holding a Bachelor of Technology (B.Tech) in Computer Science and a Post Graduate Diploma in Information Technology (PGDIT), Susheela combines strong technical expertise with strategic business insight. She was one of the co-founders of Seven Step Consulting Private Limited in 2009, contributing to its early vision of helping organisations strengthen their information security and risk management capabilities.

Her professional credentials include Certified Information Systems Auditor (CISA), Certified Information Security Manager

(CISM), Certified Data Privacy Solutions Engineer (CDPSE), ISO/IEC 27001 Lead Auditor, and Certified Scrum Master, reflecting her commitment to excellence and continuous professional development.

Known for translating complex cybersecurity and governance challenges into practical business solutions, Susheela believes that information security is far more than a technical discipline—it is a strategic business enabler that builds trust, drives innovation, and enables sustainable growth.

Beyond her professional work, Susheela is passionate about mentoring and empowering women in technology and cybersecurity, encouraging greater diversity, inclusion, and leadership within the profession. She believes that developing the next generation of cyber leaders is just as important as protecting today's digital organisations.

As co-author of the Wisdom Code Series and Seven Steps to Infosec Nirvana, she shares practical insights, proven frameworks, and real-world experiences to help executives, board members, security leaders, auditors, and aspiring professionals confidently navigate today's rapidly evolving digital landscape. Her mission is to help organisations transform cybersecurity from a compliance requirement into a strategic business advantage while inspiring professionals to lead with purpose, integrity, and resilience.

www.ingramcontent.com/pod-product-compliance
Lightning Source LLC
LaVergne TN
LVHW050925210926
848482LV00013B/544
* 9 7 9 8 9 0 5 8 4 8 0 4 9 *